# GUYANA

Edited by Arif Ali

HANSIB

Published in Great Britain 2008
Hansib Publications Limited
London & Hertfordshire, UK

Email: info@hansib-books.com
Website: www.hansib-books.com

ISBN 978-1-906190-10-1

First edition published by Hansib Publications, 2006

*Front cover*: Kaieteur Falls by Ian Brierley

*Endpapers*: (front) The road to Kurupung,
with Tiger Mountain in the distance, by Ian Brierley;
(back) Cipo Mountain, north Pakarimas, by Robert J Fernandes

Printed and bound in the United Kingdom

# Contents

# We are grateful for the support given by the following businesses and organisations:

**ABDOOL HAKH & SONS**
Rice Milling & Marketing Complex
Harlem, West Coast Demerara
Tel: 269-0027. Fax: 269-0028
Email: a.hakh&sons@solutions2000.net

**ANSA McAL TRADING LTD**
60 Betervertwagting, East Coast Demerara
Tel: 220-0455 / 0505 / 0268. Fax: 220-0796
Email: paul.chan-a-sue@ansamcal.com
Email: ansamcaltradingltd@ansamcal.com
Tel: 265-2265 (Farm East Bank, Demerara)
Tel: 333-5891 (New Amsterdam)
Fax: 333-4061

**ATTA RAINFOREST LODGE**
Wilderness Explorers
176 Middle Street, Georgetown
Tel: 227-7698. Fax: 226-2085
Email:
info@iwokramacanopywalkway.com

**AUSTIN'S BOOK SERVICES (FJT)**
190 Church Street, North Cummingsburg,
Georgetown
Tel: 227-7395. Fax: 227-7396
Email: lloydaustins@guyana.net.gy

**BANKS DIH LTD**
Thirst Park, Georgetown
Tel: 226-2491-8. Fax: 226-6523
Email: info@banksdih.com

**M BEEPAT & SONS**
100-101 Regent Street, Lacytown,
Georgetown
Tel: 226-1292 / 7380 / 227-0637 / 225-
7630 / 223-6192
Fax: 226-1930
Email: mbeepat@networksgy.com

**BUDDY'S INVESTMENTS**
Corporate Office
Brickdam, Stabroek, Georgetown
Tel: 226-8162 / 225-3983
Email: buddyshotel@guyana.net.gy

**CARIBBEAN AIRWAYS**
63 Robb Street, Georgetown
Tel: 226-5272. Fax: 227-3052
Email: cdefour@bwee.com

**CORREIA GROUP OF COMPANIES**
159 Charlotte Street, Lacytown,
Georgetown
Tel: 226-0605. Fax: 225-1171
Email: info@correiamining.com

**DIDCO (Friendship Hotel & Restaurant Holdings Ltd)**
Lot 1, Public Road, Ruimveldt, Georgetown
Tel: 226-8863 / 225-2475 / 225-1994
Fax: 225 2316
Email: didcokfc@guyana.net.gy

**EDWARD B. BEHARRY & COMPANY LTD**
191 Charlotte Street, Lacytown,
Georgetown, PO Box 10485
Tel: 227-1349 / 2526 / 0632-5
Fax: 225 6062
Email: ebbsec@beharrygroup.com

**ETEGRA INC – PETER RAMSAROOP (ROOP GROUP)**
34 King & North Road, Lacytown,
Georgetown
Tel: / Fax: 227-1053
Email: media@roopgroup.com

**EVERGREEN ADVENTURES**
159 Charlotte Street, Georgetown
Tel: 226-0605. Fax: 225-1171
Email: sales@evergreen-adventures.com

**FARFAN & MENDES LTD**
45, Urquart Street, Georgetown
Tel: 226-8130 / 226-6401
Fax: 225-8651
Email: fml@networksgy.com
Tel: 225-7373 (35 High Street,
Georgetown)

**W M FOGARTY'S LTD**
34-37 Water Street, Georgetown
Tel: 225-6870 / 5678 / 6877
Fax: 227-6381
Email: fogartystore@inetguyana.net

**GAFSONS GROUP OF COMPANIES**
Plantation Houston, East Bank Demerara
Tel: 227-5886 / 7
Email: nil@guyana.net

**GEORGETOWN PUBLIC HOSPITAL CORPORATION**
New Market Street, Georgetown
Tel: 226-1839. Fax: 226-6249
Email: gphchosp@hotmail.com

**GLOBAL BANK OF COMMERCE LTD**
Global Financial Centre
P.O. Box W1803, Friars Hill Road, St
John's, Antigua
Tel: (268) 480-2329. Fax: (268) 462-1831
Email: customer.service@gbc.ag

**GRAND COASTAL LODGE**
144 W1/2 Regent Road, Bourda,
Georgetown
Tel: 231-7674. Fax: 231-7047
Email: grandcoastal_lodge@yahoo.com

**GRAND COASTAL SUITES**
2 Area M Plantation, Le Ressouvenir, East
Coast Demerara
Tel: 220-1091. Fax: 220-1498
Email: ceo@grandcoastal.com

**GUYANA ASSOCIATION OF ALTERNATIVE MEDICINE / BAKJA HEALTH MOVEMENT**
32-33 Dr Miller Street, Triumph, East
Coast Demerara
Tel: 220-2130 / 2254. Fax: 220-5821
Email: bakja_h_m@hotmail.com

**GUYANA LOTTERY**
357 Lamaha Street, North Cummingsburg,
Georgetown
Tel: 226-0753. Fax: 225-9633
Email: tlewis@cbnco.com

**GUYANA MARKETING CORPORATION (GMC)**
87 Robb & Alexander Streets
Lacytown
Georgetown
Tel: 226-8255 / 227-5809 / 225-7808
Fax: 227-4114
Email: newgmc@guyworksgy.com

**GUYANA OFFICE FOR INVESTMENT**
190 Camp & Church Streets
Georgetown
Tel: 225-0658 / 0653 / 227-0653
Fax: 225-0655
Email: goinvest@goinvest.gov.gy

**GUYANA OIL COMPANY**
166 Waterloo Street, North
Cummingsburg, Georgetown
Tel: 225-1595-8 / 7161
Fax: 225-2320
Email: BadrieP@guyoil.com
Email: guyoil@gol.net.gy

**GUYANA SMALL BUSINESS ASSOCIATION**
160 Waterloo Street
North Cummingsburg
Georgetown
Tel: 226-7436
Email: zephent2000@yahoo.com

GUYANA STORES LTD
Lot 19 Water Street, Georgetown
Tel: 226-6171. Fax: 226-3685
Email: tonyyassin@telsnetgy.net

GUYANA SUGAR CORPORATION INC.
Ogle Estate, East Coast Demerara
Tel 222-6044
Email: marketing@guysuco.com

GUYANA TELEPHONE & TELEGRAPH
COMPANY
69 & 79 Brickdam, Georgetown
& 78 Church Street, Georgetown
Tel: 225-1315

HOTEL ARIANTZE AND SIDEWALK
CAFÉ & JAZZ CLUB
176 Middle Street, Georgetown
Tel: 226-9555 / 623-8924. Fax: 227-0210
Email: hughes@solutions2000.net

HOTEL TOWER LTD
74-75 Main Street, Georgetown
Tel: 227-2011-14
Fax: 225-6021 / 223-6019
Email: hotel.tower@solutions2000.net

INTERNATIONAL PHARMACEUTICAL
AGENCY
226B Camp Street, Georgetown
Tel: 225-0746 / 8. Fax: 225-0730
Email: ipa@guyana.net.gy

IWOKRAMA INTERNATIONAL CENTRE
77 High Street, Kingston, Georgetown,
P.O. Box 10630
Tel: 225-1504. Fax: 225-9199
Email: iwokrama@iwokrama.org

JOHN FERNANDES GROUP OF
COMPANIES
24 Water Street, Georgetown
Tel: 225-3501 / 2. Fax: 226-1881
Email: enquiries@jf-ltd.com

KARANAMBU CATTLE CO LTD
A102 Issano Place, East Bel Air Park,
Georgetown
Email: mcturk@networksgy.com

KING'S JEWELLERY WORLD
141 Quamina Street, Georgetown
Tel: 225-8570 / 226-0704 / 0984
Fax: 225-2524
Email: admin@kingsjewelleryworld.com

LAPARKAN - Freight Forwarding Division
2-9 Lombard Street, Georgetown
Tel: 226-1095 / 7. Fax: 227-6808
Email: infoguyana@laparkan.com

LE MERIDIEN PEGASUS GUYANA
PO Box 101147, Georgetown
Tel: 225-2856. Fax: 225-3703
Email: guy.pegusus@solutions2000.net

THE LINGERIE SHOP
101 Cummings Street, Georgetown
Tel: 231-3837. Fax: 227-6798
Email: saytls@networksgy.com

MINISTRY OF EDUCATION
26 Brickdam, Stabroek
Tel: 223-7900. Fax: 225-5570

MINISTRY OF TOURISM, INDUSTRY &
COMMERCE
229 South Road, Lacytown, Georgetown
Tel: 226-8695. Fax: 225-9898

MOHABIR A NANDLALL & ASSOCIATES
'Bhagwati Chambers', 217 South Road,
Lacytown
Tel: 227-2712 / 223-7487. Fax: 223-7486
Email: anil_nandlall@hotmail.com

NATIONAL MILLING COMPANY OF
GUYANA INC.
Agricola, East Bank Demerara
Tel: 233-2462. Fax: 233-2464
Email: bert_sukhai@namilcoflour.com

NEAL & MASSEY GUYANA LTD (Geddes
Grant Guyana Ltd)
5 Ruimveldt, Georgetown
Tel: 226-7291-5 / 227-2031-8. Fax: 226-
0310 / 225-7676
Email: ainlim@solutions2000.net
Email: geddesgrant@solutions2000.net

NEW GPC INC.
A1 Farm, East Bank Demerara
Tel: 265-4261. Fax: 265-2229
Email: limacol@newgpc.com or
marketing@newgpc.com

PHARMAGEN ENTERPRISES
Lot 1F Area L, Bel Air, Georgetown
Tel: 226-0776 / 227-4833. Fax: 225-6961
Email pharmagen@networksgy.com

PRECISION WOODWORKING
35 Industrial Estate, Ruimveldt, P.O. Box
10 1546, Georgetown
Tel: 225-2366. Fax: 225-6448
Email: precision@networksgy.com

PRITIPAUL SINGH INVESTMENT, INC.
McDoom Village, East Bank Demerara
Tel: 226-9934 / 223-7638 / 9
Fax: 226-7753 / 0006
Email: priti@networksgy.com

K RAHAMAN & SONS (Spare Parts)
51 Russell & Evans Streets, Charlestown,
Georgetown
Tel: 226-1778
Fax: 225-2289
Email: raheemarahaman@yahoo.com

ROCK VIEW LODGE
Annai – North Rupununi-Region Nine
Tel: 225-0605
Fax: 225-1171
Email: info@rockviewlodge.com

RORAIMA AIRWAYS INC
R8 Eping Avenue, Bel Air Park,
Georgetown
Tel: 225-9648
Fax: 225-9646
Email: ral@roraimaairways.com

R.R.T. ENTERPRISES
W ½ 107 Regent Road, Bourda,
Georgetown
Tel: 225-2237 / 231-7287
Fax: 225-1290
Email: rrt@networksgy.com

L. SEEPERSAUD MARAJ & SONS
Under the Clock, Stabroek Market,
Georgetown
Tel: 226-3469. Fax: 226-1141
Email: ramaraj@ewireless.gy.com

SPLASHMIN'S FUN PARK & RESORT
48 High Street, Werk-en-Rust,
Georgetown
Tel: 225-8066 / 223-7301 / 624-9266
Fax: 225-6052
Email: deslyn.jack@splashmins.com
Email: info@splashmins.com

TRANS PACIFIC MOTOR SPARES &
AUTO SALES
Lot 5 Good Hope, East Coast Demerara
Tel: 220-9293 / 9284 / 0985 / 0986
Fax: 220-9796
Email: transpms@guyana.net.gy
Tel: 225-7448 / 226-2103 (45 Robb &
Light Streets, Georgetown)

TWO 2 BROTHERS CORP
17 Vergenorgen, East Bank Essequibo
Tel: 260-2282 / 2014 / 4014 / 4023
Fax 260-2037
Email: info@two2brotherscorp.com

WILDERNESS EXPLORERS
Cara Suites, 176 Middle Street, Georgetown
Tel: 227-7698
Fax: 226-2085
Email: info@wilderness-explorers.com

# Acknowledgements

THANKS ARE DUE TO THE FOLLOWING FOR THEIR help and support towards the publication of the first and this second edition of *GUYANA*:

First of all, to President Bharrat Jagdeo and the Government of Guyana for commissioning Hansib to produce this book. President Jagdeo's hands-on approach to this project is much appreciated. I am also grateful to Minister Manzoor Nadir for his support in getting the project off the ground.

To Hansib's London team, especially our **Managing Editor, Kash Ali** and Project Co-ordinator, Isha Persaud; to Richard Painter of Print Resources; Shareef Ali of Graphic Resolutions; Ella Barnes and Alan Cross.

IN GUYANA: to our Co-ordinating Editor, Russel Lancaster, whose sterling work was invaluable to the project; to Indira Anandjit, Mazrul Bacchus, Hilton Chan, Geoffrey Da Silva, Nancy Ferreira, Capt. Gerry Gouveia, Cathy Hughes, Brian James, Michael Khan, Manniram Prasad, Petamber Persaud, Robert Persaud, Dolly Rahaman, and the businesses and organisations who supported the project.

TO THE WRITERS (in alphabetical order): Walter B. Alexander, Annette Arjoon, Ajay Baksh, Elsie Croal, Allan Fenty, Damien Fernandes, Desrey C. Fox, David Granger, Han Granger, Lennox Hernandez, Alim Hosein, Christobel Hughes, Michelle Kalamandeen, Marjorie Kirkpatrick, Melanie Kirkpatrick, Neil Kumar, Russel Lancaster, John Mair, Tota C. Mangar, Ian McDonald, Dr Winston McGowan, Mary Noel Menezes, C.A. Nascimento, Petamber Persaud, Ray Goble, Donald Sinclair, Kirk Smock.

TO THE PHOTOGRAPHERS (in alphabetical order): Annette Arjoon, Ajay Baksh/CI, A. Bayney, Ian Brierley, H. Castro/CI, Hilton Chan, P. DeGroot, G. Duncan, L. Fanfair, Robert Fernandes, FotoNatura, Government Information Agency (GINA, Guyana), David Granger, Guyana Tourism Authority, M. Hamilton, A. Holland, J. Martin/CI, Nick May, Stuart May, D. Phoenix, Joe Ramjohn, R. Sam, R. Thomas.

To the management and staff at Roraima Inn, Tower Hotel, Grand Coastal Inn, Hotel Ariantze and Cara Lodge; to the Caribbean Airways staff in London and Guyana, and the Immigration and Customs officers and staff at Cheddi Jagan International Airport.

To Arnon Adams, Mohamed Ali, Raki Ali, Lloyd Austin, Carl Bacchus, Sydarth Anandjit, Annalise Bayney, Lt Col (Rtd) Keith Booker, Daren Booth, June Anne Brassington, Paul Chan-a-Sue, Reuben Charles, Paul Cheong, Nicole Correia, Dr Philip Da Silva, Carlton Defour, Denise Dias, Lawrence Fanfair, Robert Fernandes, Ameena Gafoor, Uchenna Gibson, Dane Gobin, Ray Goble, Nizam Hassan, Ovid Holder, Lisa Insanally, Jessie Jenkins, Pulandar Kandhi, Afzal Khan, Ameer Khan, Farida Khan, Fizul Khan, Raheel Khan (New York), Carleen Langford, Bernard Lee Young, Tariq Mohamed, Anil Nandalal, Heson Nandalal, Allita Narine, Naseem Nasir, Gajendra Nauth Narine (Andy), Shyam Nokta, Bishwa Panday, Vibert Parvatton, Malcolm Peters, Chandani Persaud, Fidel Persaud, Oscar Phillips, Yvonne Raghoo, Kavita Ragoonauth, Reza Rahman, Christopher Ram, Dowlat Ram, Joe Ramjohn, Clement Rohee, Ted Sabat, Rackie Seecharran, Gary Serrao, Zaleena Shaw, Coralie Simmons, Chetram Singh, Alicia Spence, Pamela St Hill, Tony Thorne, Enrico Woolford, Zena Bone, Zorena and Jim Yhap, Janet Naidu, Mokesh Daby, Sheik and Elaine Asad, Derek San-Sellus, Compton Stewart, Patrick Zephyr, Oscar Phillips, Winston Browne, Kenrick Chance, Ambassador Bayney Karran and his staff in Washington, Annette Harris, Sattie Shaw, High Commissioner H.E. Rajnarine Singh and his staff in Canada, Consul General Danny T. Doobay, Moti Persaud, Habeeb Alli, Shanie Persaud, Ali Jehaludi, Baby and Shalim, Shireen Faizul, Rehana Hassan.

To the writers and photographers whose work we were unable to use, and to the scores of secretaries and personal assistants who organised and facilitated meetings with their bosses.

To the Tourism and Hospitality Association of Guyana, Wilderness Explorers, the staff at the Office of the President and State House, to Minister Jennifer Webster, Permanent Secretary Nanda Gopaul, Vic Persaud, Lt Col Francis Abraham, High Commissioner Laleshwar Singh and staff at the Guyana High Commission in London, management and staff at Guyana Lands and Survey Commission.

And, finally, to Pamela Mary for caring so much.

**Arif Ali**

# Foreword

THIS SECOND AND UPDATED EDITION OF ***GUYANA*** REFLECTS SOME OF the new developments and initiatives that were implemented at the time of the first edition, which was published in 2006.

At that time, the country was gearing up for the 2007 Cricket World Cup. This involved the construction of a new stadium and the development of new hotels to cater for the increased numbers of visitors during the competition. Guyana can now boast a state-of-the-art sports complex at Providence and can offer an even wider selection of hotels including the magnificent Buddy's Providence Hotel & Resort.

Since 2006, Guyana has also seen the commencement of construction of the Berbice river bridge; the development of the country as a yachting destination; the further promotion of its eco tourism sector; and the return to the Presidency of Bharrat Jagdeo.

This new edition marks Guyana's hosting of CARIFESTA X, a region-wide Caribbean festival that was conceived and then, in 1972, launched and hosted in Georgetown.

In his address at the launch of the first edition of GUYANA in Georgetown in July 2006, President Bharrat Jagdeo was glowing in his praise of this unique and long-awaited book. "I look at this book and I see my country", he said. "It's a book that reminds us that we live in a country of breathtaking natural beauty, with spectacular heritage sites, unmatched hospitality and a diverse, wonderful, multicultural people. I am very pleased and very proud to live in this country, and to be its leader."

Like the first edition, it is the intention of this second edition to continue to showcase the unmatched natural beauty and splendour of Guyana; to show the world what Guyana has to offer both in terms of the country as an ideal area for investment opportunities and as an idyllic tourism destination.

**Arif Ali**
**April 2008**

## DEDICATION

*This book is dedicated to my mother, Nasibun 'Sibby' Ali, 1910 – 2008*

# Message from the President of Guyana

I am pleased to be associated with this publication which introduces you to my country, Guyana; a land bursting with potential; busy in modernising its facilities and services and welcoming to visitors and investors alike.

It is my pleasure to invite you to immerse yourself in this book and discover within its pages what Guyana has to offer.

Our country, perched on the tip of South America and with close historical, political and economic ties to the Caribbean, is blessed with stupendous beauty. Within our borders are to be found breathtaking natural wonders, exotic flora and fauna and pristine rainforest. Guyana, renowned for El Dorado, the mythical city of gold and boasting of the majestic Kaieteur Falls, has the distinction of being rated amongst the top ten countries in terms of best practices in conserving our environment.

Our capital city, Georgetown, with much of its colonial architecture still intact, is alive with heritage, charming and intimate. Our greatest asset, however, is our people. Warm, friendly and of diverse ethnicities and cultures, they will shower you with our legendary hospitality and encourage you to come again and again.

Investors will find Guyana an appealing destination. Our economy is one of the most open in the Western Hemisphere, with a highly attractive incentive regime, a skilled, educated and industrious workforce, stable financial markets and laws that protect private investment and allow for the unhindered repatriation of profits and capital.

Over the past years, my government has pursued an aggressive program of economic and social reforms, complemented with prudent fiscal and monetary management that has allowed us to achieve macroeconomic stability alongside massive public investment in social and physical infrastructure.

We have laid the building blocks for the economic transformation of a small economy, based on primary products, to a more diversified value-added economy, exploiting our strategic advantage as the gateway to South America and the special relationships which we have with other countries through trading agreements. The headquarters of CARICOM, the economic grouping of fourteen Caribbean countries, including Guyana, is here in Georgetown.

We now have an improved network of roads and bridges, linking the major population centres, of the 214,969 square kilometres (83,000 square miles) of our country, and there is continuous improvement in the access to quality healthcare and social services. We are investing massively in our educational system, in the main, to turn our students of excellence with the skills necessary to meet the demands of the labour market. While our traditional sectors are being re-capitalised and restructured, new hubs of growth, especially in information technology and tourism, have mushroomed. These have provided new, well-remunerated opportunities for investment.

At the political level we continue to fortify the democratic advances made over the past fourteen years and are firmly committed to building an open and just society in which all our people can benefit and share in the fruits of economic and social progress.

Guyana is making enormous strides, and I am confident that it is destined for greatness. We invite you to our magnificent country and to share in this exciting transformation.

We welcome all of you to Guyana. Whether you are a student, a tourist, an investor, or a Guyanese returning home, you can be assured that you will always find a warm and receptive environment in our beloved country.

**Bharrat Jagdeo**
**President, Republic of Guyana**

FACING PAGE
Natural wonders such as Kaieteur Falls, in Region 8 (Potaro – Siparuni), make Guyana an attractive destination for eco and adventure tourism. The falls are within the Kaieteur National Park, a designated area which is part of one of the world's largest and most bio-diverse rainforests.   Photo: N May

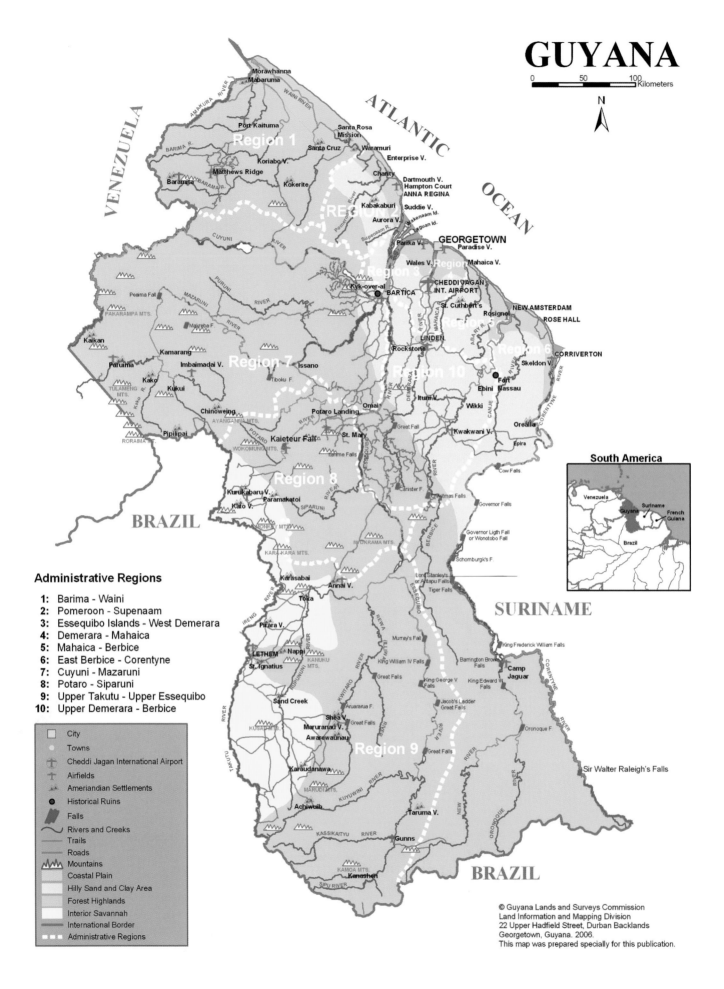

# GUYANA

0    50    100 Kilometers

N

**VENEZUELA**

**ATLANTIC OCEAN**

Morawhanna
Mabaruma
Port Kaituma
Santa Rosa Mission
Region 1
Santa Cruz
Waramuri
Koriabo V.
Enterprise V.
Matthews Ridge
Kokerite
Charity
Baramita
Dartmouth V.
Hampton Court
ANNA REGINA
Kabakaburi
Suddie V.
REGION 2
Aurora V.
Wakenaam Id.
Leguan Id.
Parika V.
GEORGETOWN
Paradise V.
Wales V. Region 3
Mahaica V.
Peaima Fall
Kyk-over-al
BARTICA
CHEDDI JAGAN
INT. AIRPORT
St. Cuthbert's
NEW AMSTERDAM
ROSE HALL
Rosignol
PAKARAMPA MTS.
Makreba F.
LINDEN
Region 6
CORRIVERTON
Skeldon V.
Kaikan
Rockstone
Kamarang
Region 10
Imbaimadai V.
Issano
Region 7
Fort Nassau
Paruima
Tiboku F.
Ebini
Kako
Wikki
Kukui
Ituni V.
Omai
Chinoweing
Potaro Landing
Great Fall
Orealla
AYANGANNA MTS.
Kwakwani V.
Pipilipai
Potaro River
St. Mary
Kaieteur Fall
Epira
RORAIMA MTS.
WOKOMUNG MTS.
Itanna Falls
Cow Falls
Region 8
Governor Falls
Christmas Falls
Kurukabaru V.
Paramakatoi
Canister F.
Governor Ligth Fall
or Wonotobo Fall
Kato V.
**BRAZIL**
MONKEY MTS.
Schomburgk's F.
KARA-KARA MTS.
IWOKRAMA MTS.
Lord Stanley's
or Aitapu Falls
Karasabai
Annai V.
Tiger Falls
Toka
**SURINAME**
Pirara V.
Murray's Fall
King Frederick William Falls
LETHEM
Nappi
KANUKU MTS.
King William IV Falls
Barrington Brown Falls
St. Ignatius
RUPUNUNI MTS.
Great Falls
Camp Jaguar
King George V Falls
King Edward VII
Sand Creek
Jacob's Ladder
Great Falls
Shea V.
Aruararua F.
Maruranau V.
Great Falls
Awarewaunau
Oronoque F.
Region 9
Great Falls
Karaudanawa
Sir Walter Raleigh's Falls
MARUDI MTS.
Achiwuib
Taruma V.
KUSAD MTS.
KASSIKAITYU RIVER
Gunns
KAMOA MTS.
Kanashen
**BRAZIL**

## Administrative Regions

**1:** Barima - Waini
**2:** Pomeroon - Supenaam
**3:** Essequibo Islands - West Demerara
**4:** Demerara - Mahaica
**5:** Mahaica - Berbice
**6:** East Berbice - Corentyne
**7:** Cuyuni - Mazaruni
**8:** Potaro - Siparuni
**9:** Upper Takutu - Upper Essequibo
**10:** Upper Demerara - Berbice

☐ City
● Towns
✈ Cheddi Jagan International Airport
⊤ Airfields
⋀⋀ Ameriandian Settlements
◉ Historical Ruins
◤ Falls
〜 Rivers and Creeks
— Trails
— Roads
⋀⋀⋀ Mountains
    Coastal Plain
    Hilly Sand and Clay Area
    Forest Highlands
    Interior Savannah
— International Border
┄┄ Administrative Regions

**South America**

Venezuela
Suriname
Guyana
French Guiana
Brazil

© Guyana Lands and Surveys Commission
Land Information and Mapping Division
22 Upper Hadfield Street, Durban Backlands
Georgetown, Guyana. 2006.
This map was prepared specially for this publication.

# Facts & Figures

**FULL NAME:** Co-operative Republic of Guyana

**AREA:** Total: 214,969 sq km (82,978 sq miles)

Land: 196,850 sq km (76,004 sq miles)

Water: 18,120 sq km (6996 sq miles)

**LOCATION:** Northern South America; bordered by Venezuela, Brazil and Suriname, with the North Atlantic at its northern coastline

**POPULATION:** 769,095 (July 2007)

**CAPITAL CITY:** Georgetown

**NATIONALITY:** Guyanese

**LANGUAGES:** English (official language)

Amerindian dialects, Creole, Hindi, Urdu

**RELIGIONS:** Christian 50%, Hindu 35%, Muslim 10%, other 5%

**ETHNIC GROUPS**

Indian 50%, African 36%, Amerindian 6%, Mixed 7%, White & Chinese 1%

**LITERACY:** 98.8%

**CURRENCY:** Guyana Dollar (GYD, G$, GUY$)

**GDP PER CAPITA:** Purchasing power parity – US$ 5300 (2007)

**EXCHANGE RATE:** US$ 1 = G$/GUY$ 203 (2008)

GB£ 1 = G$/GUY$ 400 (2008)

**GOVERNMENT:** Republic within the Commonwealth

**POLITICAL SYSTEM:** Parliamentary democracy with executive authority vested in the Head of State

**POLITICAL PARTIES IN PARLIAMENT**

People's Progressive Party-Civic (PPP/C) – Governing Party

People's National Congress-Reform (PNC/R) – Main Opposition

Working People's Alliance (WPA)

Guyana Action Party (GAP)

Rise, Organise and Rebuild (ROAR)

The United Force (TUF)

**JUDICIAL SYSTEM:** Supreme Court of Judicature consisting of a Court of Appeal, High Court and Magistrates' Courts

**LEGISLATURE:** Unicameral, 72-member National Assembly which sits for a five-year term

**HEAD OF STATE & GOVERNMENT:** President Bharrat Jagdeo

**PRIME MINISTER:** Samuel Hinds

**LEADER OF THE OPPOSITION:** Robert Corbin

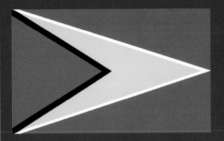

## FLAG OF GUYANA

The green background symbolises the agricultural and forested nature of Guyana; The white border symbolises its waters and rivers potential; The golden arrow symbolises Guyana's mineral wealth and its forward thrust; The black border, the endurance that will sustain the golden arrow's forward thrust into the future; The red triangle symbolises the zeal and the dynamic task of nation building, which lies before our young and independent country.

National Flower: Victoria Amazonica.   Photo: H Chan

# National Anthem of Guyana

*Words by A.L. Luker*

R.C.G. Potter

Dear land of Guy-a-na, of riv-ers and plains, made rich by the sun—shine and lush by the rains, Set gem—like and fair be-tween moun-tains and sea, Your chil-dren sa-lute you, dear land of the free.

## MAIN CITY, TOWNS & POPULATIONS (approx.)

Georgetown (capital) – 170,000

Linden (Demerara) – 30,000

New Amsterdam (Berbice) – 20,000

Rose Hall (Berbice) – 8,000

Anna Regina (Essequibo) – 3,000

## ADMINISTRATIVE DIVISIONS (ten regions)

Barima-Waini (Region 1)

Pomeroon-Supenaam (Region 2)

Essequibo Islands-West Demerara (Region 3)

Demerara-Mahaica (Region 4)

Mahaica-Berbice (Region 5)

East Berbice-Corentyne (Region 6)

Cuyuni-Mazaruni (Region 7)

Potaro-Siparuni (Region 8)

Upper Takutu-Upper Essequibo (Region 9)

Upper Demerara-Berbice (Region 10)

## INDEPENDENCE: 26 May 1966 (from Great Britain)

## MEMBERSHIP OF INTERNATIONAL ORGANISATIONS

Caribbean Community and Common Market (CARICOM)

Caribbean Development Bank (CDB)

Group of 77

Group of African Caribbean and Pacific (ACP) countries

South American Community of Nations / Rio Group

Inter-American Development Bank (IDB)

International Monetary Fund (IMF)

Organization of American States (OAS)

The World Bank

Treaty of Amazonian Co-operation

United Nations (UN)

World Trade Organisation (WTO)

International Centre for the Settlement of Investment Disputes (ICSID)

World Intellectual Property Organization (WIPO)

## TRADE AGREEMENTS

Caribbean Single Market & Economy / CARICOM

CARICOM – Colombia

CARICOM – Costa Rica

CARICOM – Cuba

CARICOM – Dominican Republic

CARICOM – Venezuela, Argentina, Brazil, People's Republic of China, Turkey and Venezuela

## PREFERENTIAL TRADE ARRANGEMENTS

EU African, Caribbean and Pacific (ACP) Agreement

US Caribbean Trade Partnership (CTP) previously Caribbean Basin Initiative (CBI)

CARIBCAN (Canada)

## NATIONAL ANTHEM

Dear Land of Guyana, of rivers and plains
Made rich by the sunshine and lush by the rains
Set gem-like and fair between mountains and sea –
Your children salute you, dear land of the free.

Green Land of Guyana, our heroes of yore,
Both bondsmen and free, laid their bones on your shore;
This soil so they hallowed, and from them are we
All sons of one mother, Guyana the free.

Great Land of Guyana, diverse though our strains,
We are born of their sacrifice, heirs of their pains;
And ours is the glory their eyes did not see –
One land of six peoples, united and free.

Dear Land of Guyana, to you will we give
Our homage, our service, each day that we live
God guard you, great Mother, and make us to be
More worthy our heritage – land of the free.

National Bird: Canje pheasant.   Photo: RJ Fernades

# The Song of Guyana's Children

*Words and Music by W. Hawley-Bryant*

## THE SONG OF GUYANA'S CHILDREN

Born in the land of the mighty
Roraima,
Land of great rivers and far stretching
sea;
So like the mountain, the sea and the
river
Great, wide and deep in our lives
would we be;

Chorus:

Onward, upward, may we ever go
Day by day in strength and beauty
grow,
Till at length we each of us may show,
What Guyana's sons and daughters
can be.

Born in the land of Kaieteur's shining
splendour
Land of the palm tree, the croton and
fern,
We would possess all the virtues and
graces,
We all the glory of goodness would
learn.

Born in the land where men sought El
Dorado,
Land of the diamond and bright
shining gold,
We would build up by our faith, love
and labour,
God's golden city which never grows
old.

Thus to the land which to us God has
given
May our young lives bring a gift rich
and rare,
Thus, as we grow, may the worth of
Guyana
Shine with a glory beyond all
compare.

**BILATERAL INVESTMENT AGREEMENTS**
People's Republic of China, Cuba, Germany, UK

**DOUBLE TAXATION TREATIES**
Canada
CARICOM countries
United Kingdom

**NATIONAL FLOWER:** Victoria Amazonica (formerly Victoria Regia) Lily

**NATIONAL BIRD:** Canje pheasant (Hoatzin)

**NATIONAL ANIMAL:** Jaguar

**NATIONAL MOTTO:** One people; one nation; one destiny

**NATIONAL HOLIDAYS & CELEBRATIONS**
New Year's Day
Republic Day (23 February 1970)
Mashramani (Mash)
Chinese New Year
Phagwah (Holi)
Youman Nabi
Eid-ul-Fitr
Good Friday
Easter Monday
Labour Day (1 May)
Arrival Day (5 May)
Independence Day (26 May)
Enmore Martyrs' Day (June)
CARICOM Day (July)
Emancipation Day (1 August)
Amerindian Heritage Month (September)
Deepavali (Diwali)
Main Big Lime
Eid-ul-Azah
Christmas Day
Boxing Day

**CLIMATE:** Tropical; hot, humid, moderated by north-east trade winds; two rainy seasons – May to June & mid-November to mid-January

**TIME ZONE:** GMT -4 hours

**NATURAL RESOURCES:** Bauxite, gold, diamonds, hardwood, shrimp, fish

**HIGHEST POINT:** Mount Roraima (2743 m / 9000 ft)

**MAIN RIVERS (Guyana has more than 1500 rivers and over 900 river islands)**
Essequibo River (832 km / 517 miles)
Berbice River (480 km / 298 miles)
Demerara River (367 km / 228 miles)

**MAIN WATERFALLS (Guyana has more than 100 waterfalls)**
Kaieteur Falls (Potaro river – single drop 226m / 741ft)
Orinduik Falls (Ireng river)
Marshall Falls (Mazaruni river)

**INTERNET COUNTRY CODE:** .gy

**TELEPHONE DIALLING CODE:** 592

# COAT OF ARMS

*The design of Guyana's Coat of Arms is interpreted as follows:*

The Amerindian headdress symbolises the indigenous people of Guyana; the two diamonds either side of the headdress represent the country's mining industry; the helmet is the monarchical insignia; the two jaguars, holding a pickaxe, a sugar cane and a stalk of rice, symbolise labour and the country's two main agricultural industries - sugar and rice; the shield (decorated with the national flower, Victoria Amazonica lily) is to protect the nation; the three blue wavy lines represent the many waters of Guyana; the canje pheasant at the bottom of the shield is Guyana's national bird.

National Animal: Jaguar.   Photo: A Holland & G Duncan

# The secret revealed

Welcome to Guyana, land of many waters, the only English-speaking country on the continent of South America and the Caribbean's southernmost state. Surrounded by three neighbours – Spanish-speaking Venezuela, Portuguese-speaking Brazil and Dutch-speaking Suriname – Guyana provides their link to the English-speaking world.

Guyana is a land of contradictions and superlatives. It boasts Kaieteur Falls, the highest single-drop waterfall in the world; one of the largest unexplored and untouched rainforests which comprises over three quarters of the country's 83,000 square miles; and a population, in direct disproportion to its size, of only 750,000 people, representing imports from Africa, India, Europe, China and with its own indigenous people, the Amerindians, who settled here thousands of years ago.

Made famous by Sir Walter Raleigh as the home of the fabled El Dorado, 'Guiana' has been under the control of the Dutch, the French and the British, and for the last forty years by its own people, all in a quest to tap into its vast natural resource of diamonds, gold and bauxite, and as yet unknown bounty, whose history revolves around the growing of sugar cane, that staple of European wealth for nearly five hundred years.

So what is it that makes Guyana such a special place and why has it remained a secret to the rest of the world for so long? The answer lies in its unique magnificence and curious history – the challenges that it has faced over the years as successive political movements have tried to grapple with its unusual combination of

**RIGHT**
Seen here at the Karanambu ranch, the world's largest water lily (*Victoria Amazonica)* is Guyana's national flower. The ranch is located near the Rupununi river in Region 9 (Upper Takutu – Upper Essequibo).

**FACING PAGE**
The waterways of Kurupung.
Photo: I Brierley

After flowing over Kaieteur Falls, the Potaro River makes its way through the rainforest valleys of Kaieteur Gorge.
Photo courtesy Guyana Tourism Authority

FACING PAGE
With more than one hundred waterfalls, Guyana is truly the land of many waters.
Photo: I Brierley

PREVIOUS PAGES 18 & 19
The breathtaking vista of Guyana's north-western region.   Photo: I Brierley

PREVIOUS PAGES 20 & 21
The road to Lethem, on Guyana's south-western border with Brazil, cuts through the savannah.   Photo: RJ Fernandes

fundamental characteristics and found that solutions to its predicaments are sometimes not easy to come by. Could this be paradise, this compelling landscape of breathless beauty and startling power, to which only the truly dedicated and deserving can come to after a long hard search for its ephemeral core? Many who look see only the external image generated by an overzealous media, and miss the true qualities for which Guyana has become renowned; its hospitality, still considered among the finest in the world, its freshness, its unspoiled natural beauty, its contradictory people, curiously both naïve and sophisticated at the same time, and among the most creative and resilient in the world. They miss the sensual energy that pervades its atmosphere and fail to notice that in Guyana the skies seem bluer, the stars seem brighter and the air is blessed with an ambrosial succulence that stirs the senses and lulls the brain into forgetting day to day concerns, as the pace slows and the outside world becomes a distant memory. Few who visit Guyana want to leave and all who have passed through long to come again.

ABOVE
Kurupung Falls.  Photo: I Brierley

RIGHT
The Timberhead Rainforest Resort is
located at Pokerero Creek, which is part
of the Demerara river.  Photo: FotoNatura

PREVIOUS PAGE
Second only to Kaieteur Falls in
popularity, Orinduik Falls is located on
the Ireng river which runs along
Guyana's western border with Brazil.
Photo: RJ Fernandes

That Guyana is special there is no doubt, as anyone who has come here can attest. Almost the size of Britain, Guyana boasts a vast network of rivers, rapids and waterfalls too numerous to catalogue, and in such an impenetrable landscape, for the most part, that only the most enduring have had the chance to lay eyes on many of them.

One starts a journey through this country in Georgetown, a capital city that is a mixture of old world charm and surprising modernity. This is where the contradictions first become apparent in a deceptively simple layout with wooden buildings and thriving greenery and where the historic sits side by side with the contemporary. In this capital can be found St George's Cathedral, the tallest wooden building in the world. It is in Guyana that the Caricom Secretariat, home to the Caribbean region's highest decision-making body, is located.

ABOVE
Local 'water taxi' passengers disembark at the stelling at Stabroek Market.
Photo: I Brierley

RIGHT
Cruise ship passengers embark at John Fernandes Wharf following their visit to Georgetown. Photo: RJ Fernandes

FACING PAGE, TOP
A novel mode of transport for one youngster.   Photo: H Chan

FACING PAGE, BOTTOM
'Lady Northcote' awaiting passengers at the stelling in Parika, a town located near the mouth of the Essequibo river.
Photo: Hansib

PREVIOUS PAGES 28 & 29
The bustling capital city at the mouth of the Demerara river.   Photo: I Brierley

**ABOVE**
The town of Anna Regina, Essequibo, is in Region 2 (Pomeroon – Supenaam).
Photo: I Brierley

**LEFT**
Bananas on sale at the docks in Georgetown.
Photo: H Chan

It is here, in Georgetown, that Guyana's highest concentration of citizens reside. And it is here that sometimes one finds it almost impossible to navigate the intricacies of the bureaucratic maze. This capital city is the nexus from which everything radiates to imprint itself on the sprawling occurrence of regional communities across the vastness that this country represents. A centralised government operating from the capital provides the framework in which the entire composite functions. Most of the population lives on the coastal belt where the fertile, continental soil provides a bounty of native vegetables and fruits and where rice and sugar have been cultivated for hundreds of years. And it is this bounty that has led to Guyana being called "the bread basket of the Caribbean".

Guyana used to be defined by three major counties: Demerara, Essequibo and Berbice until more recently when the administrative regions became the more functional way of describing the country. There are ten administrative regions with their own regional

ABOVE
Main Street is one of many tree-lined avenues which give the capital its 'garden city' feel.   Photo: I Brierley

RIGHT
A coconut estate provides a dramatic backdrop.   Photo: H Chan

FACING PAGE
The inventiveness of youth is no less uncommon in Guyana.   Photo: I Brierley

ABOVE
Constructed between 1858 and 1892, the Sea Wall keeps Georgetown and other coastal settlements protected from Atlantic high tides. The wall, which runs east from the mouth of the Demerara river, is a popular destination for afternoon walks, picnics and, sometimes, bathing.
Photo: H Chan

LEFT
The Guyanese are nothing if not resourceful.   Photo: I Brierley

democratic councils that oversee local affairs. But the major towns are still New Amsterdam in the "ancient county" of Berbice, and Anna Regina in the "Cinderella County" of Essequibo. Other towns of importance are Bartica, Corriverton, Linden and Lethem. At Lethem is the border with Brazil and the point where a bridge that will connect Guyana with Brazil is in the process of construction. This, along with an all-weather road that will be completed in collaboration with the government of Brazil, will change the face of Guyana in a very few years to come.

But Guyana's true beauty and subtle spirit can only be experienced by journeying inland to a lost world that vibrates with a magical energy and holds the secrets to universal deliverance in its yet unexplored bowels. It is here, at Iwokrama, on one million acres dedicated to sustainable living, and presented as a gift to the rest of the world, that untold mysteries are unfolding as we learn more about ways to utilise this world's resources so that they can be preserved for future generations. In Guyana, at Iwokrama, is the laboratory that may well be this earth's salvation as we search for answers to the question of our relationship with nature and our symbiotic interaction with its gifts. Guyana is also home to the giant otter and the largest open-toed sloth, and in Guyana can be found the Arapaima, the world's largest freshwater fish, and one of the world's largest cats, the jaguar.

And Guyana is the tourists' fantasy: that place in their imaginations that they have always wanted to find but could not envision until they arrive and know fulfilment. With numerous rainforest resorts catering to every taste, Guyana is fast becoming the new Mecca for a truly enervating experience. And don't think you will miss the down-to-earth in Guyana, for we love our cricket and over the years have had six Guyanese as captains of the West Indies cricket team. And because gold is so abundant here it is not unusual to find Guyanese sporting a gold tooth or two along with necklaces, earrings and rings of that precious metal. And visitors, too, get the chance to tap into this resource with exquisite pieces to add to their collections at the many jewellery stores around the country.

For those who look only for the real and profound, Guyana presents a *tabula rasa*, a clean slate on which to write your vision of paradise, miraculously transforming the way you view your existence on earth. Visit Guyana and know that you will be forever changed. Stay and be continually transformed. Ours is not an idyll for the feint of heart but a life-changing experience that will leave you renewed. Guyana is on the move and only time will allow her special qualities to be revealed to the world. ■

# So much to do, so much to see

RUSSEL LANCASTER

What to do when you're in Guyana? That question is not easily answered in that it all depends on your tastes. Guyana, for all its size and diversity, is a surprisingly simple place, with quite a lot to do if you know where to look. At the top of the list, of course, is a visit to the vast rainforest, among the largest left in the world, and with a cornucopia of flora and fauna to explore, mighty rivers, teeming rapids, and a host of resorts specifically designed to give you the best of each experience. There are cattle ranches in the Rupununi, country houses on the Essequibo, a rainforest canopy walkway at Iwokrama, to name just a few from the endless selection. And when you finish all that and return to the capital city there are restaurants, nightclubs, art galleries and the theatre, each with its own particular ambience.

Going to a restaurant for dinner is usually the exception rather than the norm for most Guyanese but there are some outstanding eateries nonetheless. The hotels, for the most part, offer dining rooms that are open to the public – foremost among these being The Essequibo Room and Brown's Café at the Le Meridien Pegasus. The Bottle Room at the Cara Lodge (originally Woodbine House that once hosted the Prince of Wales before he was crowned Edward VIII) is another example of fine hotel dining. There is the Sidewalk – an adjunct to the Ariantze hotel – which offers "real" Guyanese food: pepperpot, roti and curry, metem and cook-up rice along with every variety of local fish and fowl. The venue also presents a movie every Tuesday night and live jazz every Thursday night. Its sister restaurant, the Bourbon, is available for private functions and has an *a la carte* menu that really spices things up.

ABOVE
The ruins of Fort Zeelandia, on Fort Island in the mouth of the Essequibo, are a poignant reminder of Guyana's colonial past.   Photo: I Brierley

RIGHT
A thunderous and breathtaking vantage point from which to view Kaieteur Falls.
Photo: Guyana Tourism Authority

FACING PAGE
Guyana's vast rainforests, islands, lakes and mighty rivers are magnificent sights to behold.   Photo: I Brierley

Formerly Victoria Law Court, the High Court in Georgetown was officially opened in 1887.  Photo: I Brierley

Known locally as Brickdam Cathedral, the Cathedral of the Immaculate Conception is the seat of the Catholic faith in Guyana.  Photo: H Chan

Cove & John Ashram in East Coast Demerara.  Photo: H Chan

Other outstanding restaurants include the Dutch Bottle, located in a quaint old Guyanese cottage complete with Demerara shutters and pastiche, which offers a more Mediterranean eating experience. The Upscale restaurant is another place to find good food and entertainment, with its comedy night on Saturdays. Fogarty's Rosebud Café is a convenient place to grab a snack or meal if you're in the city centre, and you can also enjoy halal meals at Hack's Halaal. For a quick cappuccino in a delightful atmosphere, visit Oasis Café, a recent addition to the intimate eateries that are springing up around the city. For fine Chinese food there are a number of choices but those that are truly outstanding are the New Thriving chain of restaurants and the Mei Teng at Buddy's on Sheriff Street, where you can also play pool in Guyana's largest pool hall or dance the night away at their nightclub. You can also enjoy a unique dining experience at the Cellina's out on the sea wall over looking the waters of the Atlantic.

Other nightclubs that stand out are the Club Avalanche on Sheriff Street, El Club Latino on Hadfield Street, Bollywood Club, the Latino Bar at the Le Meridien, and Palm

ABOVE LEFT
Buddy's is a popular night spot in Georgetown which includes a nightclub, pool hall, gym and restaurant.
Photo: I Brierley

FACING PAGE
The Pakarima Mountains in Region 7 (Cuyuni – Mazaruni) create an impressive backdrop to the savannah.
Photo: RJ Fernandes

Court, which is also a restaurant but really comes into its own in the evening. Of course there are the ubiquitous 'rum shops', where locals go almost every day to replenish after a hard days work.

If you're interested in Guyanese art you can take a visit to the Castellani House, the National Gallery of Art, where Guyana's finest artists are on show. Also of note is the Hadfield Foundation Art Gallery that houses an eclectic collection of local artists and craftsmen. Aback of the Hadfield is the Calabash Gift shop, a must-see if you're looking for the unusual and original in Guyanese craftsmanship.

Any visit to Guyana's capital would be lacking without a stop at the Lighthouse in Kingston, the Benab and St George's Cathedral, the tallest wooden building in the world. Other sites of significance are the newly built Caricom Secretariat, the City Hall and Law Courts and the Parliament Building, the seat of the Guyanese legislature. Close by you will find St Andrew's Kirk and Stabroek Market, where it is said you can find anything "from a pin, to any other thing" you might be looking for.

ABOVE
The 'kissing bridge' in Georgetown's
Botanical Gardens is a popular
attraction. The gardens are regularly
visited by more than two hundred
species of bird making the location a
bird-watcher's paradise. The waters are
also home to the West Indian manatee.
Photo: H Chan

RIGHT
Beach volleyball at Splashmin's Fun Park.
Photo: S May

FACING PAGE
New Amsterdam in Berbice.  Photo: I Brierley

If you're going to journey outside of Georgetown, there is still much to see and do. In New Amsterdam there are discos and eateries of top class standard and the Canje Bridge. In Essequibo, visit the hot and cold lakes, the Bartica Regatta (which comes around every Easter), or the Linden Town Day and Rupununi Rodeo.

However, a trip to Guyana is not complete without visiting Kaieteur Falls, or any of the country's many spectacular waterfalls. Or maybe you just want to spend the day at Splashmin's Fun Park, Guyana's first water and entertainment facility, or visit any number of creeks where local families congregate on the weekends for picnics and parties.

The options are endless and the hospitality is renowned. It is said that if you drink creek water and eat labba, you'll always come back to Guyana. Whether you are an adventurous eco-tourist or simply wish to take a break from the daily grind, Guyana is here for your enjoyment and relaxation. ■

# Green heart of the nation

DAMIAN FERNANDES

Photo: A Bayney

Photo: R Sam

**ABOVE**
Timber and thatched accommodation at the Iwokrama International Centre.

If Guyana's true riches are its flora and fauna, then the Iwokrama Forest would be its El Dorado. Occupying approximately two percent of Guyana's landmass, the forest is the country's largest protected area and is geographically situated in the green heart of Guyana.

The reserve, and the adjacent North Rupununi wetlands, together represent an area of worldwide importance in many respects. The Iwokrama Forest plays host to a global, ten-year-old experiment in sustainable rainforest development. This concept was first presented to the international community in 1989 and was envisioned as a demonstration site for the effective conservation and sustainable use of tropical rainforests.

The Iwokrama Forest has two zones: a wilderness preserve, and a sustainable utilisation area. The latter allows for sustainable use activities, conservation and evaluation of the impacts of such activities on an intact rainforest.

Iwokrama is managed by the Iwokrama International Centre, which has worked since 1996 to develop pioneering methods for conservation and development. Since its inception, the centre has also worked closely with local communities in order to develop community-based 'green' businesses. This has included the harvesting of aquarium fish, the production of honey and crabwood oil and the sale of locally-made, indigenous crafts. The organisation is also in partnership with the local communities with the aim of developing and promoting the area's potential as a leading eco-tourism destination. A key feature in this development is the fact that Iwokrama has one of South America's few canopy walkways that is dedicated to tourism. At thirty metres high, the walkway gives visitors an unparalleled view of the rainforest canopy and its abundant wildlife.

The Iwokrama Forest is home to unique varieties of flora and fauna, many of which are only found in this part of the world. The area is also one of only two sites in South America where the river systems of the Amazon and the Guiana Shield merge. This occurs in the flooded savannahs of the North Rupununi and, as a result, the area is blessed with not only Guyanese species, but also remnant populations of Amazonian 'giants' such as the arapaima (the world's largest, scaled freshwater fish), giant river turtles, black caiman and giant otters. The reserve is also considered to have one of the highest recorded densities of jaguar and bat species in the world.

Iwokrama also has special meaning to the local Makushi people – the area's original inhabitants. The mountains feature prominently in local myths and legends and are said to be the home of great deities and spirits. Historically, the rainforests and mountains were also used as a place of refuge from warring Caribs and European slave traders. Today, the Iwokrama Forest represents an important resource area for the survival of the region's sixteen Makushi communities.

The importance of Iwokrama is unquestionable, whether from the perspective of the smallest North Rupununi village or the larger, global community. The centre marked its 10th anniversary in 2006, and continues to be at the leading edge of sustainable development and management of one of the world's few remaining rainforests. Iwokrama is, therefore, more than just Guyana's El Dorado, it is the nation's gift to the world. ∎

**FACING PAGE**
High above the Iwokrama rainforest floor, the canopy walkway provides a rare opportunity to view flora and fauna at close quarters.   Photo: R Thomas

# A multi-faceted Caribbean culture

RUSSEL LANCASTER

How do you define the culture of Guyana? By what yardstick do you measure the way a people live their lives? Guyanese are a curiously individual group with an original and creative way of connecting with life. Spirituality plays an important role in the lives of the vast majority of Guyanese whether they are Christian, Hindu, Muslim, or any other denomination, and because our parents to a large extent determine our religious foundation this contributes in no small measure to the effects of religion on our way of life.

At the other end of the spectrum is the fact that we are Caribbean people with all that presupposes – a people who love to eat, sing, dance and enjoy ourselves at the slightest provocation. With our hot sunny days, palm trees, exotic flowers and bright blue skies it is easy to want to relax and take a drink. And so what has emerged over time is an unexpectedly moralistic society that still likes to unwind and really enjoy itself.

Our history, too, cannot be discounted in this equation, as this has provided the economic and socio-political framework that defines our existence. A colonial backdrop determined how our forebears dealt with their existence and what they passed on to us, so although we've been independent for some forty years, one still feels the influence of having been a British colony. Our distinctive way of speaking, the way we dress, our love of music and our camaraderie, all hearken to earlier days – from pre-colonial times, slavery and indentureship, to the influx of different races and the mingling of their cultures – and contribute to how we see ourselves and behave as a people.

Even our public holidays reflect the multiplicity of cultures – Christmas, Phagwah, Easter, Youmanabi, Eid-ul-Azha, Diwali, all religious holidays. Mashramani, Independence, Indian Arrival Day, Emancipation Day and Caricom Day, holidays that are part of our status as Guyanese and Caribbean people.

ABOVE
Guyanese children at play.   Photo: I Brierley

RIGHT
Stabroek Market stall-holder.   Photo: H Chan

FACING PAGE
The carnival-like celebrations of Mashramani.   Photo: S May

And we like to party, throwing ourselves with gusto into any 'sport', quickly finding food and drink to entertain our friends and guests. We love to have company and our hospitality is legendary. A guest will not arrive at our doors, even an unexpected one, and not be offered something to eat and drink.

Our food is another testament to the cultural mix with cook-up, metem, pepperpot, curry, roti, cassava bread, chowmein, fried rice and garlic pork all coming from different ethnic sources. We all share these foods and find ways to make them our own. Guyanese as a whole do not eat out too much except for special occasions, but ubiquitous Chinese restaurants do a thriving business for those who want a tasty and inexpensive meal.

And we love our cricket, usually leaving work, school or any other important function to find a seat in the cricket ground where we will soon be comparing statistics with the person next to us even though we've only just met. Our general knowledge

TOP
The journey home from school.
Photo: I Brierley

ABOVE
A colourful display during the Hindu festival of Phagwah.
Photo: I Brierley

ABOVE LEFT
The sea wall is an ideal vantage point from which to view the Atlantic.   Photo: N May

FACING PAGE
Phagwah celebrations.   Photo: H Chan

ABOVE
Guyanese children of the Waini River in
Region 1 (Barima – Waini). Photo: I Brierley

LEFT
Basket-seller in Georgetown.
Photo: I Brierley

of the game is more emotional than factual, however, and arguments can go on for hours to disclaim some point of order or some arcane fact about a match we never even attended. But that is the way of Guyanese. Philosophic in the extreme as a result of circumstances over which we have little control and which we must live with if we can't or won't leave Guyana.

We love to laugh at ourselves and the rest of our brothers and sisters in the Caribbean since we consider ourselves as part and parcel with that group. Our common history and way of living make us more alike than different and we love all things West Indian – reggae, calypso, soca, mas, chutney – they're all part of our definition of ourselves.

Given these foundations, we're still a chameleon-like people with the ability to imitate and create new personas the minute we step outside our shores. A Guyanese can fit in so quickly in a new environment that if you did not see him arrive you would think that he had always been there. This having been said, Guyanese love their country and even when abroad for many years, long to come home again to experience a little of the closeness they have always felt here. For with all the tensions and struggles, we get along quite well together, with friendships lasting all of a lifetime between people of different backgrounds. Our culture is uniquely ours, and wherever we go we feel that connection to the ephemeral substance that links us. That can never be replaced no matter where we are, and regardless of what happens we know there is no better place in the world. ■

# The Amerindians: First people of Guyana

DR DESREY C. FOX

The Amerindian peoples of present-day Guyana are descendants of the first settlers who lived in the region approximately 12,000 years prior to the arrival of the first European settlers in 1492. In those early days, there were many Amerindian nations – Trios, Tarumas, Miyonggongs, Piyanogottos, Atorads, Taurepang and Kamarakoto among others. Many of these groups became extinct or fled from the region for a number of reasons such as illnesses contracted through European contact; inter-tribal wars; and forced migration by European missionaries. A great many also left because they resented colonial rule that allowed 'free nation' status to some and categorised others as slaves. The so-called free nations were the Arawaks, Akawaios, Caribs and Warraus, and the Dutch colonisers permitted them to enslave all other Amerindian groups. It was by this route that the first slave plantations operated during early colonisation. Amerindians were immediately accessible and by establishing a system to enslave them, and using their own people to make this possible, the Dutch were able to institute a structure that would last for generations.

Early Amerindian rock carvings. Photo: I Brierley

Later, after enslaved Africans were brought to the region, Amerindians provided invaluable assistance to the Dutch by helping to quell slave revolts and by recapturing runaway slaves. They also maintained security in the interior and contributed to making 'Guyana' possible by defining the geographical boundaries we know today.

The population of Amerindians in Guyana stands at approximately 70,000. However, this figure is difficult to verify because members of the various communities travel frequently between neighbouring countries and also create satellite communities both close to and far from established villages.

Guyanese Amerindians can be categorised linguistically and anthropologically into three main human and language groups: Arawakan, Cariban and Warrauan. Each of these nations has its own language and they are defined linguistically by the same categories. They also occupy relatively well-defined separate ecological niches that have influenced their distinct cultures.

The Arawak Lokono communities are settled in Region 1 (the largest area populated by Amerindians) with over 20,000 people consisting of Arawak, Carib and Warrau. The Arawaks alone are estimated to make up 15,500 of this number and are located in the Santa Rosa/Moruca sub-region.

The 7,000 members of the Wapishana community speak a language of the same name and are settled in the South Rupununi savannahs occupying lands from north to south Guyana.

The Cariban peoples, consisting of the Carib (Kari'na) and also known as the Galibi and Kalina, are concentrated in the North West District, the coastal river-heads and the coastal lowland forest. They number up to 4,000 and live in predominantly wetland forest areas.

The Akawaio (Ka'pong) are settled in the lowland and upland forests and the Mazaruni River basin and number up to 6,000. The Akawaio language is spoken within these communities while English serves as a second language and is used for instruction in schools.

The members of the Patamuna community number up to 5,000 and are located in the upland savannahs in the Pakaraima Mountains and Monkey Mountain.

The Arekuna (Pemong) peoples have communities located in the upland forested areas. Their main settlement is the border village of Paruima, which is closer to Venezuela than it is to Kamarang, the main administrative centre of the Upper Mazaruni District (Region 7).

The Makushi communities are located in the North Rupununi savannahs and they number over 7,750. Their main villages include Katoka, Yakarinta, Massara, Annai, Surama and Carasabai.

The Wai Wai community has established homelands in the extreme south of Guyana, in the dense tropical lowland forests of the Upper Essequibo River. They number just over 200 people located mainly in two villages, Masakenari and Para Bara.

The Warrau settlements are largely in the coastal swamps of the north-west region and include mixed communities of both Caribs and Arawaks. Their population stands at around 5,000.

It is the geographical location that defines these Amerindian communities: the Arawak Lokono, Carib and Warrau are coastal peoples; the Makushi, Arekuna and Wapishana are savannah peoples; and the Akawaio and Patamuna are highland/rainforest peoples.

Amerindian cultures are not homogenous and while they share many common traits they also have distinct differences. For instance, it is known that the staple food of the Amerindians is cassava bread and pepperpot. However, not all groups prepare it the same way and the end result is very distinctive and tribally specific.

The savannah peoples, such as the Wapishana and Makushi, prefer to use farine as the main staple rather than cassava bread because they consider it to be more filling and lasts longer.

The coastal groups, such as the Warrau and the Carib, use cassava bread but do not know how to make farine. The Arawaks are also fond of cassava bread but depend equally on coastal Guyanese foods and are also not knowledgeable about making farine. The Akawaio, Patamunaand and Wai Wai favour cassava bread over farine.

The 'tuma' pot (or pepperpot) is made in several different ways by varying Amerindian peoples. While the basic principle of water, pepper, meat, herbs, salt and cassareep is used, the variation on how to make the tuma remains peculiar to each group. The pepperpot that is made by Amerindians is very different to the coastal variety since spices, clove and ginger are never added to the Amerindian tuma. Instead, a lot of hot peppers are used with meat or fish and cassareep that is half-boiled. The thick dark cassareep, like that sold on the coastlands, is only used when travelling on long journeys since it has a longer shelf life.

Amerindians, today, live semi-traditional lifestyles in communal settlements that are no longer nomadic. They live in territories that are politically defined and, in many cases, on titled land that they own as a group. The political structures of these communities are linked to the local government system and village chiefs and their councillors are elected to serve for five years.

Subsistence farming guarantees the supply of food and, in most cases, the crops planted are cassava, plantain, bananas, sweet potatoes, dasheen, eddoes and yams. Some areas attempt to plant cash crops to earn money but this is often

Today's Amerindian peoples live throughout Guyana.  Photo: I Brierley

difficult because of lack of transportation, access to banks and bank loans and a stable, ready market for produce.

Guyana has some of the most educated Amerindians in the region and many now leave their communities to pursue higher education at the University of Guyana and Cyril Potter College of Education. In addition, the Hinterland Scholarship, initiated by the government, provides the opportunity for Amerindian children to attend some of the top secondary schools in Georgetown.

The Amerindian presence has been the longest one in Guyana and, therefore, as the indigenous people, they have helped to forge a nation out of an untamed land to create the foundation of what is now Guyana. As the communities interact more and more with other cultures they will redefine themselves and find new roles in this multicultural and pluralistic society.

# WORKING TOWARDS LONG TERM CONSERVATION

FOUNDED IN 2000 WITH THE MANDATE TO EFFECT SEA turtle conservation in the Shell Beach area, the Guyana Marine Turtle Conservation Society (GMTCS) realised that in order to achieve long term conservation this could not be accomplished by focusing on species conservation alone. It was mandatory that the sustainable livelihoods of the local communities, who depended on the utilisation of the natural resources in the area, should also be addressed. Therefore, in order to deal with this issue the GMTCS designed a distinctive shell-shaped label which was easily identified by most Guyanese with the Shell Beach area – best known for the four species of sea turtles that nest there each year.

The area, which is of high global importance, is a priority site for protected area status and is becoming equally well known for its organic status as it is officially designated by the government of Guyana as the country's organic region. The combination of these two unique attributes gave birth to the shell-shaped North West Organics label. Specifically

**CRABWOOD SOAP** These handmade soaps are used for a range of treatments from acne, most fungal disorders (including mange in dogs) and it is also an excellent shaving soap.

developed for products produced by north-west communities within and adjacent to the proposed Shell Beach Protected Area, communities have to meet strict quality control requirements in order for their products to earn this distinctive label. GMTCS believes in fair trade and is complying with such measures that ensure equitable distribution of benefits to the indigenous communities that produce these fine products. North West Organics products are free of chemicals and preservatives, are 100 percent organic and contribute significantly to the sustainable livelihoods of the local communities as well as conservation in the north-west of Guyana.

The Guyana Marine Turtle Conservation Society has formed conservation partnerships with retail outlets and supermarkets in Georgetown which play an invaluable role in making these organic products readily available to those customers with a discerning taste and need for healthy living and whose purchase of these fine products saves more than trees.

With the generous support of the British High Commission plans are underway to assist the farmers of Region 1 to work towards group certification of their products which, once achieved, will assist in sourcing regional and international markets. The recent trend of linking agroforestry and tourism has tremendous potential for these organic farmers. A customised tour, which combines the sea turtle watching experience with a tour of an organic cocoa plantation and a refreshing dip in the Hosororro waterfalls, which is conveniently located in the midst of the plantation, has already won accolades from first-time visitors. More information can be obtained from www.gmtcs.org.gy

ANNETTE ARJOON

**ORGANIC COCOA** Cultivated in cocoa plantations on the Hosororo hillsides, the organic cocoa, right, is also being supplied to the Prince of Wales Trust and is used in the manufacture of his Duchy Originals products. Guyana's newest café, the Oasis, has demonstrated its commitment to conservation initiatives by creating a fine organic chocolate cake from the cocoa and handmade Hosororro truffles.

# The wonders of the Kanuku Mountains

AJAY BAKSH

It is a sanctuary of life, a home to many and a mother to some; beautiful and diverse. The mighty Kanuku Mountains, located in the south-western part of Guyana in Region 9, cuts through the Rupununi and separates the north from the south like an imposing, impenetrable fort – a fort that represents one of the last remaining wilderness areas on earth. A vast area of pristine beauty, it stretches for one hundred kilometres from east to west, and fifty kilometres north to south. This 5000 sq km mountain range, with peaks as high as 1000 metres, is home to an abundant diversity of wildlife.

Larger than many Caribbean islands, the "blue mountains" of the savannah are seen as a mother to the people of the region who depend on the "Kanukus" for their existence.

For over 150 years, naturalists have been visiting the Kanuku Mountains, and the area has been recognised as one of the most biologically diverse regions in Guyana with habitats such as gallery forests, lowland forests and montane evergreen forests. Vibrant and abundant with life, the mountains are home to more than 350 species of bird – around fifty percent of all the species found in Guyana. Eighty percent of all of the species of

**BELOW**
The Rupununi in Region 9 (Upper Takutu – Upper Essequibo) is a vast area in the south-west of Guyana that comprises dry lands, sparse trees, termite mounds and wooded hills . The savannah is divided into North and South Rupununi by the Kanuku Mountains which rise to form a spectacular backdrop to the landscape. It is home to a number of Amerindian villages and a few large cattle ranches that were established in the 19th century.
Photo courtesy Guyana Tourism Authority

mammals found in Guyana can also be found there. The variation in landscape and the vast amount of resources have allowed several of the larger species of wild animals to thrive, including those that have disappeared from other regions. At least five of the South American 'giants' live in the Kanuku Mountains: the harpy eagle, black caiman, giant river otter, arapaima fish and the giant anteater.

During the Rapid Assessment Programme, conducted in 2001, it was also documented that, "The Rupununi Basin maintains one of the richest fish faunas on earth and . . . the Kwitaro and Rewa Rivers follow this trend. Plant communities here were confirmed to be among the most diverse in Guyana and show little sign of human disturbance."

The land and other resources there have been watched over for centuries by some of Guyana's first peoples – the Macushi and Wapishana – and they have made the Kanukus their home, caring and wisely using the resources in the traditional way. However, today there are several threats that face the region, putting a strain on the same resources that were once so abundant. Although the area is relatively well preserved, pressures do exist and may increase with emerging changes in land use.

CLOCKWISE FROM TOP LEFT
Traditional Amerindian fishing methods are often the most effective.
Photo: H Castro/CI

Balata latex is bled from the bulletwood tree by cutting channels into the bark.
Photo: RJ Fernandes

The rubber-like balata is fashioned into many objects such as animals and ornaments depicting traditional Amerindian settings.    Photo: I Brierley

Dotted throughout the savannah, termite nests can reach a height of around 2.5 metres (8 ft).    Photo: A Baksh/CI

In recognition of the global biodiversity value and the emerging threats, the Kanuku Mountains have been placed under legal protection by the government of Guyana. Conservation International Guyana (CIG) is the lead agency to work with the government towards achieving national consensus for establishing the mountains as a protected area. For the last five years, CIG has been engaging the relevant stakeholders, including the nearby communities and the peoples of the region, to establish the Kanuku Mountains as a protected area. This also involves maintaining and respecting the rights and traditions of the people and striking a balance between sustainable use and conservation.

The organisation has been assisting local communities (around 16,000 residents) to develop non-timber forest industries such as the production of balata craft pieces which are made from the balata latex of the bulletwood tree. As a result of this venture the community group, the Nappi Balata Artisans, was established and it has now entered the mainstream of Guyanese businesses and is providing direct economic benefit to the region. CIG continues to work with these communities and is in the process of identifying other sustainable enterprises. ■

# The African presence: Rocks upon which Guyana was built

CHRISTOBEL HUGHES

The presence of Africans in Guyana begins in the first half of the seventeenth century when a Charter was issued to the Dutch West India Company in 1621 to supply slaves from Africa. However, it was not until 1665-6, after the expulsion of the Dutch from Brazil, that the Dutch West India Company threw open the Guiana coast by inviting settlers to inhabit the area (with their slaves) on condition that they purchased their supplies from, and traded their produce in, Zeeland, a western province of The Netherlands.

The Dutch shifted their trade with the Amerindians from tobacco to sugar after tobacco prices dropped on the international market due to stiff competition from British colonies in Virginia and Maryland. With their experience in planting sugar in Brazil and their monopoly of the slave trade, the Dutch settled in Essequibo and Berbice. Plantations and infrastructure such as canals (which were constructed using slave labour) became the foundation on which a prosperous industry would rely for more than four hundred years. In the mid-1600s, some settlements were exporting as much as 74,000 pounds of sugar. From here on, the industry became inextricably linked with slavery.

For the next two and a half centuries, the African presence in Guyana was solely defined by its involvement in the sugar industry. Little credit has been given for the contribution that African people have made towards the overall development of the colony and, ultimately, Guyana as a nation. In the words of Isaac Charles of Mahaica: "The entire New World was built on the blood, sweat and tears of the African slaves. We were the beasts of burden. We were the pioneers and trail blazers, both in the North and South America."

He noted that long before Emancipation in 1838, the Africans had driven back the sea, had cleared, drained and reclaimed some 15,000 miles of swamp and forest. In short, all the fields on which the sugar estates are now based were cleared, drained and irrigated by slave labour before 1834.

Writing in 1948, the Venn Commission estimated that each square mile of cane cultivation involved the provision of forty-nine miles of drainage canals and ditches, and sixteen miles of higher-level waterways for transport irrigation. This meant that African slave labour moved millions of tons of clay, with only shovels and bare hands, to build the coastal plantations. The so-called 'Wilde Coast' was tamed and humanised by the African worker.

Although handsomely rewarded for their loss of 'property' (the slaves) after Emancipation in 1838, the plantation owners demanded a four-year apprenticeship period during which former slaves were compelled to supply free labour to their former masters. Having gained their physical freedom, the former slaves had to struggle for their economic and political freedom as well.

The period following Emancipation (1838 to 1853) has been described as one of the most remarkable in Guyanese history. The former slaves, who desired nothing more than to quit the estates, were able to accumulate funds earned during apprenticeship to purchase abandoned estates. This period saw the establishment of 'co-operative villages'. Northbrook

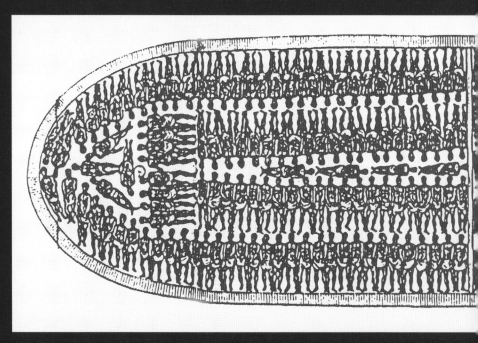

Illustration shows how captured Africans were shipped to the colonies.

(later re-named Victoria) was acquired in 1839 and became the first co-operative village. A group of around fifty or sixty former slaves would pool their resources and nominate one or two of their number to purchase the estate. They would divide the land among themselves – a house lot and a portion of farmland. It was on the basis of these democratically organised villages that the present system of land government is built. By 1840, four such estates had been established.

The outcome of the African labour strikes in 1842 and 1847 gave impetus to further land purchases on the part of the former slaves although on a smaller scale. The strikes also intensified the planters' efforts to prevent the former slaves, particularly those with the necessary financial power, from squatting on Crown lands or moving to the interior. In order for sugar to survive new tactics had to be devised and thus the nineteenth century saw the introduction of more and more restrictive legislation to control the labour market and the importation of larger and larger numbers of indentured immigrants to work on the estates. It is interesting to note that at the time of Emancipation there were 85,000 slaves in Guyana, and by 1917 there were more than 340,000 immigrants of whom over 236,000 were East Indians, over 14,000 were Chinese, more than 31,000 were Portuguese and over 55,000 were 'free Africans' from Africa and other parts of the West Indies. All, it is worth noting, were brought in to work on the estates that were prepared and cultivated by Africans three centuries earlier.

As slaves, Africans could not maintain their culture, but at the same time could not stifle their need to express themselves in a way that recalled their ancestry. The emergence of the 'masquerade' was an attempt to marry tradition with the experiences of slavery – reworking ancestral traditions while poking subtle fun at the plantocracy. Drumming was outlawed but still secretly practiced and used to transmit messages from one plantation to the next.

In the sixty years after slavery was abolished, it was a battle for economic survival and self-preservation. Despite all the obstacles and lack of credit, the Africans found outlets for their creativity. They grasped education and became the professionals, teachers, village leaders, nurses, civil servants, doctors, lawyers and ministers of religion. They pioneered the mining and forest industries and agitated for reform of the political system.

The efforts of Hubert Nathaniel Critchlow, who advocated the rights of workers and led the struggle for their empowerment, earned him the title of "Father of Trade Unionism in the Caribbean".

The beginning of the twentieth century saw the emergence of a fledgling African Guyanese culture. Folk songs and dancing began to have new meaning. Out of the collective memory, African rituals and festivals, such as Queh Queh, Obeah and Emancipation Day, began to be celebrated and practiced. Creole sayings and proverbs were more widely used and Africans began using African names. Within a century of freedom, Black poetry, plays and novels were being published in Guyana. Despite the centuries of subjugation and humiliation, the African continues to make significant contributions to life in Guyana.

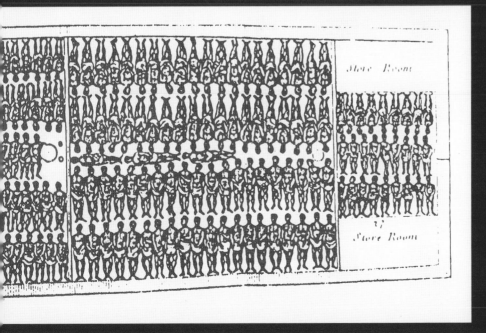

# Indian arrival: Labour to leaders

TOTA MANGAR

For over three quarters of a century Indian indentured labourers were exported from the Indian sub-continent to the West Indian colonies ostensibly to fill the void created by the mass exodus of former slaves from the plantations following the abolition of slavery and, more so, the premature termination of the apprenticeship scheme in 1838.

This influx into the Caribbean in the post-emancipation period of the nineteenth and twentieth centuries was only one segment of a wider movement of Indian labour to other parts of the world including Mauritius, Sri Lanka (formerly Ceylon), Fiji, the Strait Settlements, Natal and other parts of the African continent. Overall, where the English-speaking Caribbean is concerned, substantial numbers of indentured Indians were imported. Based on statistical evidence, Guyana (formerly British Guiana) was the recipient of 239,909 Indian immigrants up to 1917; Trinidad 143,939; Jamaica 36,412; Grenada 3,033; St. Vincent 2,472; St. Lucia 4,354; and St. Kitts 337. In addition, the non-English speaking Caribbean also imported Indian indentured labourers. For example, in the French colonies (now overseas departments) Martinique received 25,509; Guadeloupe 45,844 and French Guiana 19,276. Suriname, while under Dutch rule, imported 35,501 immigrants.

The importation of indentured labourers from the Indian sub-continent was part of the continuing search for a reliable labour force to meet the needs of the powerful plantocracy. As far as Guyana is concerned, the 'Gladstone Experiment' proved to be the basis of Indian immigration. John Gladstone (father of British liberal statesman, William Gladstone) was the proprietor of two West Demerara estates – Vreed-en-Hoop and Vreed-en-Stein – at precisely the time when the planters were beginning to experience an acute labour shortage as a consequence of the mass withdrawal of slaves from plantation labour during this period of "crisis, experimentation and change" in the 1830s. Gladstone wrote to the Calcutta recruiting firm, Gillanders, Arbutnot and

Indian indentured labourers.

Company enquiring about the possibility of obtaining Indian immigrants for his estates. The firm's prompt reply was that it envisaged no recruiting problems and that Indians were already in service in another British colony, Mauritius. Subsequently, Gladstone received permission for his scheme from both the Colonial Office and the Board of Control of the East India Company.

The first group of Indian indentured labourers arrived in Guyana on board the steamships 'Whitby' and 'Hesperus' on 5th May 1838.

This initial experiment was not confined to Gladstone's two estates but included the plantations of Highbury and Waterloo in Berbice, Bell View in West Bank Demerara and Anna Regina on the Essequibo coast.

Since their arrival in British Guiana in 1838, Indian labourers have played a significant role in the survival of the sugar industry right up to the twenty-first century. The vast majority of the workforce is Indian-Guyanese and sugar remains one of the most important foreign exchange earners in the country in the face of grave global changes. Guyanese of Indian origin are also largely responsible for the prominence of Guyana's rice industry. The indentured labourers in the late nineteenth and early twentieth centuries began to cultivate rice on a large scale and this was linked to the most exclusive Indian village settlements which emerged

Since the early 1970s, K Rahaman & Sons has supplied spare parts for private, industrial and agricultural vehicles. Dolly Rahaman (pictured) now manages the family business.   Photo: H Chan

at the time. They were integrally involved in cattle-rearing, milk-selling and cash crop cultivation.

Ever since the 1880s, Indian immigrants have also displayed high occupational profiles in a number of off-plantation activities including cab drivers, barbers, tailors, carpenters, boat-builders, charcoal-makers, goldsmiths, porters, small-scale manufacturers and fishermen.

Today, Guyanese of Indian origin are found in every sphere of activity including business, the professional class, politics and trade unions. They have ensured that there is a rich cultural heritage in the multi-cultural and pluralistic society that is Guyana. Indian values, customs and traditions have survived over the years. They brought with them their main religions: Hinduism and Islam. Approximately 83 percent of the immigrants were Hindus while fourteen percent were Muslims. The remaining three percent were Christians. Mosques and temples began to dot the coastal landscape from the late nineteenth century.

Traditional Indian wear, such as the shalwar, sari, kurta and dhoti, plays an important role in the cultural fabric. And the rituals of Indian marriage ceremonies and the importance of the extended family have been maintained with very few changes. Indian music, songs, films and art forms have taken root in Guyanese society; Indian foods, such as roti, puri, curry, dhal, polouri, bara, keer and vegetable dishes, are regularly consumed throughout the whole of Guyanese society.

Indian festivals are widely celebrated and include Phagwah, Deepavali (Festival of Lights), Ramnoumi, Shiv-Ratri, Youman Nabi, Eid-ul-Azha and Eid-ul-Fitr. Four of these festivals are now national holidays, a testimony to their significance and widespread influence. Hindus and Muslims regularly perform their religious or thanksgiving ceremonies. Within the Hindu community this devotion is reflected in the Jhandi and other flags which are displayed outside many homes throughout Guyana.

Indian immigrants and their descendants were able to thrive because of their resilience, determination, customs and traditions, and their commitment to family, which invariably promotes thrift, industry and self-esteem. They continue to make valuable contributions to the overall progress and development of Guyana.

# The Portuguese

SR (PROF.) MARY NOEL MENEZES

On 3rd May 1835, the ship 'Louisa Baillie' docked in Demerara with forty immigrants from Madeira onboard, bound for work on British Guiana's sugar plantations. They came in response to the approaching abolition of slavery and subsequent labour shortages.

However, by 1845, most of the Portuguese had moved off the plantations and had bought small plots of land and moved into the huckster and retail trades.

In the early years, it was mainly in the rum trade that the Portuguese made their mark. By 1852, more than three quarters of the country's retail rum shops were owned by the Portuguese and they retained that monopoly well into the twentieth century. The end of the 1860s and the 1870s saw the Portuguese well entrenched in the business community. Apart from being property owners, they were merchants, shop owners, importers, iron mongers, ship chandlers, leather merchants, boot and shoe makers, saddlers, coach-builders, timber merchants, brick makers, cattle owners, pork-knockers, charcoal dealers, bakers and photographers.

In 1858, the number of Portuguese in British Guiana was approximately 35,000, of which almost all were Catholic. They brought not only their agricultural expertise but their faith as well. The Madeirans were profoundly religious, and their festas were celebrated with joyful abandon and with much pomp and splendour. With the arrival of the Portuguese-speaking priests the Catholic Church advanced rapidly. In 1861, they built the Sacred Heart Church in Georgetown as well as other churches along the East Coast and East Bank, in Demerara and Essequibo. Of all the religious customs brought over by the Portuguese, the Christmas Novena continues to hold sway among Catholic Guyanese of every ethnic origin. Another Madeiran custom was the establishment of confraternities, guilds and societies for the relief of widows, orphans, the sick, the unemployed, the elderly and the imprisoned as well as for the education of the children of their members.

The Portuguese held on to their language throughout the nineteenth century and a number of Portuguese newspapers kept the community in touch with events in Madeira and in the colony. Portuguese schools were established for both boys and girls. Together with other amateur and professional groups the Portuguese entered the cultural stream of music and drama in British Guiana society. Plays and concerts were held at the Assembly Rooms and at the Philharmonic Hall.

The Portuguese were also prominent in the world of sports – boxing, cricket, cycling, rugby, football, tennis, hockey, racing and rowing. In 1898, the Portuguese formed the first cycling club, The Vasco da Gama Cycling Club. In 1952, the Portuguese Club was founded and nurtured famous tennis players of the day. Indeed, the Portuguese worked hard in their business world but they also played hard.

However much the Portuguese added to the cultural dimension, their entry into the political field took much longer. First, there was the language barrier, secondly, the majority of the Portuguese men were not naturalised British subjects, and thirdly, the government constantly cautioned the Portuguese "not to meddle with politics" but to stick to their business. Not until 1906 did the Portuguese run for office, with F.I. Dias and J.P. Santos winning seats in the Court of Policy and Combined Court. However, although the Portuguese had gained a political foothold, they were not at all welcomed with open arms into the colonial government.

By the turn of the century, the Portuguese had created their own middle and upper classes, but they were never accepted into the echelons of white European society, even though they were European. The rapid economic progress of the Portuguese, their strong adherence to the Catholic faith and their clannishness bred respect but never whole-hearted acceptance among the population in either the nineteenth or twentieth centuries. In the 1960s and 1970s, the Portuguese suffered even more discrimination and many left Guyana in search of greener pastures.

# The Chinese

MARJORIE KIRKPATRICK

A walk down any busy street or shopping centre in Georgetown would bring you into contact with "local Chinese". These are the descendants of the original Chinese who came to British Guiana as indentured labourers between 1853 and 1879.

The Chinese brought with them their love of food and ability to cook, so Chinese restaurants can be found on almost every block in the capital and in most country districts. Most of these restaurants are now run by newcomers from mainland China. In transporting their culinary expertise they transformed national foods found in Guyana by flavouring them with rum and ginger. In the case of the 'Chinee cake', the original was the Chinese bean cake, 'towsa peng', but with its local incarnation it was made with black-eyed peas. They made 'ham choy' (preserved greens) with the local mustard plant that they grew here and 'salted egg' with the local duck eggs, to replace the 'hundred-year egg'. Today, Chinese fare has been taken to new heights with the establishment of high quality eateries. The New Thriving chain has become a place of choice for Guyanese celebrations.

Over the years, the Chinese have adapted to the English customs through churches like St Saviour's Parish Church,

Traditional lion dance to herald Chinese new year.

originally known as the 'Chinese Church', when it was consecrated in 1874, as part of the parish of St Phillip's in Georgetown.

Through the Chinese Sports Club, which became the Cosmos Sports Club, and later acquired by the Guyana Motor Racing Club, Chinese boys and girls excelled at lawn tennis and table tennis giving Guyana the West Indies Championship on several occasions. Hockey was another popular sport and in the 1960s and 70s the National Team was made up almost entirely of players of Chinese origin.

Through the British Educational system, members of Guyana's Chinese community were able to make their mark as scholars, teachers, university professors, lawyers, doctors, dentists, farmers, shopkeepers, business leaders and political leaders. Many of the international businesses in Guyana are managed by Chinese.

The only Chinese customs that have withstood the test of time are practiced by individual families: wedding customs, the hospitality of the people and the celebration of any event whatsoever, by a feast of Chinese foods. Recently, with the arrival of newcomers from China, the Spring Festival (the Chinese New Year) has been making a comeback complete with lion dance and festive dinner. This has raised the consciousness of those of Chinese ancestry and allowed other Guyanese to appreciate aspects of Chinese culture that had slipped away over time.

Chinese restaurant in the heart of a busy Georgetown market.   Photo: H Chan

# Cultural glimpses of Guyana

ALLAN FENTY

Guyana's diverse heritage is a rich blend of history, beliefs and traditions that are drawn from the descendants of many nations. First came the Amerindians, who arrived from Mongolia via North and Central America. The Europeans came from Holland, Portugal, Britain, France and Spain in search of El Dorado, the mythical city of gold. Later, the Dutch and British colonisers, above all, were to bring enslaved Africans to work on the sugar plantations, followed by indentured Portuguese, Indian and Chinese labourers.

It is from that diversity of settlers that the Guyanese nation evolved. Original customs and traditions would adapt over the years to create a new culture that is uniquely Guyanese.

## FOLK FIGURES AND BELIEFS

The Amerindians, being the country's first inhabitants, can claim to have the more original and indigenous folk spirits, beliefs and customs. They also gave the country its name – 'Guiana', "the land of many waters". They tell tales of the deadly river monster, 'Massacouraman', a human-like, hairy monster that rips out human hearts and takes his victims under hinterland waters. 'Bush Dai-Dai' and the spirit of 'Kanaima' are also from Amerindian lore. 'Bacoo' and 'Ole Higue' (destructive, impish spirits) are African in creation whilst the 'Moongazer', 'Sukantie' and 'Churlie' are from the Indian imagination. 'Fairmaids' (or mermaids) and 'Jumbies' (ghosts) belong to all old Guyanese traditions.

Guyanese belief systems cannot be fully described here. They are as diverse, rich, unbelievable, complex and perplexing as those of any other peoples of the world.

## SUPERSTITIONS (that will bring 'bad luck' or 'ghosts')

If you point at funerals (bite your fingers to ward off bad luck); If you don't come indoors backwards at midnight; If you sit on a seat one has just vacated; If you don't put requisite marks on your infant; If one of two pregnant women don't walk with a stick or twig.

Both Guyanese of African and Indian descent had a tradition of Obeah, the black magic/witchcraft belief system that some now claim as religion. Life's problems can all be remedied by Obeah's applications – if you only believe. Love, too, is subject to its categories and stages – the first level being 'Typee'. Men especially are subject to these lovesick behaviours.

## FOOD FOR THOUGHT

Guyana and Guyanese can be justifiably proud that medical science from the more 'developed' societies has exploited many of Guyana's natural resources in the manufacture of drugs and medicines. Curare is a poisonous substance obtained from the plants of Guyana's rainforests, which is used in anaesthetics and antidotes for snakebites.

Guyanese used herbs, flowers, bark, roots and fruits as 'bush medicine' long before alternative medication became known to Europe and North America. For colds, diabetes, heart ailments, frigidity, blood pressure, and liver problems – many ailments could be 'cured' using bush remedies.

Everyday menus, however, feature pepperpot, the meats preserved in casareep, the brew from the bitter cassava ground vegetable. Metemgee is a meal of ground vegetables cooked in coconut milk – with or without meat. Today's Guyanese of all groups savour the Indian roti, the curries and the sweetmeats. Chinese cho-mein and lo-mein (noodles) are as ubiquitous as rice. Guyanese original cuisine is spicy, flavoured and tantalising – like the peoples who created it.

## CELEBRATIONS AND MUSIC

After thirty-six years of being a co-operative republic, Guyana's February Mashramani celebrations, to commemorate that political and constitutional status, now ranks high amongst other national observances. Republic Anniversary events climax on 23rd February with masquerades, floats, costume parades and street parties for adults and younger Guyanese.

Mashramani celebrations.
Photo: S May

Religious holidays have long been made national events – Christmas, Easter, Phagwa, Diwali (Hindu) Youman Nabi and Eid-ul-Azha (Muslim) are celebrated by all who care to, as are Freedom Day (1st August) and Indian Arrival Day (5th May).

Music, of course, drives most celebrations. Whilst the

Calypso King of the World, the Mighty Sparrow, and his Trinidad colleague, Lord Melody, once lived and learnt their craft in the Guyana of the Fifties and Sixties, Bill Rogers gave the world another African-based folk rhythm – shanto. His early tunes caught Caribbean and world attention – Harry Belafonte having to compensate the Guyanese for the use of one of his shantoes.

Decorated for Phagwa.
Photo: L Fanfair

At one time, Guyana's calypsos and steel-band music rivalled Trinidad's. Indian melodies and hybrids produced the Chutney, now borrowed by the Trinidadians. The masquerade beat struggles to survive as American and Jamaican melodies invade modern Guyana. But as soon as one lands in Guyana and goes to the right places, the musical heritage still surfaces, however briefly, and you'll know you're in Guyana!

## ON OTHER THINGS GUYANESE

Guyana has been beset by the malady of deficiency that characterised developing societies in the past. The nation, like too many developing countries, preferred to be shopkeepers, buyers and importers, instead of using the natural resources available to produce, manufacture and make.

Then a few leaders and entrepreneurs came along and showed the way – the way of creativity and innovation with products made in Guyana. Whether it is the greenheart wood of the rainforests, the blacksage shrub, used to clean teeth (later made into dental powder), the "Freshness of a Breeze in a Bottle" – Limacol, a toilet lotion that preceded most of the Western world's moisturisers, Whizz – the Caribbean's pioneering aspirin, or Ferrol Compound for coughs and colds, Guyanese can be proud that they had, indeed, discovered the science and the wisdom of manufacturing.

## OTHER PLACES, OTHER FOODS

The romance of place names in Guyana (the only English-speaking nation in South America) derives from the fact that the names came from the native Guyanese, the Amerindians. The Spanish, Dutch, Portuguese, French and English colonisers all aspired to possess the land, and later the enslaved Africans were brought in, followed by indentured Portuguese, Indians and Chinese, to work the plantations.

The country's name itself "Guyana" is of Amerindian origin, meaning "land of many waters". The era of Dutch colonisation is remembered in names such as De Kindren (the children), Ruimveldt (spacious field) and Blygezight (happy face); the Spanish left Santa Rosa and Imbotero; and the French gave us Mon Repos, Le Repentir (resting place) and La Penitence (the penitent).

English names, of course, from the long, British occupation and rule, abound. Adventure, Aberdeen, Victoria and Georgetown itself, attest to this fact. The long, coastal sea wall, however, was built by the Dutch.

Selling "sweeties".  Photo: H Chan

But the names of old-time cakes and confectionary really capture the imagination, stirred by Guyanese culinary creativity: Sweet bread, coconut biscuit, black cake, coconut roll, jackass collar, tennis roll, salara, white-eye, bull stones and Chinese cakes. The cakes were usually washed down with homemade ginger beer, sorrel, passion fruit juice, mauby or pine drink. "Sweets" or "sweetie", as Guyanese describe confectionery, included sourdrops, butterscotch, tamarind balls, nut cakes, nuttin and giant white peppermints.

And the names of the fish that Guyanese like to eat are even more exotic: hoorie, cuffum, gilbacca, packoo, patwa, hassa, tilapia, kaasie, yarrow and the ubiquitous banga Mary.

# History since European arrival

TOTA C. MANGAR

The provision of exact dates in history is often the subject of a great deal of controversy and in the case of Guyana's earliest history this is no exception. In any event it is perhaps true to say that somewhere around the 1570s non-Spanish Europeans began to take an increasing interest in exploring the Guianas as part of their challenge to Spain's New World monopoly. Moreover in 1581 the Netherlands renounced its allegiance to Spain and this act of defiance impelled her to investigate and explore trading opportunities in the region.

Uncertainly hovers around the exact date and location of the first settlement in Guyana. This vagueness is largely attributed to the obvious confusion that arose when reference was made to the settlement on the Essequibo and that on the Pomeroon in the earlier works of Hartsinck and Dalton. But the limited available evidence seemingly points to the notion that the earliest settlement was established on the Pomeroon by the end of the sixteenth century when Dutch vessels were sent out of the province of Zeeland. Hartsinck speaks of a settlement, Nova Zeelandia, established shortly after 1596 by Dutchman, Joost van der Hooge. This post, although attacked by the Spanish, paved the way for the emergence of similar ones in other parts of the country.

By the truce of Antwerp in 1609 a twelve-year armistice came into being between Spain and the Netherlands and this helped to protect Dutch settlements from further aggression. In 1613, Kyk-over-al was established by Van der Hooge on a small island at the confluence of the Essequibo, Mazaruni and Cuyuni rivers. This settlement became the first durable one under Adrianensen Van Groenwegel and it was strategically located in terms of defence. Kyk-over-al showed early signs of progress and it was boosted with the formation of the Dutch West India Company in 1621. This company assumed immediate control of the settlement and the Dutch also turned their attention towards Berbice. In 1627 Abraham Van Pere was granted permission to colonise the area.

In the initial period these settlements acted as trading posts for the thriving barter trade which emerged with the native inhabitants. Axes, knives, cloth, beads, trinkets and scissors were exchanged for cotton, hammocks, annatto, tobacco and other products. The Dutch, in order to maximise benefits out of the trading activity, entered into a deliberate policy of appeasement with these indigenous people.

As the settlements took root the Dutch extended their activity to tobacco, coffee and cotton cultivation to ensure these commodities were available in commercial quantities. To this end the Dutch West India Company began to supply the colonists with African slaves. More land came under cultivation and new settlements emerged, especially on the lower Essequibo. Berbice grew steadily under the patronage of the Van Peres.

Certain events around the mid-seventeenth century had pronounced effects on the future of Essequibo and the country in general. Firstly, by the Treaty of Munster in 1648, Spain officially recognised the independence of the Netherlands. Then in the early 1650s the Dutch West India Company declared its intention to allow private individuals, as distinct from the company, to settle in Essequibo. Of even greater significance was the eventual re-conquest of Brazil by the Portuguese. These developments led to an influx of Dutch settlers to Essequibo with much needed capital and expertise. Sugar cane cultivation started on an export basis and Kyk-over-al was transformed from a trading post to a central market. This apparent prosperity was short-lived as during the second Anglo-Dutch War of 1665-67 the English, under Major Scott, ravaged Kyk-over-al and Pomeroon.

The colonies continued to experience "adverse fortunes of war which led them to a precarious level of existence." The French, under Du Casse, attacked Berbice and Pomeroon in 1689; Essequibo suffered at the hands of Antoine Ferry in 1708-1709 and in 1712 Berbice was bombarded by Jacques Cassard. During these attacks heavy ransoms were demanded from the Dutch.

Following the attacks on Berbice, administration of the colony was placed in the hands of some Amsterdam merchants who subsequently formed a joint-stock company, the Berbice Association. In 1718, the Council of Policy and Justice became the most important political institution in Essequibo. Both colonies recovered rapidly from the French attacks and by the 1730s more lands along the sea coast were put under sugar, coffee and cotton cultivation. In the case of Essequibo its larger islands experienced a proliferation of estates.

Dutch colonisation was greatly enhanced through the strenuous efforts of Laurens Storm Van Gravensande who became Commander of Essequibo in 1743. He quickly embarked on a "deliberate and thoughtful policy of development and exploration of Demerara". He obtained permission for settlers from abroad to assist in the venture and the result was an influx of Englishmen from Barbados and Antigua with the necessary capital and expertise. Groups of German, Spanish, French, Swedish and Danish settlers took up the challenge. It was this marked migration to Demerara that gave rise to the unchallenged dominance of the sugar industry for several decades as it "laid the foundation of the wealthy plantocracy."

Such was the phenomenal rise of the new colony, Demerara, that by 1769 it had 206 plantations and 5,967 slaves as compared to 92 plantations and 3,986 slaves in Essequibo. Regarding its growing prosperity, Gravesande revealed, "When one returns to Demerara after a year's absence one is astonished at the progress that has been made." Such a view was partly supported by Pinckard when he writes, "From the nature of the land, the crops upon the coast are very abundant and are far more regularly productive than in any of our settlements in the West Indies." In any event, it was clear that before the close of the eighteenth century Demerara had eclipsed the older colonies. To Im Thurn it was a case where "the daughter soon swallowed the mother." In 1774, its capital, Borselen, was removed to the present capital site and renamed Stabroek.

Meanwhile, in 1763, Berbice was rocked by a major slave uprising. Chronic shortages of supplies, cruel treatment and a fierce desire for freedom were among the principal causes of the revolt. For several weeks the rebels under Cuffy were evidently gaining the upper hand in the confrontation as plantation after plantation fell into their hands. In the end a lack of sustained attacks, disunity and the timely arrival of reinforcements all contributed to a reversal of the situation with the Dutch regaining control.

In 1781, the British captured Essequibo, Demerara and Berbice. This was the beginning of a period of uncertainty and fluctuating fortunes as the colonies were tossed back and forth. In 1783, the French seized them but they were eventually restored to the Dutch. They were again captured by the British in 1796 and occupation lasted until 1802 with restoration to the Dutch. The following year the British completed their final conquest of the colonies. Formal cession was effected by the 1814 Treaty of Paris. In 1831, the colonies were united into the "colony of British Guiana" and Stabroek was renamed Georgetown.

As a consequence the British inherited the Dutch system of government and this remained in force until 1891. Such a situation persisted through Article 1 of the 1803 capitulation treaty which stated that the colonies were to retain the existing laws, customs and political institutions.

The nineteenth century witnessed fluctuating fortunes within the sugar industry. The abolition of the slave trade in 1807 and slave emancipation in 1834 brought fear, uncertainty and gloom to the plantocracy. This state of affairs worsened with the

The 1763 Monument in Georgetown depicts Cuffy who led the slave rebellion in Berbice in 1763. Photo: I Brierley

PREVIOUS PAGE 74
Fort Zeelandia was established as a trading post by Dutch settlers in the seventeenth century. The ruins are located on Fort island in the mouth of the Essequibo river. Photo: RJ Fernandes

ABOVE
Early twentieth century photograph of
New Amsterdam in Berbice.

ABOVE RIGHT
Victoria Law Courts in Georgetown circa
early twentieth century.

Stabroek Market was built in 1881 and
retains the name of the original Dutch
capital prior to the colony becoming
British Guiana.

termination of the apprenticeship system in 1838 as there was a marked exodus of former slaves from the plantations to newly acquired villages and a consequential loss of labour. The village movement quickly gained momentum and by around 1850 over 42,000 former slaves were in the newly created villages which emerged throughout the coastal belt. Added to this, planters began to feel the effects of the 1846 Sugar Duties Act which ended their monopoly on the British market. In fact even before its implementation, the Act had engaged a lively debate in the House of Commons between "metropolitan defenders of the monopoly arrangement," and opponents of such "preferential treatment".

The grave labour shortage led to the importation of indentured labourers. In the initial years of change and crisis small numbers of European immigrants including those of German, Irish, English, Scottish, Welsh and Maltese nationalities were brought in, but these failed to make any significant impact on the plantations. As early as 1835 forty Portuguese immigrants were introduced from Madeira and this was followed by a group of 429 a year later.

State-aided Portuguese immigration commenced in 1841 and lasted until 1882 by which time over 31,000 had arrived. Many of these immigrants eventually branched off into commercial activities. Immigration of Africans was encouraged by the British Government and between 1841 and 1863, 14,060 mostly "Liberated Africans" from Sierra Leone and St Helena came to the colony. Creole immigrants were also tried and a steady stream of Barbadians, estimated at 40,656 arrived between 1835 and 1893. This type of labour had "qualitative advantages" as it provided a relatively cheap source of experienced labourers. Chinese immigration was another experiment. Between 1853 and 1913, 15,720 Chinese came to the colony.

East Indian immigrants greatly outnumbered all other groups. Under the "Gladstone experiment" the first group from India arrived in May 1838 but ill-treatment, sickness and high mortality rate led to a temporary suspension of the scheme. Large-scale immigration began around the mid-nineteenth century and lasted until 1917. By that time over 239,000 immigrants had arrived. In the main it was this source of East Indian indentured labour that saved the sugar industry from complete collapse in the nineteenth century.

The 1856, Portuguese riots, during which business places were attacked, cast a cloud over future race relations while the 1870 sighting of Kaieteur Falls by Charles Barrington Brown subsequently brought fame to the colony. Gold was discovered in significant quantities in the 1870s and the gold industry made tremendous strides under the administrations of Henry Irving and Lord Gormanston during the last decades of the century. Increasing numbers of concessions to interior locations were granted to the several gold mining companies which emerged.

This period also witnessed improved techniques in both sugar cane cultivation and in sugar manufacture. Muscovado processed sugar was becoming more and more unacceptable to the overseas sugar market. The local industry faced the challenge by changing over from muscovado processing to that of vacuum pan manufacture. This latter process involved steam heating and boiling at a lower temperature than before and it led to a greater quantity of crystallised sugar being produced. Such was the transformation that the industry was described as "technologically most advanced" in the region.

In the area of education 1876 marked the year when the Compulsory Education Bill was introduced. Under it the labouring class was compelled to send their children to school. Schools fell into two categories: (a) "aided schools" which were under the management of religious bodies, and (b) "colonial schools" which were under direct government supervision.

By the 1890s, there was a gradual movement from the estates as East Indian immigrants began to buy, rent or even squat on lands along the coastal plain. This process accelerated from the turn of the century and within a few decades many immigrant settlements emerged in the rural districts and these became inextricably bound up with the emergent rice industry.

In 1891, after years of struggle, the constitution underwent major reform. Some of the material changes included the enlargement of the Court of Policy, the abolition of the College of Electors, direct election of the unofficial section of the Court of Policy, the widening of the franchise and the right of the Governor to dissolve the Court of Policy at any time. According to Lutchman the changes "resulted in a situation in which the planters had lost the stranglehold they possessed in the nineteenth century."

As gold exploitation intensified in the 1890s uneasiness appeared in the Venezuelan camp. Venezuela's relationship with Great Britain became strained. This situation led to an international tribunal to define the boundary between British Guiana and Venezuela and hence the Arbitral Award of 1899. Immediately before the colony attained independence in 1966, Venezuela revived her claim to the Essequibo territory and deemed the 1899 award "null and void". This controversy resulted in the 1966 Mixed Commission and the Protocol of Port of Spain, which terminated in 1982.

ABOVE
Nineteenth century artist's impression of the Public Building which was later adopted as the Parliament building.

BELOW
The statue of Hubert Nathaniel Critchlow, 'Father of Trade Unionism in the British Caribbean', stands in the grounds of Parliament in Georgetown.   Photo: S May

Cheddi Jagan became prime minister in 1961. He was elected president in 1992 in what was considered to be Guyana's first free and fair elections since independence in 1966

Forbes Burnham was prime minister when Guyana achieved independence in 1966. In 1980, he became the country's first executive president

Arthur Chung was president from 1970 to 1980 and is, to date, the country's longest-serving president

A series of strikes gripped the colony in the early twentieth century as workers found it hard to survive. Working class organisation was boosted with the formation of the British Guiana Labour Union in 1919 by the "Father of Trade Unionism in the British Caribbean," Hubert Nathaniel Critchlow. This was followed by an upsurge of trade unions. Agitation for further political reform led to Crown Colony status in 1928 as the Court of Policy and Combined Court were replaced by a Legislative and Executive Councils.

In 1946, Dr Cheddi Jagan, a dentist, founded the Political Affairs Committee, an organisation primarily aimed at fostering political awareness of the masses. Shortly afterwards he won a seat in the Legislative Council. In 1950, Jagan teamed up with Forbes Burnham, a barrister, and other leaders to form the People's Progressive Party. Elections were held under a new constitution in 1953 and the party swept to power. That triumph was, however, only short-lived. The fear of Communist threat caused Great Britain to suspend the constitution, dispatch troops and declare a state of emergency. With the toppling of the legally-elected government an interim one was imposed. The country received a further set-back with the split in the PPP in 1955. "Ideological, racial and personal factors" were all associated with the split into 'Jaganite' and 'Burnhamite' factions of the party. This unfortunate development was to have serious repercussions later, and from which the country is yet to fully recover.

When the elective principle was restored in 1957, Jagan's PPP won the elections. The same year Burnham's faction was renamed People's National Congress. At fresh elections in 1961, Jagan retained power. The colony was gripped with serious political and racial unrests between the turbulent 1962 and 1964 period.

In a very tense atmosphere general elections were held in 1964 under a new system of proportional representation. The PPP won 24 seats, the PNC won 22 and the United Force obtained seven. With no party securing a majority Forbes Burnham and the UF leader, industrialist Peter D'Aguiar, entered into a PNC/UF coalition and formed the

## Members of the British Guiana Legislature following the 1953 General Elections

| NAME OF SUCCESSFUL CANDIDATE | CONSTITUENCY |
| --- | --- |
| W.A. Phang (Independent) | North-West District |
| Theophilus Lee (Independent) | Essequibo Islands |
| Charles Carter (Independent) | Upper Demerara River |
| Thomas Wheatling (Independent) | Pomeroon |
| Eugene Correia (National Democratic Party) | Bartica and Interior |
| W.O.R. Kendall (National Democratic Party) | New Amsterdam |
| Janet Jagan (PPP) | Western Essequibo |
| Fred Browman (PPP) | Demerara Essequibo |
| Jenarine Singh (PPP) | West Bank Demerara |
| J.P. Lachhmansingh | East Bank Demerara |
| Ashton Chase (PPP) | Georgetown South |
| Clinton Wong (PPP) | Georgetown South-Central |
| Jessie Burnham (PPP) | Georgetown Central |
| Frank Van Sertima (PPP) | Georgetown North |
| Forbes Burnham (PPP) | Georgetown North-East |
| B. Ramkarran (PPP) | West-Central Demerara |
| Sydney King (PPP) | Central Demerara |
| Jane Phillips-Gay (PPP) | East-Central Demerara |
| Sam Persaud (PPP) | Mahaica Mahaicony |
| Balli Lachhmansingh (PPP) | West Berbice |
| Adjodia Singh (PPP) | Berbice River |
| Robert Hanoman (PPP) | Eastern Berbice |
| Cheddi Jagan (PPP) | Corentyne Coast |
| Mohamed Khan (PPP) | Corentyne River |

SOURCE: As published in *The Argosy*, April 23, 1953 and *Daily Chronicle*, April 23, 1953

government. The country achieved political independence on 26 May 1966 with Guyana as its name, and on 23 February 1970 it was proclaimed a Co-operative Republic. That year also marked the opening of the new premises of the University of Guyana at its Turkeyen Campus and the nationalisation of the Demerara Bauxite Company, a subsidiary of the Canadian-based Alcan. In 1975, Jessels Sugar Holding was nationalised. The nationalisation of Bookers Holdings followed in 1976.

In 1980, Prime Minister Burnham became Guyana's first Executive President following general elections under an extremely controversial new constitution. By the early 1980s, it was clear that the country was heading towards a serious economic crisis. The pillars of the economy – sugar, rice and bauxite – experienced declining production and fuel prices rose drastically. With a depletion in foreign currency reserves, shortage of raw materials and spares, and a rising national debt, living standards fell dramatically. Migration to neighbouring Suriname, Venezuela and Brazil, to the Caribbean and North America rose at an alarming rate.

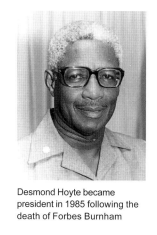

Desmond Hoyte became president in 1985 following the death of Forbes Burnham

Samuel Hinds has been prime minister of Guyana almost continuously since 1992

Following the death of Cheddi Jagan in 1997, his wife, Janet, was elected president

Leader of the opposition, Robert Corbin

## GENERAL ELECTION RESULTS FROM 1957 TO 2006

| DATE OF ELECTIONS | PARTY | SEATS | GOVERNMENT |
|---|---|---|---|
| 12 August 1957 | People's Progressive Party (PPP, "Jaganite") | 9 | PPP |
| | People's Progressive Party (PPP, "Burnhamite") | 3 | |
| | United Democratic Party (UDP) | 1 | |
| | National Labour Force (NLF) | 1 | |
| | TOTAL SEATS | 14 | |
| 21 August 1961 | People's Progressive Party (PPP) | 20 | PPP |
| | People's National Congress (PNC) | 11 | |
| | United Force (UF) | 4 | |
| | TOTAL SEATS | 35 | |
| 7 December 1964 | People's Progressive Party (PPP) | 24 | PNC / UF Coalition |
| | People's National Congress (PNC) | 22 | |
| | United Force (UF) | 7 | |
| | TOTAL SEATS | 53 | |
| 14 December 1968 | People's Progressive Party (PPP) | 19 | PNC |
| | People's National Congress (PNC) | 30 | |
| | United Force (UF) | 4 | |
| | TOTAL SEATS | 53 | |
| 16 July 1973 | People's Progressive Party (PPP) | 14 | PNC |
| | People's National Congress (PNC) | 37 | |
| | Liberator Party (later assumed by UF) | 2 | |
| | TOTAL SEATS | 53 | |
| 15 December 1980 | People's Progressive Party (PPP) | 10 | PNC |
| | People's National Congress (PNC) | 53 | |
| | United Force (UF) | 2 | |
| | TOTAL SEATS | 65 | |
| 9 December 1985 | People's Progressive Party (PPP) | 8 | PNC |
| | People's National Congress (PNC) | 54 | |
| | United Force (UF) | 2 | |
| | Working People's Alliance (WPA) | 1 | |
| | TOTAL SEATS | 65 | |
| 5 October 1992 | People's Progressive Party / Civic (PPP / C) | 28 | PPP / C |
| | People's National Congress (PNC) | 23 | |
| | Working People's Alliance (WPA) | 1 | |
| | The United Force (TUF) | 1 | |
| | TOTAL SEATS | 53 | |
| 15 December 1997 | People's Progressive Party / Civic (PPP / C) | 29 | PPP / C |
| | People's National Congress / Reform (PNC / R) | 22 | |
| | The United Force (TUF) | 1 | |
| | Alliance for Guyana (AFG) | 1 | |
| | TOTAL SEATS | 53 | |
| 19 March 2001 | People's Progressive Party / Civic (PPP / C) | 34 | PPP / C |
| | People's National Congress / Reform (PNC / R) | 27 | |
| | The United Force (TUF) | 1 | |
| | Guyana Action Party (GAP) / WPA | 2 | |
| | Rise, Organise and Rebuild Guyana (ROAR) | 1 | |
| | TOTAL SEATS | 65 | |
| 28 August 2006 | People's Progressive Party / Civic (PPP / C) | 36 | PPP / C |
| | People's National Congress / Reform (PNC / R) | 22 | |
| | Alliance for Change (AFC) | 5 | |
| | Guyana Action Party (GAP) / ROAR | 1 | |
| | The United Force (TUF) | 1 | |

WITHIN THE LAST YEARS, A NUMBER OF COSTLY PROGRAMMES WERE EMBARKED UPON. THESE INCLUDE THE EAST DEMERARA-WEST BERBICE HIGHWAY, THE CHEDDI JAGAN INTERNATIONAL AIRPORT MODERNISATION PROJECT, THE TAIN BERBICE CAMPUS, THE CARICOM SECRETARIAT HEADQUARTERS, THE INTERNATIONAL CONFERENCE BUILDING, THE NEW AMSTERDAM HOSPITAL, THE SKELDON MODERNISATION AND EXPANSION PROJECT AND THE RENOVATION OR BUILDING OF NUMEROUS SCHOOLS AND HEALTH CENTRES. PROGRESS HAS ALSO BEEN MADE IN THE RURAL POTABLE WATER SUPPLY, ELECTRICITY GENERATION AND THE CREATION OF SEVERAL NEW HOUSING SETTLEMENTS COUNTRYWIDE.

**ABOVE RIGHT**
Bharrat Jagdeo became president in 1999 following Janet Jagan's resignation due to health reasons. He was re-elected in 2001 and 2006.

In August 1985, President Burnham died at the Georgetown Hospital after undergoing surgery and Hugh Desmond Hoyte became his successor. In 1989, in the face of a worsening economic situation, the Hoyte administration embarked on an Economic Recovery Programme through agreement with the International Monetary Fund (IMF) and the Support Group of Countries. A massive devaluation that year led to shock, public outcry and strikes.

The early 1990s witnessed an intensification of the struggle for the restoration of democracy. In October 1992, under free and fair elections and internationally supervised, Dr Jagan made a triumphant return to office after a prolonged period in the political wilderness. He promptly embarked on the arduous task of nation-building and good governance. Unfortunately, Dr Jagan died in March 1997, a critical period in the overall recovery and rebuilding process.

The country was briefly administered by Samuel Hinds and following elections of December 1997, Mrs Janet Jagan was elected President. The immediate post-1997 period witnessed a wave of anti-government protests which were followed by CARICOM intervention, the Hermanston Accord and the St Lucia Agreement.

In 1999, Janet Jagan resigned the Presidency due to ill-health and she was succeeded by Bharrat Jagdeo. At the 2001 General Elections, the PPP/Civic was returned to office under the leadership of President Jagdeo.

Post-elections violence was followed by the emergence of the dialogue process with Desmond Hoyte in 2001. The following year there was the Camp Street Prison jail-break and a subsequent increase in crimes including murder, robberies and kidnappings and the village of Buxton emerged as a haven for heightened criminal activity. Desmond Hoyte died the same year and Robert Corbin emerged as the Leader of the PNC/Reform.

Within the last years, a number of costly programmes were embarked upon. These include the East Demerara-West Berbice Highway, the Cheddi Jagan International Airport modernisation project, The Tain Berbice Campus, the Caricom Secretariat Headquarters, the International Conference Building, the New Amsterdam Hospital, the Skeldon Modernisation and Expansion Project and the renovation or building of numerous schools and health centres. Progress has also been made in the rural potable water supply, electricity generation and the creation of several new housing settlements countrywide.

In these early years of the 21st century, Guyana continues to face the daunting challenges of survival against the background of the harsh realities of globalisation. On the local front, the country has to intensify its efforts to ensure ongoing national progress and development, social and economic justice and national unity. ∎

# Significant events in the history of Guyana

COMPILED BY PETAMBER PERSAUD

**1596** Publication of Sir Walter Raleigh's book, *The Discoverie of the Large, Rich and Bewtiful Empyre of Guiana* (sic) leads to the search for the mythical El Dorado and subsequent exploration and colonisation of Guyana by various European nations

**1600** Dutch settle on Kyk-over-al (meaning 'see-over-all') at the confluence of three rivers – Mazaruni, Cuyuni and Essequibo

**1621** The Dutch West India Company is founded, paving the way for Dutch colonisation

**1627** Abraham van Pere establishes the first Dutch settlement in Berbice

**1664** First sugar mill established (in Essequibo)

**1671** Abary River becomes the agreed boundary between the two existing colonies of Berbice and Essequibo

**1689** French privateers attack the Dutch settlement in Berbice

**1708** French privateers plunder the Dutch on the Essequibo

**1738** A Christian mission is established by the Moravians among the Amerindians in Berbice

**1743** Capital of Essequibo moved from Kyk-over-al to Fort Island

**1753** Borselen Island, located about 32 km from the mouth of the Demerara River, made capital of Demerara

**1763** Slave rebellion in Berbice, led by Cuffy. This event was to become the symbol of Guyana's Republic status in 1970

**1772** Major slave rebellion in Essequibo

**1775** The digging of Canal #1 linking the Demerara River to the Essequibo River

**1781** Essequibo, Demerara and Berbice captured by the British; the city of Georgetown is laid out by Governor Kingston

**1790** The first printing press arrives in Guyana (then Demerara)

**1793** The first newspaper launched

**1807** Slave trade abolished

**1808** The arrival of Rev. John Wray leads to the Christianisation of the slaves

**1812** Stabroek renamed Georgetown

**1813** The first major fire in Georgetown

**1815** The arrival of Josiah Booker leads to the founding of the 'Booker Empire'

**1823** Slave rebellion in East Coast Demerara

**1831** Merger of Demerara-Essequibo and Berbice to form British Guiana

**1834** Emancipation of slaves throughout the British Empire; protests, in Essequibo, against the subsequent four-year apprenticeship period following emancipation

**1835** Arrival of indentured Portuguese labourers

**1837** Establishment of a Mayor and Town Council in Georgetown

**1838** Apprenticeship period ends; arrival of East Indian indentured labourers; first bank opened

**1839** Formation of the Police Force

**1842** Formation of the British Guiana African Association

**1844** Queen's College founded

**1847** St Rose's High School opened

**1848** Demerara railway opened

**1853** Arrival of Chinese indentured labourers

**1858** Georgetown Cricket Club formed

**1866** Catholic Grammar School founded

**1870** Kaieteur Falls sighted by C. Barrington Brown

**1871** Telegraph system opened

**1872** Devonshire Castle uprising by Indian indentured labourers

**1876** Georgetown Water Works inaugurated

**1881** Stabroek Market opened

**1882** Guiana Scholarship founded

**1883** Constitutional reforms place 'whites' in full control of political power

**1887** Victoria Law Courts opened in Georgetown

**1893** St George's Cathedral opened in Georgetown

**1899** Town Hall opened in Georgetown

**1901** Electric tram service established

**1903** First rice exports

**1909** Public Library opened in Georgetown

**1913** Local air service established

**1916** Formation of the British Guiana East Indian Association; work commences on the east coast sea defences

**1917** The Common Law of England adopted as the Common Law of British Guiana

**1918** Epidemic almost decimates the population of Georgetown

**1919** British Guiana Labour Union founded by Hubert Nathaniel Critchlow

**1922** British Guiana Girl Guides Movement established in New Amsterdam

**1928** Constitutional changes take place; Government Teachers Training Centre opened

**1929** Income Tax introduced

The African Liberation Monument in Georgetown commemorates the people who lived and died under slavery and those who fought to gain Emancipation.
Photo courtesy Government Information Agency (GINA)

**1934** Great floods on the East Coast of Demerara

**1935** First privately-owned commercial radio station opened

**1946** Establishment of the first women's political body, the Women's Political and Economic Organisation

**1948** The deaths of five Indian sugar workers leads to the annual Enmore Martyrs commemoration

**1950** Formation of the People's Progressive Party (PPP)

**1952** Georgetown Zoo opened

**1953** Universal Adult Suffrage introduced; elections held on 23 April in which the PPP won 18 of the 24 seats with Cheddi Jagan as Leader and Forbes Burnham as Chairman of the party; Cheddi Bharrat Jagan becomes first Chief Minister; suspension of the Waddington Constitution, and the ousting of the PPP after 133 days in government; a nominated interim government is introduced

**1955** A split in the PPP leads to a division into two factions, one led by Cheddi Jagan (PPP – Jagan) and the other led by Linden Forbes Sampson Burnham (PPP – Burnham)

**1957** National elections held which were won by PPP – Jagan; formation of the People's National Congress (PNC) led by Forbes Burnham

**1960** Formation of United Force Party (UFP)

**1961** General elections won by the PPP

**1963** Establishment of the University of Guyana

**1964** General elections held; Coalition government formed between the PNC and UFP with Forbes Burnham as Chief Minister

**1966** British Guiana gains independence from Britain with Forbes Burnham becoming Guyana's first Prime Minister

**1970** Guyana becomes a Co-operative Republic

**1972** First Caribbean Festival of Arts (Carifesta) held in Guyana

**1974** Formation of the Working People's Alliance (WPA) with Walter Rodney as leader

**1978** 913 members of the People's Temple commit suicide/ were murdered in the so-called "Jonestown Massacre"

**1980** Walter Rodney killed on 13 June

**1981** Forbes Burnham installed as Guyana's first President under the new 1980 constitution

**1985** President Forbes Burnham dies on 6 August; Hugh Desmond Hoyte ascends to the Presidency

**1987** Guyana Prize for Literature established

**1992** PPP returned to power with Cheddi Jagan as Head of State after 28 years in opposition

**1997** President Cheddi Jagan dies on 6 March; Sam Hinds ascends to the Presidency; Janet Rosalie Jagan (wife of the late President Jagan) becomes President after elections in December and becomes the country's first woman President

**1999** Bharrat Jagdeo becomes President following the resignation of Janet Jagan. His appointment, at 35 years old, made him the world's youngest Head of State

**2001** Bharrat Jagdeo returned to the Presidency following victory at the polls by the PPP/C

**2002** Desmond Hoyte dies on 22 December; Robert Corbin becomes Leader of the PNC and Leader of the Opposition (PNC/R)

**2006** Bharrat Jagdeo returned to the Presidency

**2007** Commencement of the Berbice Bridge Project

**2007** Completion of the new sports stadium at Providence, East Bank Demerara

WELCOME
TO
CITY HALL

# A nation's history reflected in architecture

L.J. HERNANDEZ

Prior to European colonisation in the early seventeenth century, the only inhabitants of Guyana were Amerindian peoples. They lived in dwellings made from the abundant timber and grasses. These structures were simple, but are acknowledged as being climatically efficient. Built with rounded poles and 'troolie' roofing (a form of thatch), they offered some cool relief against the tropical climate. Some were rectangular in shape with a double pitched roof – a style favoured by the Arawak peoples; others were circular with a conical roof – a structure preferred by the Wai Wai peoples.

A fine example of Amerindian architecture in Guyana is the Wai Wai 'benab', located near Le Meridien Pegasus hotel in Georgetown. The Umana Yana (its official name) or 'meeting place', was built in 1972 to host the first meeting in this hemisphere of the Non-Aligned Movement of Third World Nations. The venue is still used for important functions and is renewed every few years to the original design.

The first European settlers in Guyana were Dutch. They built a small fort (Kyk-over-al) on an island in the Mazaruni River close to where it branches off from the Essequibo River. The Dutch built solid structures such as forts and administration buildings.

Evidence of the Dutch presence in Guyana can be seen on Fort Island near the mouth of the Essequibo River. Built in the mid-18th century, Fort Zeelandia is a former administrative complex that also housed a church and a court. Built of brick, this fort defended the capital of the Colony of Essequibo until 1784 when the capital was moved to Stabroek (now Georgetown).

Historic buildings in the capital date mainly from the 19th century – a period marked by the profusion (and confusion) of fashions in art and architecture.

FACING PAGE
City Hall was built in 1889 and is arguably the most impressive building in the capital.
Photo: I Brierley

RIGHT
Built in the style of a traditional Amerindian dwelling in 1972, the Umana Yana ("meeting place") in Georgetown belongs to the National Trust.
Photo: I Brierley

For Christian religious buildings, the Anglicans used the gothic revival style of architecture, whereas the Catholics mainly employed the classical style, including that of Italian Renaissance architecture. A lasting reminder of this period is the impressive wooden structure of St George's Cathedral, built in 1894, which is the world's tallest wooden building.

However, many of Georgetown's original timber buildings were destroyed by fire. Destruction by fire was, and still is, a great threat to the capital's timber buildings. In 1913, when the timber-built St Mary's Roman Catholic Cathedral was destroyed, it was decided not to rebuild using wood. Hence, the solid ferro-concrete Cathedral of the Immaculate Conception was constructed on the same site and opened in 1925) on Brickdam. Huge and imposing, the building is still without its tower and spire.

Georgetown's public buildings exhibit both gothic revival and neo-classical architecture. The City Hall (1889) designed by Fr Ignatius Scoles, probably Guyana's most distinguished 19th century architect, is reminiscent of the gothic chateau along the River Danube in central Europe.

The traditional Georgetown house is distinctive and was derived from the homeland of the European settlers, but constructed of timber and adapted to suit the climate and frequent flooding. This resulted in elevated structures with many windows and verandas.

ABOVE
St George's Cathedral in Georgetown is the Mother Church of the Anglican Diocese in Guyana. At a height of 143 feet, it is the world's tallest wooden building.   Photo: H Chan

FACING PAGE
Formerly Victoria Law Court, the High Court in Georgetown was officially opened in 1887.   Photo: I Brierley

ABOVE
The Cheddi Jagan Research Centre in the capital is a 19th century colonial-style building which displays fine examples of 'Demerara' windows.
Photo: I Brierley

RIGHT
Home to the Young Men's Christian Association (YMCA), this building was erected in 1925 and donated to the association by local firm Wieting & Richter.
Photo: I Brierley

FACING PAGE
Built in 1881, the distinctive four-faced clock tower of Stabroek Market in Georgetown dominates the skyline.
Photo: I Brierley

One of the many fine examples of this type of building is located on Main Street and now houses the Walter Roth Museum of Anthropology. Built in the last decade of the 19th century, it is thought to have been the residence of the eminent legislator and barrister, Duncan McRae Hutson. The timber building features a portico entrance, timber columns and mouldings, internal arches, and the 'Demerara' windows, so typical of domestic houses of the late 19th and early 20th centuries.

Indian immigration to the colony began in 1838, but it was not until after 1850 that the Indians established more settled places of worship. And it was not until the last two decades of the 19th century that permanent structures of brick and stone were built.

The Hindu Shiv Mandir at Woodley Park, West Coast Berbice, is one of four existing examples of this Eastern architecture. During the early 20th century, the Hindu temple became a larger structure able to accommodate a congregation, a shrine and a tower (sikhara) rising above the roof of the building. These early Hindu temples displayed elements of the colonial architecture of the period. However, after 1950, an awakening

The Hindu temple, above, and mosque, left, are both located in Corriverton. The town is situated in Region 6 (East Berbice – Corentyne) at the mouth of the Corentyne river.

Photos: I Brierley

of Indian tradition and a quest for classical Indian forms effectively destroyed any further development of this new architecture. Two important examples of the local Hindu temple are the Albouystown Temple in Georgetown (1922) a linear temple, and the Providence Temple (1932) East Bank Demerara, a central plan temple.

The development of the mosque, in turn, also appears to have gone through a period of reflecting the elements of colonial architecture, but to a lesser degree than the Hindu temple. The open-air mosque at Cumberland in Berbice, is more in keeping with homeland tradition. The original structure, built of bricks in the late 19th century, was demolished in 1932 and re-built using blocks and concrete. In Georgetown there is the Queenstown Mosque, the oldest place of Islamic worship in the city. Established in 1896, albeit incomplete, the original structure was made of timber and has three domes (gumbars). In the 1940s, a roofed gallery was added in the colonial architecture style with balustrade handrails and turned timber columns. However, repairs and renovations in 1963 saw the removal of the timber walls and the colonial style giving the solid and less decorative, but unique, structure we see today. ■

# A wealth of natural treasures

DAMIAN FERNANDES

Although the fabled El Dorado was never found, Guyana's true riches may well be its flora and fauna. The country is made up of three basic natural regions, which include forests, savannahs, and coastal ecosystems. As a result of these diverse habitats, Guyana's collection of flora and fauna is unlike anything else in the world.

Approximately 75 percent of Guyana is forested, compared to an average of only 59 percent for other South American countries. These forests make up a major part of the Guiana Shield, which is one of the world's four remaining areas of significant tropical rainforests. About 35 timber species are harvested commercially in the country, of which only eight to fifteen are currently intensively utilized. These include the greenheart, which is world renowned for its durability. Guyana is the primary source of this wood, since its distribution is mostly limited to this country. The crabwood tree is also a well-known timber species, as well as the only source of crab oil, which is used to produce soaps, candles and shampoos. The manicole palm, although not a major wood source, is used to produce 'heart of palm'. This culinary delicacy is canned in Guyana and exported to European markets. Other tree species provide the raw materials used in the handicraft of Guyana's indigenous Amerindians. These include the fibres from the ite palm and mucru, which are used in weaving and basketry, and the resin from the bulletwood tree, used to sculpt balata ornaments.

More than 5,500 flowering plant species have been collected in Guyana's three natural regions, of which 284 are found nowhere else on earth. Numerous varieties of heliconias and bromeliads add a splash of vivid colour to the green of the forest, and are a regular feature in the local floral industry. Orchids, which account for 523 species, are the largest family in the country and are found in both savannahs and forested areas. As a survival mechanism, some orchid species have evolved flowers that only attract certain insect varieties. In return, these insects almost exclusively feed on the nectar of its flowers and thus ensure the plant's pollination. In comparison, the sedges, grasses and shrubs of the savannahs have developed ingenious ways of coping with the area's seasonal dry spells. These species often have hair-like projections on their leaves, thick stems and root tubers, all serving to trap and store water. These adaptations also aid in the resistance and recovery of grassland species from regular savannah fires. Not surprisingly, many of Guyana's plants are yet to be documented, and may represent species new to science.

This abundance of plant life provides both the habitat and food to support an amazing variety of indigenous fauna. Relatively little wildlife research has been conducted in Guyana to date, and as such the true amount of animal species in the country is largely uncertain. The best current estimates point to a diversity of species that is difficult to imagine. They include more than 800 species of birds, in excess of 220 mammal species, over 200 species of reptiles and amphibians and more than 800 species of freshwater fish. Studies conducted in the Iwokrama Rainforest, Kanuku Mountains and the North Rupununi Floodplain, have identified these areas as being globally unique in respect to their proliferation of species. The Iwokrama Rainforest in central Guyana and the Kanuku Mountains in the Rupununi have the highest diversity of bat species ever recorded in

TOP
The sloth is a solitary, forest-dweller that spends almost all of its life in the trees.
Photo: FotoNatura

ABOVE
Passion flower. Photo: H Chan

LEFT
The Victoria Amazonica (the national flower) is the largest of all the water lilies. The leaves can grow to three metres in diameter on stalks which may reach lengths of up eight metres. Photo: H Chan

PREVIOUS PAGE 92
The tiger-striped leaf frog lives in the forest canopy. Photo: FotoNatura

**ABOVE**
Jaguars on the banks of the Rewa river, which flows through Region 9 and into the Essequibo river.
Photo: A Holland & G Duncan

**RIGHT**
The red howler monkey is known for its distinctive 'howl' which can be heard at sunrise and sunset. Photo: RJ Fernandes

**FAR RIGHT**
The formidable jaws of the elusive jaguar.
Photo: FotoNatura

**BOTTOM RIGHT**
Forest butterfly. Photo: RJ Fernandes

**MAIN PICTURE**
Tarantula.  Photo: A Holland & G Duncan

**LEFT TOP**
Known locally as the 'watrass', the capybara is the world's largest rodent. This semi-aquatic animal inhabits the river and lake areas of interior.
Photo: RJ Fernandes

**LEFT MIDDLE**
A pair of nine-banded armadillos.
Photo: FotoNatura

**LEFT BOTTOM**
The tapir is known locally as the 'bush cow' and is one of largest mammals to inhabit the South American continent.
Photo: RJ Fernandes

**FAR LEFT**
Prehensile-tailed porcupine.
Photo: FotoNatura

The freshwater crab is found primarily in the forests and wetlands of the interior. Photo: S May

This blossom is known locally as 'bottle brush flower'. Photo: I Brierley

Heliconia marginata. Photo: I Brierley

MAIN PICTURE
Squirrel monkey. Photo: I Brierley

the world, with more than ninety of Guyana's 121 species of bats found at each of these two sites. While the vast network of waterways of the North Rupununi Floodplain is home to over 420 species of freshwater fish, the world's highest concentration of species for an area of this size.

It may be the water, the wide open spaces or the abundant food source, but for some unknown reason Guyana is home to several 'giant' species. Sometimes referred to as the "Giants of El Dorado", these species inhabit the land, sky and water of the remote hinterland and are in most cases threatened or endangered. The 'giants' that stalk the land include the capybara, which can weigh up to 150 pounds and is the largest rodent in the world, the giant anteater which is the largest of this species in the world and the magnificent jaguar, which is the largest member of the cat family in the western hemisphere. There is no shortage of giant reptiles, as the bushmaster is the largest of the pit vipers and the anaconda is one of the biggest snakes in the world. This tendency towards gigantism even extends to invertebrates. Guyana's bird-eating spider is the world's largest, with a 'leg-span' of up to 28 cm (11 in), or the size of a dinner plate. Not to be outdone, the waterways of the interior are also inhabited by their share of giants. The

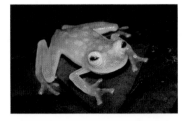

LEFT
Green iguana. Photo: H Chan

TOP
Glass frog. Photo: FotoNatura

ABOVE
West Indian manatee. Photo: I Brierley

ABOVE
Heliconia nickeriensis. Photo: I Brierley

RIGHT
Great egret. Photo: I Brierley

FACING PAGE
Corkwood tree. Photo: I Brierley

**ABOVE**
Coconut plantation. Photo: H Chan

**RIGHT**
When fully-grown, the leaves of the lotus lily are used during Hindu wedding ceremonies. Known locally as 'puri leaf' or 'kamalgatta', the leaves are used like plates upon which food is served.
Photo: H Chan

**FACING PAGE**
Forest bloom. Photo: RJ Fernandes

**TOP**
Highland forest canopy with Tepui (aka Tabletop) Mountain in the background.
Photo: I Brierley

**ABOVE LEFT**
Known locally as the 'ant bear', the giant anteater is the largest of Guyana's three species.  Photo: FotoNatura

**LEFT**
The king vulture is the largest and most colourful of Guyana's three species.
Photo: RJ Fernandes

**FAR LEFT**
The arapaima is the world's largest, scaled freshwater fish and may grow to a length of three metres (10 ft) and weigh more than 200 kg (440 lbs).
Photo: A Holland & G Duncan

**TOP**
The common caiman is found throughout
Central America and northern South
America. It spends most of the day
floating on the surface and becomes
more active at night. Photo: S May

**ABOVE LEFT**
The yellow oriole is known locally as the
'yellow plantain'. Photo: RJ Fernandes

**ABOVE CENTRE**
With a wing-span of 1metre, the false
vampire bat is the largest bat in the
Americas. Photo: FotoNatura

**ABOVE RIGHT**
The anaconda spends most of its life
partially submerged in shallow water. It is
the world's heaviest snake and usually
feeds on capybara and deer.
Photo: I Brierley

giant river turtle, arapaima, black caiman and giant otter, are each in their own right, the largest of their species in the world. Patrolling the skies, the harpy eagle by day and the false vampire bat by night, are both the largest of their kind in the Americas. Another winged oddity is Guyana's national bird, the hoatzin or canje pheasant. This rare bird is limited to only a few countries of northern South America, where it is found in isolated, swampy areas. It is often called the "missing link" of the bird world, since its hatchlings are born with paired claws on the tips of their wings.

From the uppermost reaches of its greenheart forests, to the depths of its black caiman-infested rivers, Guyana's flora and fauna are beyond compare. The relatively unspoilt status of Guyana's plants and animals is in stark contrast to the degradation being experienced in other countries. For instance, current estimates suggest that one and a half acres of the earth's remaining rainforests are lost every second. Guyana, therefore, represents a natural refuge of global importance. The challenge now is for the country to identify ways of sustainably benefiting from its unique flora and fauna, rather than following the global trend of exploitation and destruction. In the end, the legend of El Dorado pales in comparison to the reality of Guyana's natural treasures. ■

# Bird watching in Guyana

KIRK SMOCK

Bird-watching in Guyana has, over recent years, gained popularity with both locals and visitors alike. This largely untapped attraction is among the many natural resources that the country has to offer. While Guyana may not have the white-sand beaches that are synonymous with other Caribbean destinations, it does boast an unmatched eco-tourism experience.

The Guyana Birding Tourism Program (a joint initiative between the Guyana Tourism Authority and the United States Agency for International Development / Guyana Trade and Investment Support project) is dedicated to promoting Guyana as a leading bird-watching destination. With more than eight hundred species, from seventy-two different families, birding in Guyana is developing into an accessible and enjoyable pastime which offers regular sightings of some of the most sought-after species.

Geographically, Guyana is located within the neo-tropics – an area that encompasses Central America, the Caribbean and northern South America. Within Guyana itself, the main habitats are the coastlands, rainforests and savannahs that are home to over seventy of the more than one hundred species that are prevalent in the Guiana Shield.

Keen birdwatchers will encounter many key species including those from larger families such as heron; hawk and eagle; falcon and caracara; rail; sandpiper; gull, tern and skimmer; parrot; nighthawk and nightjar; swift; hummingbird; woodpecker; ovenbird; woodcreeper; antbird; tyrant flycatcher; cotinga; finch; and New World blackbird.

Many species can be seen on a daily basis throughout the country, but there are some specific locations that are considered to be ideal for the more complete bird-watching experience.

The Iwokrama Centre for Rainforest Conservation and Development boasts around 500 bird species which may be spotted on rivers, in dense rainforests, along the road corridor, or from 100 feet above the forest floor on the Canopy Walkway. Iwokrama is renowned for its numerous fruit-eating birds and many prized species such as the harpy eagle, crimson topaz and the hoatzin (the national bird of Guyana).

Just south of Iwokrama's boundaries is the village of Wowetta, which has adopted a community-based tourism project. The programme included the construction of a trail through primary forest which has provided access to species such as the Guianan cock-of-the-rock, red and green macaw, golden-handed manakin, toucanette, capuchin bird, green oropendola, rufous-winged ground cuckoo and black curacao.

Karanambu Ranch is well-known for the work of its owner, Diane McTurk, in the rehabilitation of orphaned giant river otters. However, birdwatchers have been flocking there for many years to see some of the more than three hundred species of bird supported by the Rupununi River and nearby wetlands. Highlights include the jabiru stork, tyrant manakins, capuchinbird, bearded tachuri, green ibis and rufescent heron.

Further south, in the Rupununi, is the famed Dadanawa Ranch. Here, birdwatchers can head-out on horseback to look for harpy eagle nests, Guianan cock-of-the-rock and the rare red siskin.

Other popular birding destinations include Kaieteur Falls, which offers the spectacular sight of thousands of white-collared swifts that nest behind the falls. Shanklands

TOP
Red-shouldered macaws.   Photo: S May

ABOVE
The kiskadee is a common sight in
Georgetown.   Photo: I Brierley

LEFT
The wattled jacana is known locally as
the spur wing.   Photo: S May

FACING PAGE
Nests of the crested oropendola.
Photo: I Brierley

PREVIOUS PAGE 104
The unusual hoatzin, or Canje pheasant,
is Guyana's national bird. The habitat of
this tree-dwelling bird extends from the
Mahaica River to the Canje Creek.
Photo: RJ Fernades

ABOVE
The Guianan cock-of-the-rock is found only in northern South America. Photo: P DeGroot

RIGHT
Common terns are frequently seen off the seawall in Georgetown. Photo: RJ Fernandes

BELOW RIGHT
The striking scarlet ibis. Photo: A Arjoon

FACING PAGE
Found only in Central and South America, the rare harpy eagle, or "flying wolf of the rainforest", is the world's largest eagle.
Photo: RJ Fernandes

BELOW
Ecologist, environmentalist and 'birdman', Gajendra "Andy" Narine is the epitome of a true conservationist. After spending many years travelling throughout Guyana and studying with some of the world's leading bird experts, he set up the eco-tourism business, Guyana Feather Friends. Specialising in city and hinterland tours, and customised trips to the remote parts of the country, Andy is an indispensable tour guide.

Rainforest Resort on the Essequibo River is prized for accessible bird-watching of species such as the tropical kingbird, swallow-winged puffbird, common tody-flycatcher, red-bellied toucan, violaceous trogon and white-plumed antbird.

The nation's capital, Georgetown, is, itself, home to more than two hundred species of bird as well as the Guyana Amazon Tropical Birding Society (GATBS). The organisation runs trips to nearby birding locations such as the Botanic Gardens and the newly-refurbished Promenade Gardens where it is not uncommon to see upwards of fifty species in just a few hours. *For more information, visit www.guyanabirding.com.*

# Safe haven for marine turtles

MICHELLE KALAMANDEEN / Photos: A ARJOON

Set in a tropical wilderness where the Caribbean meets South America, Guyana is a captivating country that boasts the legend of El Dorado – "the city of gold" – and a landscape that inspired Arthur Conan Doyle's *The Lost World*. It is home to one of the world's last four remaining areas of rainforest and is host to an abundant natural world.

One of the best places to witness this natural bounty is along Shell Beach, a fairly remote area along the north-western coast of Guyana. This ninety-mile stretch of beach is an ecological paradise teeming with spectacular wildlife. The beach, itself, consists entirely of seashells (after which the region is named) and actually encompasses nine beaches.

The diversity of birds is one of the richest in Guyana, supporting over 250 species including crested eagles, ospreys, parrots, macaws, scarlet ibises, Caribbean flamingos, frigate birds, Muscovy ducks and harpy eagles. The mammalian inhabitants include manatees, tapirs, deer, jaguars, giant otters, howler monkeys, squirrel monkeys, wedge-capped and brown capuchins, porpoises and anteaters.

Shell Beach is also an exceptional and beautiful ecosystem that comprises more than 1400 species of plants and extensive mangrove forests, lowland swamp forests and seasonally-flooded palm savannahs.

From March to August, Shell Beach plays host to nesting marine turtles. Large and ungainly on land, four of the world's eight endangered species of marine turtle – leatherback, green, hawksbill and olive ridley – come to the beach to lay their eggs.

After crawling ashore under cover of darkness, the female digs a deep pit above the high-tide mark into which she lays 100-150 eggs. She then covers the pit and returns to the sea. The eggs hatch about 6-8 weeks later and the young turtles then have to make

A leatherback turtle hatchling makes the perilous journey to the sea.

LEFT
A leatherback turtle makes its way up Shell Beach to lay its eggs.

BELOW
After laying its eggs and covering the pit, the turtle returns to the sea.

**ABOVE**
Shell Beach is a ninety-mile ecological paradise and the nesting ground for marine turtles. Located in Region 1 (Barima – Waini), it is Guyana's most northerly coastline.

**BELOW**
Conservationists measure and tag a leatherback turtle. This species is the most endangered of all marine turtles.

their way down the beach to the water. However, many fall victim to beach predators such as crabs and seabirds before making it to the sea.

An uncertain future lies ahead for the hatchlings as they leave the shores of Shell Beach. The numbers of marine turtles have plummeted over the years due to commercial fishing, which has taken its toll because sea turtles are accidentally caught in fishing nets, and the loss of habitat and pollution of the oceans. As a consequence, only a fraction of turtles visit Shell Beach today compared to levels in the past, and no olive ridleys have been seen here since 2002.

Recognising the increasing threat to sea turtles, a leading turtle biologist and two Amerindian former turtle fishermen, took steps to promote marine turtle conservation at Shell Beach. In the 1980s, a pilot project was launched with funding from the Florida Audubon Society aimed at protecting nesting turtles with the help of local communities. Over the years, alternative protein projects were undertaken to discourage harvesting of marine turtle meat and eggs by local communities and an environmental education programme was implemented.

In recognition of the conservation efforts at Shell Beach and the region's unique and rich biodiversity, the Government of Guyana identified the wider Shell Beach area as a site for protection and one of national importance.

Today, Shell Beach remains one of the world's best-kept secrets. As the Spanish sought to find El Dorado in days gone by, the lure of a different kind of treasure entices many to the shores of Guyana. As the human population and its environmental impact increases, Shell Beach holds in trust a wealth of biodiversity for the world and its future. ∎

# Rising tide of sports development

NEIL KUMAR

Sport has always played a major role in the lives of the Guyanese people and over the years, the country has demonstrated that it can produce outstanding sports men and women. From the earliest colonial times, all have indulged in some form of competitive, physical activity.

Cricket, established by the British, has been played by every ethnic and social group in Guyana, and in many ways it has transcended those classifications. Over the years, no fewer than six Guyanese captains have led the West Indies cricket team, the most notable of which being Clive Lloyd. Arguably one of the world's greatest cricketers, and certainly one of the greatest captains, he led the West Indies to cricketing victories in the first two World Cup Series.

But sport is so much more than cricket, and the Guyanese have a taste for all forms. From rugby to horseracing, swimming to squash, boxing to badminton, and football to kung fu, Guyanese like their sports and they come out in great numbers to support their players. This enthusiasm has been rewarded over the years with international class athletes. In 1980, Michael Anthony Parris won a bronze at the Olympic Games; Andrew "Sixhead" Lewis captured the nation's first ever boxing World Title and was soon followed by Wayne "Big Truck" Braithwaite and "Vicious" Vivian Harris. More recently, Gwendolyn O'Neil also won a World Title.

In cricket, two of the world's leading batsmen are Shivnarine Chanderpaul and Ramnaresh Sarwan, both Guyanese. The West Indies Under-19 Captain for the 2006 ICC U/19 Cricket World Cup was Leon Johnson, also Guyanese.

**RIGHT**
Rohan Kanhai in action during his excellent 157 runs against England at Lord's in 1973. His captaincy marked the beginning of the rise of West Indies cricket.

**FAR RIGHT**
Seen here in 1983, Clive Lloyd was an inspirational team leader and the most successful captain of the West Indies.

**FACING PAGE**
Shivnarine "Tiger" Chanderpaul reaches a century during the Test between the West Indies and Australia at Bourda in Georgetown in April 2003.

Photos: Getty Images

As the nation grows, a genuine effort is being made to secure facilities that will assist the development of sport in Guyana. The Cliff Anderson Sports Hall plays host to basketball, volleyball and table tennis competitions at international standard. Table tennis training is accomplished under the watchful eye of Chinese coach, Zhou Ping. The Colgrain and Castellani swimming pools are fully utilised allowing Guyana's young swimmers to acquire the skills needed to compete on the international stage. The Sports Programme being implemented by the National Sports Associations and Federations, the Guyana Olympic Association and the National Sports Commission, are continuing to show progress.

A brand new stadium was built to host the Super 8 matches of the 2007 World Cup Cricket competition. Supported by the government of India, at a cost of US$ 25 million, the new venue took Guyana's sporting facilities to another level.

Ramnaresh Sarwan in action against South Africa. Photo: Getty Images

### GUYANA-BORN CRICKETERS WHO REPRESENTED WEST INDIES AT TEST MATCH LEVEL

| | Career | Matches | Runs | Avg | Wkts | Avg |
|---|---|---|---|---|---|---|
| BACCHUS, S.A.F. | 1977-1982 | 19 | 782 | 26.06 | | |
| BAICHAN, L. | 1974-1976 | 3 | 184 | 46.00 | | |
| BUTCHER, B.F. | 1958-1969 | 44 | 3104 | 43.11 | | |
| BUTTS, C.G. | 1984-1988 | 7 | 108 | 18.00 | 10 | 59.50 |
| CAMACHO, G.S. | 1967-1971 | 11 | 640 | 29.09 | | |
| CHANDERPAUL, S.* | 1993-2007 | 108 | 7182 | 46.63 | 8 | 105.62 |
| CHRISTIANI, C.M. | 1934-1935 | 4 | 98 | 19.60 | | |
| CHRISTIANI, R.J. | 1947-1954 | 22 | 896 | 26.35 | | |
| CROFT, C.E.H. | 1976-1982 | 27 | 158 | 10.53 | 125 | 23.80 |
| DE CAIRES, F.I. | 1929-1930 | 3 | 232 | 38.66 | | |
| DEONARINE, N. | 2005-2007 | 4 | 107 | 21.40 | | |
| FERNANDES, M.P.* | 1928-1930 | 2 | 49 | 12.25 | | |
| FREDERICKS, R.C. | 1968-1977 | 59 | 4334 | 42.49 | | |
| GASKIN, B.B. | 1947-1948 | 2 | 17 | 5.66 | 2 | 79.00 |
| GIBBS, G.L. | 1954-1955 | 1 | 12 | 6.00 | | |
| GIBBS, L.R. | 1957-1976 | 79 | 488 | 6.97 | 309 | 29.09 |
| HARPER, R.A. | 1983-1994 | 25 | 535 | 18.44 | 46 | 28.06 |
| HOOPER, C.L.* | 1987-2003 | 102 | 5762 | 36.46 | 114 | 49.42 |
| JONES, C.E.L. | 1929-1935 | 4 | 63 | 9.00 | | |
| KALLICHARRAN, A.I.* | 1971-1981 | 66 | 4399 | 44.43 | | |
| KANHAI, R.B.* | 1957-1974 | 79 | 6227 | 47.53 | | |
| KING, R.D. | 1998-2005 | 19 | 66 | 3.47 | 53 | 32.69 |
| LAMBERT, C.B. | 1991-1999 | 5 | 284 | 31.55 | | |
| LLOYD, C.H.* | 1966-1985 | 110 | 7515 | 46.67 | | |
| MADRAY, I.S. | 1957-1958 | 2 | 3 | 1.00 | | |
| McGARRELL, N.C. | 2001-2002 | 4 | 61 | 15.25 | 17 | 26.64 |
| McWATT, C.A. | 1953-1955 | 6 | 202 | 28.25 | | |
| MENDONCA, I.L. | 1961-1962 | 2 | 81 | 40.50 | | |
| NAGAMOOTOO, M.V. | 2000-2003 | 5 | 185 | 26.42 | 12 | 53.08 |
| PAIRADEAU, B.H. | 1952-1957 | 13 | 454 | 21.61 | | |
| RAMDASS, R.R. | 2004-2005 | 1 | 26 | 13.00 | | |
| SARWAN, R.R.* | 1999-2007 | 67 | 4303 | 38.76 | 23 | 46.73 |
| SHIVNARINE, S. | 1977-1979 | 8 | 379 | 29.15 | | |
| SOLOMON, J.S. | 1958-1965 | 27 | 1326 | 34.00 | | |
| STAYERS, S.C. | 1961-1962 | 4 | 58 | 19.33 | 9 | 40.44 |
| STUART, C.E.L. | 2000-2002 | 6 | 24 | 3.42 | 20 | 31.40 |
| TRIM, J. | 1947-1952 | 4 | 21 | 5.25 | 18 | 16.16 |
| WIGHT, C.V. | 1928-1930 | 2 | 67 | 22.33 | | |
| WIGHT, G.L. | 1952-1953 | 1 | 21 | 21.00 | | |
| WISHART, K.L. | 1934-1935 | 1 | 52 | 26.00 | | |

* Denotes captains of the West Indies.

*Statistics to December 2007 compiled by Ray Goble*

FACING PAGE
Cricket is so ingrained in the psyche of the Guyanese people that impromptu games can take place almost anywhere.
Photo: I Brierley

**BOXING:** Guyana has had its share of title-holders over the last few years and continues to excel in this sport. "Vicious" Vivian Harris and Wayne "Big Truck" Braithwaite, both former world title-holders, are looking to regain their supremacy along with Gwendolyn O'Neal who will be fighting Laila Ali to reclaim her spot on the world stage. Two up-and-coming boxers of which to take note are Pamela London and Gary Sinclair.

Champion boxer Gwendolyn O'Neal.
Photo: I Brierley

**FOOTBALL:** There is heavy investment in football with some sixteen million dollars having been provided in the development of 32 clubs in order to upgrade their systems and to improve facilities. Local football is one of the most popular sports and spectators are willing to travel great distances to support their teams. One of the more successful franchises (established by Kashif and Shaghai) attracts growing sponsorship and large crowds to its tournaments.

**RUGBY:** Over the past few years, spectacular successes have been recorded in the highly-organised field of rugby. The country's under-19 squad has been the defending champions in the Caribbean for the past three years. Kit Nascimento, following up on his leadership of Guyana rugby, has gone on to be elected to the presidency of the regional body.

Women's rugby is gaining ground and it is hoped that it will eventually mirror the successes of the men's game. Photo: S May

**TABLE TENNIS:** Under the guidance of a Chinese coach for the past three years, table tennis in Guyana has shown a marked improvement. It has become one of the most popular sports for youngsters who attend practice sessions at the Cliff Anderson Sports Hall. Guyana has performed well in competitions throughout the Caribbean, especially at junior level.

**BADMINTON AND SQUASH:** Guyana has made great steps in both of these sports. Its players have been invited to participate in the Surinamese Badminton Championships and, in squash, Guyana won the Caribbean Junior Championship.

**CYCLING:** Hassan Mohamed has, almost single-handedly, encouraged and promoted the sport of cycling in Guyana. While there is great deal of interest in the sport among both younger and older riders, it has been the dedication and commitment of Mohamed and the National Sports Commission that sees continuing tournaments being held across the country.

**MOTOR RACING:** Motor racing is one of the most popular spectator sports in Guyana recording mammoth crowds at both local and international meetings. Considered to be the finest in the Caribbean, the South Dakota Motor Racing Circuit can trace its origins back to 1953. It was at this time that a group of motorcyclists staged their first meet at the Number Sixty-three Beach. From this humble event emerged the British Guiana Motor Racing Club and with it some of the sport's leading exponents. Names such as Pat Holder, Kit Nascimento, Ashim Hack and Eric Vieira – the club's first president who went on to serve for twenty years – are etched into Guyana's motor racing history. The venue was eventually changed to the South Dakota Circuit from where motor racing is still enjoyed today. There have been many outstanding moments in the world of Guyanese motor racing including the first locally-created car ("The Beast"), and the rise of one of the finest female drivers, Gabriel Koenig.

**HORSE RACING:** Over the years this 'sport of kings' has become an increasingly popular spectator and betting activity. It has seen the establishment of a number of turf clubs in the Berbice region at Port Mourant, Bush Lot and West Coast Berbice and, more recently, in Georgetown with the establishment of the Demerara Turf Club at Mocha.

**MARTIAL ARTS:** Because of its Chinese heritage, the people of Guyana have always had a keen interest in martial arts. The sport's leading lights are Frank Woon-a-Tai and Monasingh. With the exchange of skills from the Chinese government, Guyana is grooming a new breed of martial artists in the art of Wu Shu, a fighting skill akin to Tai Chi.

**BASKETBALL:** A number of programmes are being run to encourage the development of basketball and there are regular competitions between local teams.

**SWIMMING:** The swimming programme in Guyana has seen a vast improvement with the introduction of clubs across the country. In Georgetown, Stephanie Fraser has been instrumental in encouraging the development of skills at the Colgrain and Castellani pools. Guyana participates annually at the Inter Guyana games between Guyana, Suriname and French Guiana and recently participated at the Commonwealth Games.

**VOLLEYBALL:** Guyana has a well-organised programme for volleyball, which is co-ordinated by former national player, Lennox Shuffler.

The country's sports bodies, including the Olympic Association, the National Sports Commission and other national sports associations, are all committed to fostering the highest levels of sporting excellence with the ultimate goal of winning medals at the Olympic Games. Guyana is working towards producing sportsmen and women who are dedicated and capable of competing at international level. With the support of the government, and the continued interest and commitment of the Guyanese people, the levels of sporting ability will continue to rise. ■

# Artistic reflection of social issues

ALIM A. HOSEIN

The achievement of independence in 1966 unleashed the full creativity of Guyanese artists. These artists – Stanley Greaves, Ron Savory, Aubrey Williams, Donald Loncke, Marjorie Broodhagen, Emerson Samuels among the best-known – had been preparing themselves since the end of the 1950s under the renowned teacher E.R. Burrowes. They drew inspiration from such precursors as Hubert Moshett, Reginald Phang, Golde White and Vivian Antrobus who had begun turning the painting techniques of the Europeans to the service of truly depicting the local landscape and life from as far back as the 1930s. While this ferment was brewing in Georgetown, the sculptor and painter Philip Moore, in Berbice, was receiving mystical inspiration which commanded him to create art. These developments also define the great currents in Guyanese art: sculpture and painting, which would alternate dominance of the local scene in the ensuing decades.

Guyana achieved independence in an international climate that was conducive to cultural development. Global aspirations for liberation from colonialism, and such developments as the Black Power movement and Non-Alignment, lent urgency and legitimacy to artistic exploration. The government well-understood the importance of art to the development of Guyanese and Caribbean consciousness, and it provided conditions for art to flourish. In 1972, Guyana broke new ground by initiating CARIFESTA, the Caribbean Festival of Arts. In 1974, a Director of Art in the shape of Denis Williams was appointed, and in 1975, a local school of art named after E.R. Burrowes, was established. The new dispensation gave artists encouragement and

ABOVE
This well-known photograph depicting traditional Amerindian fishing methods was taken by Robert Fernandes. Its evocative subject matter and popularity over the years has confirmed its place in Guyana's annals of contemporary art.

LEFT
The Hadfield Gallery was established at the beginning of the 1990s.

security to explore new ways of depicting the local landscape. The many different directions taken – Donald Locke's experiments with Amerindian motifs; Stanley Greaves' lattice effect; Ron Savory's hinterland landscapes; Marjorie Broodhagen's paintings of local scenes and issues; Stephanie Correia's use of Amerindian motifs on ceramics – illustrate the artistic ferment of the time. The new directions in art were even given explicit national political approval: Aubrey Williams' Timehri murals executed in 1970 boldly announced Guyana's uniqueness to people arriving at Guyana's new international airport, and Philip Moore's 1763 Monument, unveiled in 1976, crowned a decade of political and cultural independence.

Further indications that Guyana had shaken off the cultural baggage of the West appeared in a locally-grown free-style form of sculpture from a new generation of artists, many of whom were untutored. This sculpture seemed to have decisively shifted the epicentre of Guyanese art away from the West, allowing the Director of Art to proudly declare in 1981: "No one can really say today that Guyanese artists are still trying their hands at Western art". Its chief exponent, Gary Thomas, pioneered this style in beautifully carved, sensuous pieces, and Omowale Lumumba added a metaphysical dimension to it. The opening of a dedicated gallery, the Roots and Culture Gallery, in 1986, indicates the importance of this development. It showcased this new generation including sculptors Thomas, Lumumba and Roderick Bartrum, painters Dudley Charles, Basil Thompson, Angold Thompson, leather craftsman Winston Strick, and others. Unlike many of the previous generations of artists, these had close connections with the ordinary people, and their work had a greater sense of untutored invention. Two major styles mark their work: the free-form sculpture, and a controlled, naïve manner of landscape painting typified by the work of V. Budhram and later on, Seunarine Munisar. Although it eventually lost its vitality and finally ceased to be a major force, this style, especially the sculpture, lives on in a street-art culture which it had done much to inspire.

Other artists were also emerging, among them George Simon, Francis Ferreira, Ras Ita, Linden Jemmott, Mervyn Wilson, Terrence Roberts – some self-taught and many from the Burrowes School of Art – making the period of the 1980s one of great variety. The re-emergence of the Guyana Women Artists Association in 1988, after sixty years of dormancy, added to the variety since it gave exposure to long-standing women artists such as Broodhagen, Correia, Leila Locke and Doris Rogers, and lesser-known ones such as Valerie Cox, O'Donna Allsopp, Josefa Tamayo and Irene Gonsalves, and also widened the scope of the art to include textiles, jewellery and ceramics.

But conditions of life in the country had been deteriorating, and this was forcefully highlighted by Bernadette Persaud in her brave inaugural exhibition in 1984. This marked a change in the art, although subsequent political art was not as pointed as Persaud's. In 1987, Desmond Ali came on the scene with a drastically different approach in his double-sided, high-relief sculpture which harkened back to Pre-Columbian times and had a distinct theme of political liberation. Oswald Hussein won the sculpture prizes at the National Exhibition of the Visual Arts in 1989 and 1993 for his powerful sculpture which was rooted in his Amerindian heritage. Hussein and other Amerindian artists such as Lynus Clenkien and Roland Taylor powerfully announced the imagination of their Lokono people in a series of exquisite exhibitions beginning in 1991. Also emerging at this time was Winslow Craig, who is gifted with an astonishing talent for carving wood into exquisitely realistic forms which he used to portray messages of corruption and salvation.

The essential development from the middle of the 1980s was therefore an art of deeper spirit. In the hands of Winslow Craig and Oswald Hussein it has a religious aspect. In Bernadette Persaud and Desmond Ali, it is deeply political. The off-centre artists such as Bryan Clarke, Ohene Koama, Ras Ita and Linden Jemmott found a natural connection with this spirit, doing so through a series of exhibitions focusing on themes such as national unity, respect for diversity, liberation, ethnic consciousness, peace and justice. Even the work of Stanley Greaves, who had been working in Barbados for a

ABOVE
The 1763 Monument features Cuffy, one of Guyana's national heroes. Sculpted by Philip Moore (pictured above), it was unveiled in 1976 and commemorates the slave uprising of 1763 which was led by Cuffy (or 'Kofi'). Photos: I Brierley

# CARIFESTA COMES FULL CIRCLE FOR 2008

The Caribbean Festival of Creative Arts (CARIFESTA) is a three-week exposition of art in all its forms. This all-embracing event includes exhibitions, concerts, demonstrations, recitals and plays featuring the music, dance, drama, sculpture, painting, literature, craft, photography and folk art of the region.

The festival was conceived in 1970 following a regional gathering of artists who were participating in a writers' and artists' convention in Guyana's capital. Two years later, the first CARIFESTA was staged (also in Georgetown) and attracted creative artistes from more than thirty Caribbean and Latin American countries.

Since (and including) its inaugural event in 1972, there have been nine such festivals, with the tenth being held in 2008 – again in Georgetown. CARIFESTA X will carry the theme, "One Caribbean, one purpose – our culture, our life" and like all previous festivals will be a confluence of the nations of the Caribbean Community (CARICOM), the wider Caribbean, Latin America and a representation of Africa, Asia, Europe and North America.

## CARIFESTA SINCE 1972

**CARIFESTA I**    Year: **1972**    Venue: **Guyana**
*The artist in society with special reference to the Third World*

**CARIFESTA II**    Year: **1975**    Venue: **Jamaica**
*A hallmark of cultural extravagance*

**CARIFESTA III**    Year: **1979**    Venue: **Cuba**
*A rainbow of peoples under one Caribbean sun*

**CARIFESTA IV**    Year: **1981**    Venue: **Barbados**
*Living images of the sun*

**CARIFESTA V**    Year: **1992**    Venue: **Trinidad and Tobago**
*Together is strength*

**CARIFESTA VI**    Year: **1995**    Venue: **Trinidad and Tobago**
*The world's best cultural mix*

**CARIFESTA VII**    Year: **2000**    Venue: **St Kitts and Nevis**
*Caribbean arts and culture: reflecting, consolidating, moving on*

**CARIFESTA VIII**    Year: **2003**    Venue: **Suriname**
*Many cultures: the essence of togetherness of the spirit of the Caribbean*

**CARIFESTA IX**    Year: **2006**    Venue: **Trinidad**
*Celebrating our people, contesting the world stage*

**CARIFESTA X**    Year: **2008**    Venue: **Guyana** (22-31 Aug)
*One Caribbean, one purpose – our culture, our life*

---

number of years, reflects this character in his politically satirical paintings. Thus, Guyana's art since the late 1980s is more sombre and less excited, more conservative in style but deep in its currents. It is sarcastic and scathing in Persaud, revolutionary in Ali, magical in Hussein, religious in Craig, hopeful and reconciliatory in the off-centre artists, but the targets are the same: liberation, ethnic and cultural recognition, personal growth, the environment, national unity, and redress of history. While it may be said that the art reflects the restless, end-of the-century period, more importantly, it reflects the political and social changes in Guyana itself.

Meanwhile, the new government, which took office in 1992, did much to secure the heritage of Guyanese art by establishing the first national art museum and gallery, Castellani House, in 1993. Castellani has showcased the national collection and the works of contemporary artists, and has also created regular competitions in watercolours and drawing in order to develop these arts. The opening of the Hadfield Gallery at the beginning of the 1990s is also important. In a difficult period, this gallery, with an avant-garde air, mounted many important exhibitions, including the first exhibition of Amerindian Art in 1991.

Today, Guyanese art is vitally caught up in the larger national question of identity and belonging. In a positive way, artists are asserting cultural identities and suggesting solutions to national and even global problems. Often, there are gentle reminders of the beauty around us in time and space, as in the photography of Robert Fernandes, the nostalgic countryside reminiscences of Maylene Duncan, and the sculpture of Josefa Tamayo. Perhaps more than any other time in our history, our art is reflecting issues close to the common citizen. Thus, contemporary Guyanese art continues to evolve, living, as do so many other aspects of local life, in the space between anguish and beauty. ■

Published by Hansib, *The West Indian Digest* produced a souvenir issue of its monthly magazine to mark the launch of Carifesta in 1972

# MUSIC – FOOD FOR THE SOUL

GUYANESE HAVE ALWAYS BEEN A VERY MUSICAL people, and over the years this has expressed itself in both the folk arena and the more formal musical genres. Growing up as a child in Guyana in the sixties and seventies, it was the pattern for those who lived in Georgetown to attend music lessons. This created an environment where music came to be seen as an adjunct to living, a necessary part of an existence that was both balanced and exploratory.

The roots of this commitment were the potpourri of cultures that formed an integral part of the Guyanese landscape, and which would eventually influence each other to create new modes of musical expression and maturity. In the bigger towns and in the capital among the upper and middle classes, the more formal tools were employed; the theory of music in the European tradition, and the playing of pianos and violins. English folk songs were sung in the schools and local folk songs were relegated to private gatherings. In the more remote villages, on the other hand, be they Amerindian, Indian or African, traditional instruments were the universal connection to an earlier time and were the carriers of a culture that for many was changing with exposure to other cultures. In these the sound of the drum, distinct and unique in its myriad forms, arbitrated a dialogue among peoples originating in many parts of the world who now called themselves Guyanese. The Chinese and the Portuguese, too, had their distinctive musical forms and while for the former these were shared with other Guyanese at certain times like the Chinese New Year, in the case of the Portuguese, this usually found expression through their church festivals and family gatherings.

Musical development is linked directly to the historical environment in which it emerges and the beginnings of a Guyanese musical expression can be seen in the spirit of the fifties and sixties when the themes of independence and self-sufficiency first appeared. The calypso, as a tool of social commentary, and a Caribbean staple, had its birthplace in the connection between musicians from across the region who saw Guyana as a Mecca for the arts during that time, and came here in their droves to explore and express their musical urgings. Shanto, a particularly indigenous form of the genre, was made popular by Bill Rogers, and his 'Weed Song' is still one of the more recognised pieces that uses the style to deliver its message. There is a hot debate over the origins of another Caribbean musical icon, the steelpan, with both Guyana and Trinidad claiming to be the originators of this uniquely modern instrument. Even if we did not create it, it soon became an integral part of our way of life in the 1940s when it first appeared.

The sixties also saw Guyanese seeking to enter the mainstream of the international music scene and many singers emerged who were trying to sound and express in the format of their American and English counterparts. They did not see Guyana as their playing field and most left to pursue musical careers abroad. Amerindian David Campbell and his 'Kabakaburi Children' is a notable ballad of the period. The fact that it was produced outside of Guyana in no way reduces its relevance and connection to its indigenous heritage.

The most notable musician on the international scene of Guyanese heritage is Eddy Grant whose group, the Equals, single-handedly eclipsed any other bands of the period in which it was popular. Born in Guyana, he migrated to England in 1960 with his parents and there emerged as a force with his combination of pulsating base guitar and gravelly voice. In the late 1960s his song 'Baby Come Back' was Number 1 on the British charts.

Much has been happening in the past few years in Guyana, as the natural tendency towards self-expression has led to more and more artists creating and performing their works for the consumption of the public. An innovative phenomenon has been the fusion of Indian and Caribbean styles that proclaims itself as 'chutney' music. This genre enervates with its scintillating rhythms and topical and down-to-earth lyrics.

The other focus of interest is the beginnings of a local music industry with the major players representing a growing number of enterprising young writer/singer/performers who are searching for a medium to express their triumphs, frustrations and feelings about life in Guyana.

The future looks promising as we move towards an opening of barriers with the rest of the Caribbean. Guyana is poised for its re-emergence as one of the leading Caribbean lights and a centre for arts and culture. As it has been since the arrival of the first slave ship, our music is an expression of our people, their dreams and aspirations, their struggles and challenges, their joys and triumphs. Our music is the food that feeds our souls and it will play on.

RUSSEL LANCASTER

# The development of Guyanese literature

PETAMBER PERSAUD

Literature written about Guyana and by Guyanese has existed since colonial times with the earliest examples being produced by European explorers, missionaries and administrators. These first writings were mainly travelogues and histories of which the most famous of that period was *The Discoverie of the Large, Rich and Bewtiful Empyre of Guiana* by Sir Walter Raleigh, published in 1596. The next body of writings was the history books of the nineteenth century by William Brett, Henry Dalton, Everard Im Thurn and the Schomburgk brothers. Over the years, many more history books would be added to this prodigious list including James Rodway (1912) and C.A. Clementi (1937), and in more recent times the work of Dwarka Nath, Peter Ruhomon, Mary N. Menezes, M. Kwok Crawford, Brian Moore, James Rose and Dale Bisnauth. Cheddi Jagan's *The West on Trial*, which falls into this category, also stands out as being in the top position of autobiographies by a Guyanese.

The literary imagination and the exploration of its vistas saw its initial expression in the mother of all literature: poetry. And in Guyana in 1832 the 'Colonist' published his *Midnight Musings in Demerara* in the city of Georgetown. In 1838, Simon Christian Oliver was writing to celebrate the end of slavery. Dr Henry Dalton can be credited as being the first to concentrate on local themes with his *The Essequibo and its Tributaries* published in 1857. Thomas Don's *Pious Effusions* followed in 1873 and Egbert Martin's *Poetical Works* in 1883. Walter McArthur Lawrence contributed many works between 1896 and 1942. Four fictional works stand out from that period: Edward Jenkins' *Lutchmee and Dilloo* (1877), James Rodway's *In Guiana Wilds* (1899), W.H. Hudson's *Green Mansions* (1904) and A.R.F. Webber's *Those that be in Bondage* (1917).

The 1800s also saw the emergence of the first East Indian writings. The first of these were letters sent home to India. Later came the letters to the press, of which a leading exponent was Bechu of Enmore Estate. Around that same period, John Ruhomon, who was born in Guyana (then British Guiana), came to prominence as a journalist and lecturer.

In 1882, the National Geographic and Commercial Society founded *Timehri* in order to record important discoveries, and social and cultural happenings. The *Christmas Tide*, founded in 1893, was more of a literary magazine, an outlet for the imaginative outpourings and recordings of civic functions and cultural affairs. Those two (the latter ceased in 1956 and the former in 1978) gave identity to the new state of British Guiana and helped to preserve its cultural heritage.

Other literary magazines eventually emerged: the *Chronicle Christmas Annual* (now *The Guyana Annual*) was founded in 1915 and is still being published today. The *Caribia* and the *Pepperpot*, published by British Guiana Lithographic, were short-lived. Their influence on popular literature, however, was important for they fostered emerging voices and encouraged the growth of short fiction in preference to the novels produced by British publishers. Included in the extremely long list of such short story writers are Edgar Mittleholzer, Wilson Harris, Sheik Sadeek, Basil Balgobin, Sheila King, Cecile Nobrega, Doris Harper-Wills and J.A.V. Browne. In more recent times the news

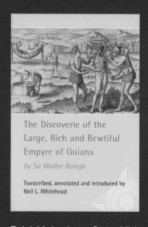

Raleigh's book was first published in 1596 and is acknowledged to be the earliest book on Guyana. This transcribed edition was reprinted in 1997

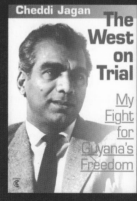

First published in 1966 by Michael Joseph Ltd, Jagan's book is one of the leading autobiographies by a Guyanese. It was re-published in 1997 by Hansib

The Guyana Annual was founded in 1915 and is still published today.

David Dabydeen's Coolie Odyssey was first published by Hansib in 1988 and reprinted in 2006

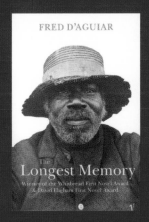

The Longest Memory won Fred D'Aguiar the Whitbread and David Higham First Novel Awards

magazine *Guyana Review* has become the most prolific journal with more than 144 monthly issues published since 1993.

The turn of the twentieth century saw the upsurge of intellectualism in Guyanese society encouraging the formation of literary circles and social groupings like the British Guiana Literary Society, the British Guiana Dramatic Society and the British Guiana Union of Cultural Clubs. Some of these organisations boasted their own literary journals like the *Indian Opinion*, founded by the British Guiana East Indian Association in 1916.

For over one hundred years it was poetry that would stir the imagination and lead to an outpouring of work from Walter McArthur Lawrence, A.J. Seymour, Ivan Van Sertima, W.W. Persaud, Ramcahritar-Lalla, J.W. Chinapen and the Ruhomon brothers. By 1931, there was quite a large body of poetry, leading to the next logical step: an anthology which appeared under the title *Guianese Poetry 1831-1931*, edited by the indomitable litterateur, N.E. Cameron. This was soon followed by *An Anthology of Local Indian Verse*, edited by Ramcahritar-Lalla in 1934. Some other anthologies worthy of mention are *A Treasury of Guyanese Poetry*, edited by A.J. Seymour in 1980, *Independence Ten, Guyanese Writing 1966-1976*, produced by the National History and Arts Council in 1975, *An Introduction to the Poetry of the East Indian Diaspora 1901-1991*, edited by Kampta Karran in 1991, *They Came In Ships*, Indo-Guyanese prose and poetry selected by Laxhmi Kallicharran, Joel Benjamin, Lloyd Searwar and Ian McDonald in 1998, *Just a Number*, edited by Roopnandan Singh in 2001 and *The Lure of the Mermaid and other stories*, edited by Janet Jagan in 2002.

While poetry dominated the literary landscape, the Guyanese novel would define and illuminate it. The work of Edgar Mittleholzer was seen as the pioneering effort that encouraged other writers to lend their pens to the creation of an indigenous voice. Jan Carew, Christopher Nicole, Wilson Harris, E.R. Braithwaite, Peter Kempadoo, O.R. Dathorne, Dennis Williams, Sheik Sadeek, Rooplall Monar and many others made contributions to this growing collection.

A few publishing houses have been responsible for allowing Guyanese writers to see their books in print. Peepal Tree Press, established in 1980 in the UK, has produced over seventy Guyanese titles; Hansib Publications, also UK-based and established in 1970 to publish newspapers and magazines, later turned to book publishing. In 1988, Hansib published a series of titles to mark the 150th anniversary of the arrival of East Indians in Guyana. Bogle-L'Ouverture, Dido Press, the Free Press and the Association of Guyanese Writers and Artists have all made contributions. And Sheik Sadeek stands out as a pioneer in local publishing.

The Cheddi Jagan Gold Medal for Literature was the literary accolade of the 1950s and 1960s, which was a fertile period for local writing. There were three active journals during this period: *Kyk-over-al*, edited by Seymour, *Kaie*, edited by Celeste Dolphin, and *New World*, edited by David DeCaires. In 1987, Desmond Hoyte established the Guyana Prize for Literature, which gave a boost to local writing. Internationally, Guyanese writers have excelled and won the Commonwealth Poetry and Fiction Prize, the Whitbread Prize, the Casa de las Americas Prize, the T.S. Eliot Poetry Prize and the Raja Rao Award. David Dabydeen, Fred D'Aguiar, John Agard, Harry Narain, Pauline Melville, Grace Nichols, Wilson Harris, Sasenarine Persaud and Paloma Mohamed, are among the winners of some of these prestigious honours.

Our literary heritage is rich and varied, influenced by the experiences and cultural miscellany that informs our existence. It has encouraged the flow of ideas, fostered debate and research and helped to promote tolerance among our peoples as it continues to inspire and engender creativity. Where it goes from here will depend largely on the new and emerging writers who must take up the torch and carry it on into the future. They have a great legacy on which to build and an abundance of sources on which to call. Our voices will be heard as our literary works continue to find their place in the world.

# THE GEORGETOWN PUBLIC HOSPITAL CORPORATION

THE GEORGETOWN PUBLIC HOSPITAL CORPORATION, Guyana's premiere heath institution was established in the late 1800s. Since then it has undergone significant and numerous transformations. In 2000, the management was changed and it became a non-profit corporation with an independent board and government representation. Six directorates make up the hospital. These include: Administrative, Medical and Professional Services, Internal Audit, Nursing Services and Facilities Management.

The corporation has been undergoing massive infrastructural development over the last few years at a cost of more than US$ 7.2m. The first major renewal project was the Ambulatory Care and Diagnostic Centre (ACDC) building, at a cost of some US$ 6m. This building is home to the medical, surgical, paediatric, obstetrics and gynaecology, diabetic, ear, nose and throat, audiology, speech therapy and intensive care clinics. The High Dependency Unit, main operating theatre, Skin Clinic, Bio Medical Unit, Eye Clinic, X-ray Unit, the main pharmacy, Orthopaedic Department and Accident and Emergency Unit also occupy this building.

Photo: J Ranjohn

The improved design for the Georgetown Hospital began in the mid 1980s with financing from the International Development Bank. However, construction began in earnest between 1992 and 1995. This included the construction of the Accident and Emergency area, main operating theatres, Intensive Care and High Dependency Units. A new pharmacy and the first Burn Care Unit in the Caribbean were also part of the new ACDC building. To date, this remains the only such facility in the Caribbean. This project also included the construction of other support service buildings, such as the power plant, dietary section and laundry.

The male medical unit was constructed between 1998 and 2000. Remedial works were carried out on the maternity building a few years ago at a cost of some US$ 25m.

The medical research library, the interns and doctor-on-call residence are all to receive massive upgrade in the near future. A new Reference Testing Laboratory is also to be constructed.

The programmes to be instituted are aimed at providing an improved quality and more complete health care services at all levels. Along with the infrastructural upgrades, the human resources at the institution as well as the equipment will be improved. The GPHC offers almost all of the services comparable with other CARICOM countries. The institution even offers a comprehensive chemotherapy program to cancer patients, which were expanded in 2005 to include

treatment of children with leukaemia. Through an agreement with the Global Imaging Services of Chicago, a new state-of-the-art Cancer Treatment Centre, equipped with the latest technological features to treat the disease, is to be opened soon. Under the agreement with the Chicago company, a comprehensive radiotherapy program will be provided to Guyanese living with cancer. The US-based company will operate the centre and provide its own specialists, which will include an oncologist.

A new state-of-the-art Cardiac Unit for bypass surgeries and angioplasty is now operational at the Georgetown Public Hospital. Up until now, those who required heart surgery were forced to go overseas since Guyana did not have the facilities to conduct such complex procedures. This project was facilitated through an agreement between Guyana's Health Ministry and a US-based medical team. The contractual arrangement entailed an initial US$ 2m investment by the Guyana government. Not only does this project allow for the expansion of services at the GPHC but it is also a major accomplishment for Guyana.

With the new Cardiac Unit, Guyanese will be able to access complex surgery and other treatments at a cost which will be subsidised to a large extent by the Guyana government. At the moment, local doctors are benefiting from the expertise of the many Chinese and Cuban specialists who complement the services offered at the GPHC.

# Sustained investment for improving healthcare

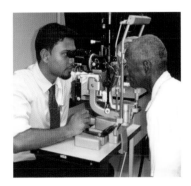

Healthcare across Guyana has been steadily improving, and with the introduction of the National Health Plan in 2002, there are broad based efforts to ensure that it responds to the needs of all Guyanese. A government initiative, the Health Plan emerged out of consultations with stakeholders at every level of the society and is a comprehensive strategy to tackle the complexities of catering to the nation's healthcare needs.

Improvement of infrastructure, along with a greater number of qualified healthcare professionals at every level, and making the society more aware of issues that affect good health, is leading to a population that is more and more capable of maintaining good health for longer periods. This is in keeping with the mission statement of the National Health Plan that seeks the improvement of the spiritual, physical and mental health status of Guyanese. This holistic approach means that healthcare is being viewed in a much more comprehensive manner than it was in previous times.

The guiding principles of the plan are linked to this overall concept and revolve around equitable distribution and utilization of healthcare services, effectiveness and quality of services provided, efficiency, sustainable financing and inter-sector collaboration and community participation. The general goal is the improvement in the health and quality of life of all Guyanese.

The country has four major public hospital complexes located in Georgetown, New Amsterdam, Linden and Essequibo, with many smaller health centres and cottage hospitals distributed throughout the country. The healthcare given by doctors and nurses is provided free of charge for citizens.

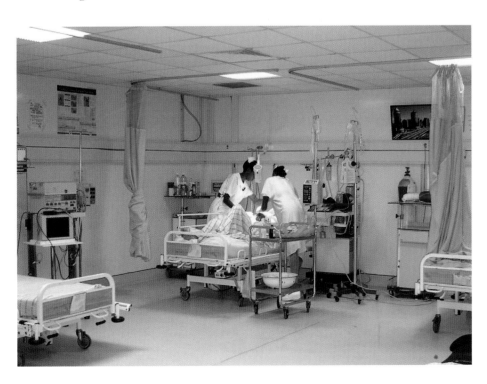

ABOVE & RIGHT
Patient care at the Georgetown Public Hospital Corporation is of the highest standard.   Photos: J Ramjohn

# RAISING MILLIONS FOR GOOD CAUSES

SINCE ITS LAUNCH IN AUGUST 1996, THE GUYANA Lottery Company has raised over two billion dollars for many social causes that include health and educational programmes and sports and cultural projects. It also provided assistance during the devastating floods that affected Guyana in 2005, in particular, in the form of help for senior citizens' and children's homes and with the donation of much-needed supplies. Funds raised by the Lotto also help towards the provision of medical equipment to public hospitals and also to support the local fight against HIV/AIDS.

Twenty-four percent of the money raised goes to the government for allocation to good causes. Funds are generated by instant ticket games as well as through such competitions as the Lotto, 3D and Play De Dream.

The Guyana Lottery Company is owned by Canadian Bank Note Company Inc. It has extensive manufacturing operations for printing currency, passports, visas, lottery tickets, postage and other related products as well as the manufacture and supply of card readers and lottery terminals.

Locally, the company employs more than thirty people as well as approximately 150 agents throughout the country.

# A PIONEER IN THE PHARMACEUTICAL INDUSTRY

PHARMAGEN ENTERPRISES EMERGED TO MEET THE needs of a society that needed the best products available to maintain a healthy lifestyle at a time when such products were not widely available. This family-owned business is now a leading pharmaceutical importer in Guyana.

In 1987, Carl Bacchus and his wife Jaiwantie (both pharmacists) established a retail outlet under the name of Medicare Pharmacy. Although this was not the first privately-owned pharmacy, it soon became synonymous with quality practices. The decision to expand to become a major importer was taken in 1991, and a wholesale division was set up under the name of Pharmagen Enterprises.

The company is now an importer and wholesale distributor of a wide range of products from the UK, North America, Europe and the Caribbean.

## HOSPITALS IN GUYANA

| | | |
|---|---|---|
| Aishalton District Hospital | South Rupununi | Region 9 |
| Balwant Singh Hospital (Private) | East Street, Georgetown | Region 4 |
| Bartica Hospital | Bartica | Region 7 |
| Charity Hospital | Charity, Essequibo | Region 2 |
| Davis Memorial Hospital (Private) | 121 Durban Backlands, Georgetown | Region 4 |
| Fort Canje Hospital (Psychiatric) | Fort Canje | Region 6 |
| Fort Wellington Hospital | Fort Wellington | Region 5 |
| Georgetown Medical Centre (Private) | Middle & Thomas Street, Georgetown | Region 4 |
| Georgetown Public Hospital Corporation | Thomas & New Market Streets, Georgetown | Region 4 |
| Kumaka District Hospital | Moruca | Region 1 |
| Kwakwani Hospital | Berbice River | Region 10 |
| Leguan Cottage Hospital | Leguan | Region 3 |
| Leonora Cottage Hospital | Leonora, West Coast Demerara | Region 3 |
| Lethem Hospital | Rupununi | Region 9 |
| Linden Hospital | Riverside Drive, McKenzie | Region 10 |
| Mabaruma Hospital | Mabaruma | Region 1 |
| Mahaica Hospital | Mahaica, East Coast Demerara | Region 4 |
| Mahaicony Hospital | Mahaicony | Region 5 |
| Mahdia District Hospital | Mahdia | Region 8 |
| Medical Arts Hospital (Private) | 265 Thomas Street, Georgetown | Region 4 |
| Mibikuri Hospital | Mibikuri, Black Bush Polder | Region 6 |
| New Amsterdam Hospital | Main & Garrison Roads | Region 6 |
| Pakeira Hospital | North West District | Region 1 |
| Port Kaituma Hospital | Port Kaituma | Region 1 |
| Port Mourant Hospital | Berbice | Region 6 |
| Skeldon Hospital | Skeldon, Berbice | Region 6 |
| St Joseph Mercy Hospital (Private) | 130 Parade Street, Kingston, Georgetown | Region 4 |
| Suddie Hospital | Public Road Suddie, Essequibo Coast | Region 2 |
| Upper Demerara Hospital | Blue Berry Hill, Wismar, Linden | Region 10 |
| Wakenaam Cottage Hospital | Belleplain, Wakenaam | Region 3 |
| West Demerara Regional Hospital | Bess, West Coast Demerara | Region 3 |
| Woodlands Hospital (Private) | 110 Carmichael Street, Georgetown | Region 4 |

**ABOVE**

Mabaruma is one of the most northern towns in Guyana and is situated near the country's border with Venezuela. The local hospital serves the residents of Region 1 (Barima – Waini).   Photo: I Brierley

## PLAYING A VITAL ROLE IN HEALTHCARE

LOCATED AT EAST BANK DEMERARA, NEW GPC INC. carries on an eighty-five year tradition as the Caribbean's oldest and largest manufacturer of pharmaceuticals and household products of the highest quality. Today, the company manufactures in excess of three hundred products as diverse as classics like 'Limacol', 'Whizz' and 'Ferrol', to life-prolonging drugs and treatments such as its range of anti-retrovirals. These world-class products are marketed throughout the Caribbean, North America and the United Kingdom.

Through its continued pioneering research and development activities, governmental and non-governmental collaborations and technological and human capital development, New GPC Inc. continues to lead the regional pharmaceutical industry and plays a vital role in the lives, health and traditions of West Indians, at home and abroad.

In Georgetown, the flagship of the healthcare system is the Georgetown Public Hospital Corporation, which is in the process of refurbishment that will make it one of the most modern facilities in the Caribbean. Its new Eye Clinic is helping to provide a more wide-ranging service for a broader cross section of Guyanese. In New Amsterdam, the hospital there was rebuilt with a loan from the Japanese Government, and the West Demerara hospital was also modernized.

Dental service has always been of the highest quality in Guyana with former President Cheddi Jagan practicing in that field before going on to lead the country. Over the years, assistance from the government of Cuba has enabled Guyanese to train in the field of dentistry. The Cheddi Jagan Dental Centre boasts some of the most advanced equipment in this part of the world, and many Guyanese who live abroad still come home to have their dental work done.

Private hospitals and medical practitioners are other facets of the health care options available to Guyanese. With five well known private hospitals: St Joseph's Mercy Hospital, Woodlands, Davis Memorial, Prasad's Georgetown Medical Centre, Medical Arts and, more recently, Balwant Singh's Hospital, there are many alternatives to using public facilities. In dentistry and optical services, as well, there are many private practitioners.

Funding to improve healthcare, and especially in the fight against HIV/AIDS, continues to flow into Guyana with the major donor being the United States government. This, along with the technical assistance provided, is beginning to stem the tide in the fight against these pandemics. The government is committed to working with all stakeholders, donors and citizens to create a better quality of life for Guyanese, and in the implementation of its Health Care Plan, it is beginning to see the results. ∎

# Education since 1953

WALTER B. ALEXANDER

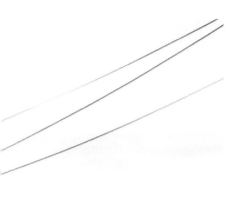

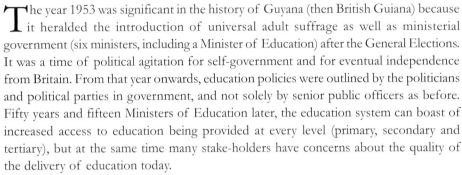

The year 1953 was significant in the history of Guyana (then British Guiana) because it heralded the introduction of universal adult suffrage as well as ministerial government (six ministers, including a Minister of Education) after the General Elections. It was a time of political agitation for self-government and for eventual independence from Britain. From that year onwards, education policies were outlined by the politicians and political parties in government, and not solely by senior public officers as before. Fifty years and fifteen Ministers of Education later, the education system can boast of increased access to education being provided at every level (primary, secondary and tertiary), but at the same time many stake-holders have concerns about the quality of the delivery of education today.

In the primary school sector the most dramatic change in the past half of a century was the complete take-over of all schools by Government in 1976. From that year to about 1992, no private school was allowed to operate in the country. Previously, about one quarter of the four hundred schools were government primary schools, the rest being denominational schools managed by the churches under a system of dual control. This hybrid system, born of the historical development of education in the then colony, permitted the churches to control the appointment of head teachers and teachers, while the state was responsible for the curriculum, teachers' emoluments and the payment of grants for maintenance of school buildings. Therefore, in the light of the attainment of independence in 1966, and the need to have an integrated and efficient education system in a country with diverse ethnic groupings, the then government, in one fell swoop, took control of all the church schools.

One of the immediate consequences was that a teacher could now be promoted on the basis of merit and seniority, and not including adherence to the particular denomination. Understandably, the churches protested the loss of their input in the moral and spiritual development of the pupils, but in an age of expansion of secular education, the will of the state prevailed. Just two years later (in 1978) the Teaching Service Commission was established which, under the Constitution of Guyana, is an independent body with responsibility for the appointment and discipline of teachers. Today, the state sector has 440 primary and 82 secondary schools, to which seventy percent of the more than seventeen thousand candidates, who write the Secondary Schools Entrance Examination, are awarded 'free' places.

However, by the last decade of the twentieth century there was a noticeable decline in the quality of education being delivered in the state sector, with a consequent demand for the re-establishment of private schools. The government conceded. Today, the education system has come full circle with the existence again of private nursery, primary and secondary schools established mainly by religious bodies and private individuals. Private schools are now located in Georgetown as well as in Regions Two, Three, Four, Five, Six and Ten. A few are officially established, while most others (more than sixty in number) are unregistered.

The highest tertiary institution is also part of the cycle. It influences the school system, which, in turn, determines the student input of the University of Guyana. This

ABOVE
Turkeyen Nursery School.   Photo: H Chan

RIGHT
Travelling to school along the Waini River in Region 1 (Barima – Waini).
Photo: I Brierley

FACING PAGE, TOP
School children at the Saxacalli Mission which is located twenty-five miles from Parika on the left bank of the Essequibo.   Photo: I Brierley

FACING PAGE, BOTTOM
A short break for teacher and pupils in the north-eastern town of Corriverton.
Photo: I Brierley

PREVIOUS PAGE 130
Minibuses known as 'tapirs' ferry pupils to and from school in Corriverton.
Photo: I Brierley

was the vision when the institution was established in 1963 after the decision was taken to break away from the University of the West Indies (UWI) and to establish a separate body that would prepare graduates for secondary school teaching, the civil service and other professions. From a mere 164 students in three faculties (Arts, Natural Sciences and Social Sciences) in 1963, and in borrowed accommodation at Queen's College, the University of Guyana has grown into a university with its own campus at Turkeyen. Since 1969, the university has grown in size and stature, and now has an enrolment of more than five thousand students and an additional three faculties (Education, Technology, Agriculture and Health Sciences) for full-time and part-time courses. The university also attracts students from the wider Caribbean who work, largely, towards degrees in Medicine and Law; would-be teachers, enrolled on degree and diploma courses, come mainly from the local secondary schools. ■

# The safety and defence of the nation

DAVID GRANGER

Guyana became independent in 1966 in a state of emergency. Externally, the new state's neighbours – Venezuela to the west and Suriname to the east – renewed claims to large swathes of its territory and sea-space, and internally, the population had been riven by ethnic and political rivalry and communal violence.

The security of the nation from external aggression and the safety of the population from the threats of criminal violence and terrorism became the chief priorities of the government.

Although at present Guyana's 2,500 km land frontier and coastline are relatively secure, defence against external aggression has always been a pressing concern. Just prior to independence, the colonial, part-time British Guiana Volunteer Force was demobilised and a regular army – the Guyana Defence Force (GDF) – was established under the Defence Act.

A unitary body, the GDF comprises a regular force which includes the Coast Guard, Air Corps and Women's Army Corps, and a reserve force, formerly known as the Guyana People's Militia, made up of citizen volunteers. The 2,500-member GDF is responsible for "the defence of, and maintenance of order in Guyana" among other duties. The President of the republic, in addition to his ceremonial title of Commander-in-Chief of the Armed Forces, is Chairman of the Guyana Defence Board, the governing authority of the GDF, and also has ministerial responsibility for defence.

Traditionally, the GDF has also been employed as a labour-rescue force during national emergencies such as the floods of 2005 and 2006. The Civil Defence Commission (CDC), the main disaster mitigation agency, is usually headed by a military officer. The Force has frequently travelled to other Caribbean countries – Antigua and Barbuda, Grenada, Jamaica, St Kitts-Nevis and elsewhere to assist in reconstruction after natural disasters, and to Haiti as part of an international stabilisation force. Although Guyana is not a signatory to the Regional Security System (RSS) Treaty, the GDF and the GPF participate in the annual US-sponsored Caribbean Exercise Tradewinds security manoeuvres.

As with other countries on the South American continent and in the Caribbean Basin, crime, resulting mainly from the narcotics trade, intensified during the last decade of the 20th century. The country's main crime-fighting and law-enforcement agency, the Guyana Police Force (GPF), has been in existence since 1839. Today, under the Police Act, the 3,000-member Force is responsible for "the prevention and detection of crime; the preservation of law and order; the preservation of peace; the repression of internal disturbance; the protection of property; the apprehension of offenders; and the due enforcement of all laws and regulations with which it is directly charged."

The Police Force possesses a Tactical Service Unit (TSU) which enables it to respond rapidly to emergencies and to conduct mobile counter-crime operations across any terrain, in the hinterland and on the borders. It also has a large auxiliary unit called the Special Constabulary and is assisted by scores of Community Policing Groups (CPG) made up of citizen volunteers. The Force covers the entire country through more than seventy stations and outposts and has active co-operation agreements with Brazil, Suriname,

TOP
Police headquarters in Georgetown.
Photo: I Brierley

LEFT
Ruimveldt Police Station.   Photo: H Chan

Venezuela, the United States, Caribbean states and other countries for the suppression of illegal, trans-border trade in narcotics and other crimes.

Given the importance of the campaign against trafficking in narcotics, the Police Force has a counter-narcotics branch, which concentrates on the eradication of narcotics production countrywide and also co-operates with the Customs Anti-Narcotics Unit (CANU), which focuses on ports of entry. Indeed, the vast size of the country in relation to its small population of just over 750,000 persons, its numerous rivers which flow northwards into the open Atlantic Ocean, its long coastline and borders, and the numerous aerodromes throughout the hinterland, all present challenges to the security and law-enforcement agencies to prevent the entry of contraband commodities and illegal aliens.

Most buildings in Guyana are made of wood, an abundant natural resource, but also the source of many costly fires. The Guyana Fire Service (GFS), previously a part of the Police Force, was established as a separate service in 1957 under the Fire Service Act. The duties and responsibilities of the GFS are, essentially, fire prevention, fire fighting and the protection of life and property from destruction by fire. The GFS is concentrated in coastal towns, settlements and aerodromes where the threat of fire is greatest.

TOP
Central Fire Station in Georgetown.
Photo: I Brierley

MIDDLE
The Women's Army Corps is part of the
Guyana Defence Force.   Photo: D Granger

BOTTOM
Internal security patrols are carried out
by the Guyana Defence Force.
Photo: D Granger

The Guyana Prison Service (GPS), established under the Prison Act, ensures the safe and secure custody of persons in accordance with the orders of the courts. The core function of the Prison Service is to ensure the safe custody of offenders who have violated the law of the land and are placed in physical confinement in order to protect society. The main prisons are located in the capital, Georgetown, at New Amsterdam (mainly for women), and at Mazaruni, in the hinterland.

The Police, Fire and Prison services are all administered by the Ministry of Home Affairs, which is charged with responsibility for public safety and public order.

With limited human, material and financial resources, Guyana embarked on aggressive diplomatic action by pioneering the creation of the Caribbean Community (CARICOM) and by participating actively in the Commonwealth, Organisation of American States (OAS), Non-Aligned Movement (NAM) and the United Nations. Guyana also established, equipped and trained agencies and forces capable of responding to the challenges to its territorial integrity and national security. Diplomacy, therefore, has been an important factor in preserving this country's national defence and security. ■

# A burgeoning media landscape

JOHN MAIR

Since the beginning of British rule in Guyana (then British Guiana), the country has had an active, privately-owned and government-controlled, press. Titles such as *The Argosy* and *Daily Argosy*, *Berbice Gazette & British Guiana Advertiser*, *The Colonist*, *The Creole*, *Daily Chronicle*, *Demerara Daily Chronicle*, *Guiana Chronicle and Demerara Gazette*, *Guiana Graphic* (later the *Guyana Graphic*), were established in the earliest years of the 19th century and post-Dutch rule. By the 1960s, many newspapers were being published.

By the 1970s the number of newspapers had dwindled until the last remaining private newspaper was the *Guyana Graphic*, owned by the Thompson Group. When the group decided to pull out of Guyana in 1973, the shares in the publication were offered for sale to the public. At the eleventh hour, however, the then Prime Minister, Forbes Burnham, introduced legislation which required state permission for the sale of company shares. Burnham refused to give permission, and the shares were subsequently bought by the government!

The *Guyana Graphic* was renamed *Guyana Chronicle* and was heavily controlled by the state and the ruling party. This was the country's only newspaper until the launch of the *Stabroek News* in November 1986. Set up by two lawyers, David Decairies and Miles Fitzpatrick, its arrival heralded a more liberal political climate following the death of President Forbes Burnham and his replacement by Desmond Hoyte. The *Stabroek News* soon developed a firm readership and an independent and often robust voice on Guyana's political scene.

The *Guyana Chronicle* is published seven days a week and is still under state control. However, its readership has diminished in recent years following the appearance of other newspapers.

The so-called "new kid on the block" is the *Kaieteur News*. Set up by shoe shop magnate, Glen Lall in 1996, this daily newspaper is a populist and regularly sensationalist tabloid. Of the three leading newspapers in Guyana, *Kaieteur News* has the highest circulation, followed by *Stabroek News* and the *Guyana Chronicle*.

*Guyana Chronicle* is published seven days a week and until the mid-1980s was the country's only newspaper.

The launch of *Stabroek News* in 1986 heralded the arrival of a more liberal political climate.

The daily *Kaieteur News* is a populist and regularly sensationalist tabloid.

Radio in Guyana is served by the state-owned NCN Radio. This monopoly of the airwaves has been often questioned but has remained relatively unchanged for the last thirty-five years.

In the beginning was Radio Demerara, a British-owned broadcaster with British content. It dominated throughout most of the 1950s until a second station – BGBS – was launched in December 1958. Ten years later, BGBS was nationalised and renamed GBS (Guyana Broadcasting Service). Ten years after that, both radio stations were taken into state ownership under the banner of the Guyana Broadcasting Corporation (GBC). That provided two channels – one national and one regional, followed in 1998 by a third channel, Hot FM.

In 2004, GBC merged with GTV to form the National Communications Network (NCN). Today, NCN Radio broadcasts one AM frequency (Voice of Guyana) and one FM frequency (Hot FM). It is still government controlled.

Guyana is a veritable 'wild west' where television broadcasting is concerned. It has been like this for more than a decade and shows no signs of changing in the foreseeable future. The country has developed a large number (twenty four at last count) of 'Television stations'.

The industry grew by stealth, beginning in 1990 with Tony Viera, the scion of an old sugar barony, who petitioned the then President, Desmond Hoyte, to be allowed to bring TV to Guyana. His wish was granted and Viera started an encrypted service for

## LARGEST RESOURCE BUILT ON EXPERIENCE AND SERVICE

AUSTIN'S BOOK SERVICES IS THE LARGEST AND MOST comprehensive resource for books and related products in Guyana. The company is the brainchild of Lloyd Austin who has been involved in the marketing of books for over 30 years.

Guyana had suffered from a shortage of good reading material for a number of years and Lloyd Austin, seeing the need, established the company to fill the gap. He has forged major links with all of the major book distributors worldwide and his store is the first choice for anyone looking for almost any type of book.

The company has become the leading source for textbooks from nursery to university and beyond, and you can find tomes in all of the major fields of human endeavour; from history to law, music to science, and gardening to decorating. There are books for children, adult reading, self-help and do-it-yourself. You can also find a wide selection of greetings cards, toys and games.

Austin's Book Services has proven over the years to be committed to its customers and an outstanding corporate citizen, giving back to the community through sponsorship and promotions. Realising that education is key to national development, Austin's Book Services will often go out of its way to source hard to get texts for specific buyers. This hands-on approach has allowed the company to build a strong customer base.

As a family-run business with a reputation for integrity, the bookstore is poised for growth and recently added a

second floor for the expanded product range now offered. With experience and understanding of the requirements of their customers, Austin's has more than earned its reputation as the nation's foremost resource for reading matter.

paying subscribers. However, it wasn't long before local Guyanese expressed their dissatisfaction with having to 'pay' for their television viewing, and the service was eventually made 'free to air'.

But Viera had set the 'purchasing' template for others to follow. Large satellite dishes, which were situated in the grounds of his former estate manager's house at Versailles, 'pulled down' US programmes and then rebroadcast them along the coast.

Post 1992, Viera's VCTV soon found itself joined on the TV broadcasting landscape by Rex Mackay's Channel 7. The diet brought to Guyanese viewers by Channels 28 and 7, and later by Jacob Rambarran's Channel 13, remains an almost entirely US affair.

Throughout the Nineties, many new TV stations were established throughout Guyana. Three were launched in Berbice (Little Rock, DTV and Corentyne Broadcasting); one in Essequibo (Tarzie); one in Linden (LTV); and one in East Coast Demerara (Hala Gala TV). In Georgetown, even more were established: Sharma, GWTV, MTV, NTN, Sancharra, Yuman Yassin, and Blackman TV. Today, Guyana has no fewer than 24 television stations.

Guyana's media landscape, which serves a population of just over three quarters of a million people, is nothing if not crowded. And although many flowers have been planted, they do not always have the prettiest blooms. ■

# Agricultural backbone of the nation

ELSIE CROAL

Agriculture is one of the principal forms of economic activity in Guyana and it has been called "the backbone" of the country, an appropriate designation, since approximately seventy percent of the population is primarily dependent on agriculture-related activities as a source of income. Growth in the sector averaged 5.4 percent from 1993 to 1999, and 4.3 percent to 2004, with output accounting for 32 percent of total Gross Domestic Product (source: Ministry of Agriculture).

Currently, most of the agricultural activity takes place on the narrow coastal plain, comprising less than ten percent of the total land, which is below sea level and requires the construction and maintenance of dykes and a sea wall for protection against inflows from the sea. The Dutch originally constructed these during the eighteenth century to utilise the fertile clay soils available on the coast, after reduced productivity on the former riverine estates made them unprofitable. The riverine areas continue to be used by small farmers for subsistence-level farming.

There are approximately 500,000 hectares of land under crops or 2.3 percent of total land area. Of this about 30.2 percent is irrigated. There are on-going efforts to make greater use of the soils in some of the other areas of the country such as the intermediate and interior savannahs for crops other than sugar and rice.

## THE HOME OF DEMERARA SUGAR

World renowned and genuine 'Demerara Sugar', which is only produced in Guyana, was introduced to the world in the mid-18th century – the name perpetuating, forever, a former name of the country. Sugar production has continued uninterrupted since then. Most of the sugar plantations were owned by British landlords and were eventually coalesced into ownership by two companies – Booker Sugar Estates Limited (nine estates) and Jessel Holdings (two estates). These estates were responsible for the production of the majority of the sugar cane produced but a small percentage was contributed by peasant cane farmers who sold their produce to the nearest sugar factory, a practice that continues to this day.

In 1976, the sugar industry was nationalised by the government and a state company – the Guyana Sugar Corporation (GuySuCo) – was formed to cultivate sugar cane and produce sugar. The corporation continues to produce one of the world's finest raw sugars. Sugar accounts for approximately twenty percent of Guyana's GDP and forty percent of agricultural production. Genuine Demerara sugar is exported to countries within the European Union, the United States and CARICOM countries such as Trinidad and Tobago, Suriname, St Lucia, Grenada, Antigua and Barbuda, Dominica, Barbados, St Vincent and Jamaica.

Since its formation, GuySuCo has implemented such restructuring as was considered necessary for efficient sugar production and the holdings now consist of five sugar estates and eight factories. The company's major product is Genuine Demerara sugar, exported in bulk form and shipped to the European Union under quotas specified by the ACP/EU Sugar Protocol, the Special Preferential Sugar Agreement and the US Quota. Sales are also made to Trinidad and Tobago under a Common Export Tariff

# IF IT'S NOT FROM DEMERARA, IT'S NOT 'DEMERARA'

IN 1832, AT THE VREED-EN-HOOP SUGAR ESTATE ON the west bank of the Demerara River, an innovative process involving the use of a vacuum pan with steam energy was introduced in the manufacturing of sugar. The crystals produced were so refined and of such superior quality that they could no longer be categorised as 'muscovado' sugar – the dark, sticky sugar commonly produced in the British colonies at the time. As a result, the product was re-classified by the British authorities as 'Demerara crystals' and subsequently referred to as "Demerara sugar".

Since then, there have been many incarnations of Demerara sugar, with the name, 'Demerara' being adopted by sugar producing countries throughout the world. Even beet sugar manufacturers are producing 'Demerara' sugar, and the term has become generic for just about any type of brown sugar. Indeed, much of the 'Demerara' sugar sold internationally is actually refined sugar coated with molasses.

Legal recognition of the term "Demerara sugar" as a sugar produced in the Demerara region of British Guiana was ended in November 1913 by a decision of the High Court of Justice in London. A magistrate dismissed the case against the sale of sugar described as "Demerara sugar" (but not the genuine article) on the grounds that the expression had become a "conventional term for the yellow crystal sugar not necessarily produced in Demerara".

The Oxford English Dictionary defines 'demerara sugar' (without initial capital, ed.) as "light brown cane sugar" – origin: from the region of *Demerara* in Guyana. Ninety years after the court ruling, the Guyana Sugar Corporation Inc. (GuySuCo), the only producer of genuine Demerara cane sugars, took steps to revalidate the dictionary's definition of the term 'demerara sugar' and regain global recognition of the product's original source.

In 2003, the corporation launched its first branded, pre-packaged sugar, 'Demerara Gold', a natural brown sugar made from the finest quality canes. Since then, Demerara Gold has established itself as the premium sugar in Guyana and many Caribbean countries as well as obtaining new and burgeoning markets in the US and UK. The corporation hopes that in time, and under the new dispensations for global trade and intellectual property recognition, the world will come to recognise that if it does not come from Demerara, it is not 'Demerara'.

Harvesting sugar cane is thirsty work

TOP
Harvesting paddy.   Photo: H Chan

ABOVE
Loading sugar cane into punts for
transportation from field to factory.
Photo: RJ Fernandes

PREVIOUS PAGES 146 & 147
Empty canal punts await the next sugar
cane harvest.   Photo: I Brierley

PREVIOUS PAGE 144
Irrigation canal running through a
coconut estate at Greenfield.
Photo: RJ Fernandes

Agreement and to the US. Molasses, a by-product of the sugar extraction process, is used locally in the production of rum and exported in bulk form to several Caribbean countries.

The corporation diversified its production and established a livestock complex in 1986, and a cheese and butter plant in 1989. The utilisation of bagasse (another by-product obtained after the juice has been extracted from the canes) for power generation in the factories is now being planned. This is part of the proposed strategy to improve productivity and to help counter the effects of the severe price cuts in sugar of 36 percent over a four-year period under the ACP/EU Sugar Protocol, due to take effect in 2006. The corporation has also developed pre-packaged sugar in the form of sachets and packages of 500g, 1kg, 2kg, 5kg and 10kg for sale to consumers, retailers, food services and the tourism industries.

GuySuCo has a strong history of training and research. Through its Apprenticeship Training Scheme and Management Training Centre the corporation is assured of a constant supply of trained personnel at all levels. Company research led to the introduction of smut disease-resistant varieties in 1974 and the varieties most utilised in current sugar cane production. Various technological advances have also been introduced over the years including superior environmental standards, programmes for insecticide and agrochemical stock reduction, use of chemical ripeners for increased yields, high density planting and the production of small acreages of organically-produced sugar.

## RICE – A SUCCESSFUL TRANSPLANT FROM THE EAST

It is reported that in 1738, rice (paddy) was introduced as a crop into Essequibo (then a Dutch colony, now Region 2, Pomeroon-Supernaam) to provide a staple food for the slaves on the sugar estates. Following Abolition, and the departure of the slaves from the estates, labour was sought through an indentureship scheme that brought workers from India to what was then British Guiana. Many of these labourers remained in the country after completion of their indentureship and rice cultivation increased through their efforts. The first recorded exports of rice from British Guiana were to Trinidad in 1889.

Due to reduced imports into the region during the First World War, British Guiana was afforded the opportunity to increase both rice production and rice exports, and by the end of the Second World War had a virtual monopoly on exports to West Indies markets, exporting 22,991 tons. Marketing was centralised through the British Guiana Rice Marketing Board – the forerunner of the current Guyana Rice Development Board – and by 1956, the country had gained the title, "breadbasket of the Caribbean" (source: *Our Rice Industry* by L Ramgopal).

Rice is the second major crop grown in Guyana, accounting for four percent of the GDP. In 2004, 74 percent of the crop was exported. Approximately 100,000 people (about thirteen percent of the population) rely on this industry.

Rice is grown mainly by small farmers with cultivations averaging 10-20 acres. Approximately 10,000 families depend on paddy production as the major income earner and there are numerous part-time paddy producers. The paddy produced on the farms is milled into rice in some 105 privately-owned mills, one of which is owned by a foreign company.

Over the past fifteen years, rice production generally increased both in acreage and yield per acre. The highest production (365,000 tonnes) in the history of rice production in Guyana was achieved in 1999. Production decreased somewhat until 2003 when the downward trend was reversed. Production in 2004 was 325,592 tonnes, and export increased to 243,093 tonnes or US$55,066,534, the highest export value since 1999. The industry is, therefore, recovering from the decline in export values in the recent past, which were due mainly to difficulties in both the CARICOM and EU markets. Rice is

ABOVE
Farmers drying paddy on the road.
Photo: H Chan

FACING PAGE
Unloading paddy at the Alesie complex.
Photo: I Brierley

# PROMOTING THE COUNTRY'S AGRICULTURE

GUYANA MARKETING CORPORATION (GMC) IS A government corporation established under section 46 of the Public Corporations Act, Cap 19:05 of the Laws of Guyana that has been working assiduously to promote the cultivation and export of Guyana's non-traditional agricultural crops.

The GMC is sometimes referred to as "New GMC" because in 1985 the policy of the organisation was changed. The corporation stopped its buying and selling operations, and a mandate to provide market information to the private sector for the export of non-traditional agricultural produce, facilitate local market development, develop and disseminate post-harvest technology to farmers, was adopted.

In 1997, GMC resumed the buying of farmers' produce and processed agricultural products and other locally-manufactured items. This was part of the corporation's effort to make Guyanese produce and products more accessible to consumers as well as to assist local agro-processors with the distribution of their products.

In 1999, to complement the efforts of creating a greater awareness for Guyanese products, GMC launched its 'Made in Guyana, Grown in Guyana' campaign. This promotion was taken to all parts of the country and the highlight of the campaign was the 'Guyana Nights' that are held in various regions.

Guyana Marketing Corporation's stall at one of the many agricultural fairs attended by the organisation

Apart from these activities, GMC also has the responsibility of overseeing developments in the non-traditional agricultural sector. The corporation provides exporters of non-traditional agricultural products with marketing and technical information, assistance for sourcing supplies, harvesting, cleaning, packaging and facilitating logistical arrangements for exports.

exported to the European Union through a quota shared with Suriname, and to other markets such as the wider Caribbean, South and Central America and West Africa.

Rice production is supported by an active rice research programme focusing on, among other activities, the production of rice cultivars resistant to blast disease, and to the production of pure line seed paddy for sale to farmers.

The industry faces several potential challenges. In recent years the coastal plain has been subject to both floods and droughts due in part to the El Nino and El Nina phenomena. Increased production and productivity in many rice-exporting countries has resulted in a decrease in global rice prices in recent years, and the ongoing increases in oil prices are a significant factor in this highly mechanised industry (source: Guyana Rice Development Board).

## FROM THE EXOTIC TO THE MUNDANE

A diverse range of other non-traditional crops is produced including peanuts, legumes, bananas, plantain, cassava (manioc), pineapple, citrus and vegetables. These are all exported in small quantities, as are more exotic products for which niche markets have been identified. Several of these are largely unknown in international trade but are in great demand in those developed countries which have large immigrant populations. Lesser-known produce such as passion fruit, 'dry coconut', awara, bilimbi, bora, carilla, ochro, cerasee tea, breadfruit, saeme and sapodilla are commonplace in Guyana but are not easily available to Guyanese communities overseas.

Some production highlights in this sub-sector include the start made with organic farming in Mabaruma-Hososoro (Region 1, Barima-Waini) where 100 acres of cocoa were rehabilitated with support from the Prince of Wales Fund and with identified marketing opportunities in the UK.

A peanut production programme is ongoing in the hinterland area of Upper Takatu-Upper Essequibo (Region 9) to provide a quality product for local and overseas markets and to provide a livelihood for residents of the region who are mostly Guyana's indigenous Amerindians. Cashew nut production and processing is another exotic crop initiative in this region, producing nuts through an innovative roasting system. The nuts are sold locally in supermarkets and other retail outlets.

Coconut remains an important crop in certain regions, especially Pomeroon-Supenaam (Region 2), where an oil mill was commissioned in 1999 capable of processing all the copra produced in the region into edible oil for local consumption and for export. Small-scale initiatives in 'other crops' in several regions include beekeeping for honey, cut flowers, oil palm and cassava.

## LIVESTOCK

The country's largest livestock herds were once found on the rolling savannahs of the Rupununi, bordering Brazil, where some of the oldest soils on earth are found. Here, cattle grazed on the lush savannah grasses, moving at will between the two countries and identifiable only by their owners' brands. In those days, animals destined for the coastal markets were driven along a well-known cattle trail, arriving on the coast, weeks later, after journeying through the length of the country, herded by the local cowboys or vaqueros (in Spanish).

Air transport has superseded this method of supply and now the coastal herds have increased so that the largest herds, both private and commercial, are now on the coast. This situation is due, in part, to the success of a National Dairy Development Programme

ABOVE
Gathering coconuts in the north-eastern town of Corriverton.  Photo: I Brierley

ABOVE LEFT
A Georgetown stall-holder demonstrates his technique for preparing water coconuts.
Photo: H Chan

FACING PAGE
Transporting crabwood seeds.
Photo: I Brierley

(NDDP) that is intended to achieve national self-sufficiency in milk and milk products in the shortest possible time through improved pasture availability, improved breeding and herd management practices, and education and extension activities among cattle rearers. As a result of these efforts national milk production has increased from 2.8 million gallons in 1983 to 8.75 million gallons in 1993, a saving of GUY$3.5 billion. The national herd is now estimated to be between 260,000 and 275,000 animals, of which 200,000 are for beef production and 70,000 for dairy produce. Milk is collected and processed locally into pasteurised milk, flavoured milk products and related dairy products such as yoghurt and cheese at a number of milk plants. Three regions are on the verge of self-sufficiency in milk.

The Ministry of Fisheries, Crops & Livestock implements a more detailed Livestock Development Programme which focuses on promoting efficiency in the rearing of poultry, cattle, swine, sheep and goats with the aim of increased production and

# HIGH STANDARD OF SERVICE AND BUSINESS PRACTICE

ESTABLISHED IN 1981, AND SPECIALISING IN ESSENTIAL foods such as poultry meats, groceries and dairy products, DIDCO Trading Company Limited has since grown into one of the nation's largest commercial establishments and is now a household name.

As Guyana embarked upon its course of national development, DIDCO took the initiative to establish the Integrated Poultry Strategy. This comprehensive programme involved the establishment of a highly technological feed mill, state-of-the-art hatchery, poultry farms and poultry processing plant. This project has seen an increase in annual production to approximately 18.5 million pounds of poultry meat and has positioned the company as the largest poultry producer in Guyana.

In addition to its interests in meat production, DIDCO has established its own shipping arm with its own wharfing, bond and warehousing facilities. Specialising

in ocean freight, the company also acts as agents for other shipping lines such as Carolina Line and Associated Transport Line.

Further diversification saw the company enter into tissue paper production in 2000. It currently produces the local brands 'Unique' and 'Gentle' and it has plans to expand its distribution into other Caribbean markets.

The DIDCO Group of Companies has continued its expansion with the establishment of Friendship Hotel and Restaurant Holdings Limited. This company has the national franchises for the KFC and Pizza Hut brands, which are the largest fast-food establishments in Guyana.

The group now employs over five hundred full-time staff as well as many contract and part-time employees. It has a firm commitment to the further development of Guyana and constantly strives for the highest standards of service and business practice.

productivity, attaining national self-sufficiency and promoting the export of livestock and livestock products.

Guyana's sheep population numbers 200,000 and the national goat herd is approximately 100,000. Animal quality benefited immensely through the supply of breeding rams and improved management techniques obtained during a project sponsored by the Caribbean Agricultural Development Institute (CARDI) during the 1990s. The country is self-sufficient in mutton, a very popular meat which is especially in demand for certain Muslim religious observances. Goats are reared for domestic consumption and local sale.

The country is self-sufficient in chicken and eggs, importing only small quantities of exotic poultry such as Cornish hens and turkeys. Hatching eggs and baby chicks are imported and broilers and layers are produced locally by small-scale producers and larger commercial farms. Poultry production in 2005 was 22,699,412 kg with table egg production at 24,123,726.

Production of Peking and Kunshan ducks became popular over the past fifteen years through co-operation with China which supplied hatching eggs. Peking, Kunshan and Muscovy ducklings are produced at the Livestock Farm managed by the main agricultural research institute, National Agricultural Institute (NARI), and sold to farmers. In 2001, 86,000 ducklings were sold but this number decreased in 2002 due to ageing of the parent stock. With the replacement of the parent stock in 2003 the numbers of ducklings sold have begun to increase.

# A LEADER IN GUYANA'S FISHING INDUSTRY

PRITIPAUL SINGH INVESTMENT INC. WAS ESTABLISHED in 1999 when its founder and Managing Director, Pritipaul Singh, rented the ageing facilities of Guyana Fisheries Ltd at Mc Doom, East Bank Demerara. The company's operations are now conducted at two self-sufficient, integrated facilities, which are both, located along the Demerara River close to the main port and capital city of Georgetown.

Mr Singh and his Finance Director, Ronald Deen, originally sought and obtained financing from C. Phillip Jones and Co. Ltd of the United Kingdom and the local National Bank of Industry and Commerce. An investment programme of US$32 million was implemented and resulted in the purchase of the facility and its development and modernization. The company's technical staff then made it into one of the largest, most modern and diversified shrimp and fish processing complexes in Guyana.

At the nine-acre, Mc Doom location (Mid Atlantic Seafoods), there are three ice machines, generators, a dry

Seabob trawlers

Workers load seabob into a bulk tank prior to peeling

dock, an extended wharf that adjoins the plant, blast and plate freezing facilities and peeling machines. The fleet of vessels consists of fifteen seabob trawlers, twenty red snapper vessels and fifteen other wooden fishing vessels, all providing raw material to the plant. Fish is also purchased from artisanal fishermen throughout the coast of Guyana. The plant has the capacity to process forty-five tons of seabob and sixty tons of fish every day. Peeled frozen seabob and fish in various forms are exported from this location to North American and Caribbean markets.

The six-acre, Providence location (Bee Gee Shrimp) was acquired following the purchase of the former Georgetown Seafoods and Trading Company in May 2005. The facilities are similar to those in Mc Doom, with the exception that there are no plate freezers and the fleet consists of thirty-one prawns trawlers. This plant produces and exports headless shrimp (prawns), peeled shrimp (prawns) and squid to North American markets.

Dry-dock at the Mc Doom plant

One of the company's ice plants

## FISHERIES

The potential of fishery products has long been recognised in Guyana and development of the sector proceeded apace during the 1980s. By the end of the decade shrimp had become the third leading earner of foreign exchange after sugar and bauxite. Production totalled 45,000 tons in the mid-1980s, of which 3,600 tons was shrimp, the most valuable portion. Shrimp exports for 2001 were 25,800 metric tons (m/t) but this figure has slipped since then and in 2004 total shrimp exports were only 18,605. However, total fin fish exports continued to increase from the 2001 figure of 24,700 m/t to 37,073 m/t in 2004. More exotic fish products exported include dried fish glue, salted shark, shark fin, shark bones, live crabs, crab meat, squid, ornamental fish and live aquarium fish. The total value of fish products exported in 2004 was over GUY$12.6 billion.

Special attention is being paid to development of the aquaculture industry and three species of tilapia fingerlings are offered for sale to potential freshwater farmers. The cultivated acreage under fish farming has risen tremendously from 2.5 acres in 1997 to over 2000 acres.

## SUPPORTING INSTITUTIONS

As befits a major sector, agriculture in Guyana is supported by a number of institutions and support services. Training at the tertiary level is offered at the University of Guyana's Faculty of Agriculture, the Guyana School of Agriculture, the Agricultural In-Service Training and Communication Centre and the GuySuCo Management Training Centre. The GuySuCo Apprentice Scheme offers training for operatives in all areas relevant to the sugar industry and the corporation conducts research in sugar.

The Guyana Rice Development Board is responsible for rice research and more general agricultural research is conducted by the NARI, which seeks to maintain and increase productivity and quality in crop and animal practice, and to integrate knowledge with agricultural production, processing and marketing into systems which optimise resource management and facilitate the transfer of technology to users. The institute replaced the former Central Agricultural Station which operated under the authority of the then Ministry of National Development and Agriculture in 1964, to more effectively

ABOVE
The hassar is a member of the catfish family and is found in coastal rivers. It is a popular addition to the Guyanese menu, especially when curried.
Photo: I Brierley

ABOVE RIGHT
Fishing boats awaiting their next outing.
Photo: H Chan

utilise the available scientific research personnel. The institute maintains field stations serving various functions at locations covering different ecological zones and conducts several research programmes including the Root, Tuber and Other Food Crops Programme, the Vegetable and Seed Production Programme, the Biotechnology, Plant Genetic Resources and Crop Protection Programme, and the Livestock and Pasture Programme, with each of these broad categories having a number of sub-programmes.

The Ministry of Fisheries, Crops and Livestock offers co-ordinating and administrative services and provides extension services for farmers and fishermen countrywide in collaboration with local (regional) government bodies. It also co-ordinates plant health matters such as plant and animal quarantine, to protect the nation from the unintentional import of diseases which could damage the country's production and to ensure that only disease-free, high-quality agricultural products are exported.

The Lands and Surveys Commission is responsible for the survey and mapping of the country's land and water resources, and are the custodians of all public lands, which are administered in the public interest. This entity processes all applications for the distribution of State and Government land for agricultural purposes. Land is available to individuals for agricultural purposes through annual permissions, licences or leases under specific terms.

A marketing advisory service is offered by the 'new' Guyana Marketing Corporation which is charged with provision of market facilitation services to the private sector for the export of non-traditional crops. This function is carried out through the facilitation of local market development, the dissemination of post-harvest technology and the provision of appropriate market research. The agency became 'new' in 1986 when its policy was changed from an operation responsible for buying and reselling farmers' produce to the mandate outlined above. In 1997, the purchase of farmers' produce was resumed at prices negotiated directly with farmers and manufacturers, for products of high quality and for which there was a ready market. In 1999, a 'Made in Guyana, Grown in Guyana' campaign was launched and taken to all parts of the country to create greater awareness of Guyanese products. The highlight of this campaign is the popular Guyana Night extravaganzas, held in various regions to showcase the country's primary and secondary agricultural products.

Activities undertaken by the New GMC include the provision of market and marketing information, advice on the availability of produce, freight and other marketing matters,

ABOVE
Harvesting coffee beans in the Pomeroon area of northern Region 2 (Pomeroon – Supenaam).
Photo: RJ Fernandes

ABOVE LEFT
Guyanese fruit stalls offer a wide and abundant variety of produce. Photo: H Chan

FACING PAGE
Undeveloped roads such as this are known locally as 'back-dams' and lead through the paddy fields.
Photo: RJ Fernandes

a one-stop desk for export documentation of non-traditional agricultural produce, advice on the availability of trade and business opportunities and facilitation of the registration of exporters with the US Food and Drugs Administration (FDA).

The agency also conducts market studies for the local and export markets and participates in trade fairs and other exhibitions to promote Guyana's fresh fruits, vegetables and processed products.

The peculiar situation of Guyana's coastal belt (several meters below sea level) requires constant vigilance. This is supplied by the National Drainage and Irrigation Board (D&I Board), which deals with all public matters pertaining to the management, improvement, extension and provision of drainage, irrigation and flood control infrastructure in declared areas of the country.

Water control is accomplished through several conservancies along the coast, each managed by a Board, or in the case of the Abary Conservancy, the Mahaica-Mahaicony-Abary Agricultural Development Authority (MMA-ADA), and each collaborating with the D&I Board to reduce the flooding to which the coast is so prone. The MMA Authority is particularly important for agricultural production in Mahaica-Berbice (Region 5). This is a three-phase project intended to facilitate the development of about 450,000 acres of land for agricultural purposes, between the Mahaica and the Berbice Rivers. Under the scheme, water control is to be provided for the coastal lands to a distance of some thirty miles inland by impounding surface waters in reservoirs (conservancies) located in the upper reaches of the rivers. Drainage and irrigation would be provided through engineering infrastructure at appropriate times for crop cultivation. Construction works for Phase 1 of the project were completed, making available 37,524 acres for the growing of paddy and facilitating a further 20,000 acres of private lands for similar cultivation. Extensive livestock rearing and some sugar cultivation have also been made possible through the works. This area supports nearly half of the national rice production and about 30-35 percent of national sugar production (source: Mahaica-Mahaicony-Abary Agricultural Development Authority).

ABOVE
Market stall-holders ply their trade in the shadow of the clock tower at Stabroek Market. Photo: H Chan

## WHAT LIES AHEAD?

Guyana's potential in the agricultural sector has long been recognised and indeed highlighted in the well-deserved term "the breadbasket of the Caribbean". In recent decades both production and export have increased despite the constraints.

The Ministry of Fisheries, Crops and Livestock, established in 1997, is the government agency with responsibility for the development of the sector. The Ministry's mission statement envisions the formulation and implementation of policies and programmes to facilitate the development of agriculture in Guyana. This focus is expected to contribute to the enhancement of rural life and the improvement of incomes of producers and others involved in agricultural production and marketing. The Ministry's programmes emphasise the removal of constraints to production and trade, as an important prerequisite for the infusion of new local and foreign investment in the sector, to increase production and productivity and to encourage the expansion of currently under-capitalised agro-related industries. Priority has been given to measures expected to promote new technical knowledge, the reformation and strengthening of agricultural support services, and improving accessibility to land for agricultural use.

Success is expected to result in the creation of new jobs, increased self-employment in the production area, the revitalising of crops such as coffee, cocoa, cashew, and the development of new crops and products.

Failure is not an option in this endeavour. Too many lives in this high potential but still developing country depend on ongoing success. ∎

## From cowboys to rodeo stars

FROM THE FOOTHILLS OF THE PAKARAIMAS to the base of the Kanukus, this land that Makanaima (the great spirit of the Amerindian peoples) once walked was from the 1920s to the early 1970s ruled by cattle. The first animals were brought from Brazil in the 1860s by a Dutch trader, de Rooie. By the end of the century he was joined by the Scotsman H.P.C. Melville and by the 1920s cattle dominated the landscape.

Here, the livestock was worked by Amerindians, gentlemen, rogues and vagabonds alike creating a culture steeped in local traditions and pitted with Brazilian and English jargon.

The trail to the coast ranged from Dadanawa in the south, heading north to Surama, across the Essequibo at Kurupukari, on to Canister Falls in Demerara and finally ending at the Berbice River where a steamer would bear the cattle to Georgetown. Nourished on fareen (grated and parched cassava) and tasso (dried salt beef) the vaqueros (cowboys) would regale 'coast-landers' with encounters of animals prehistoric in magnitude, of magnificent plants, and demon spirits of mythic lore and untold treasures.

The days of the cattle barons are gone; unfavourable political attitudes and harsh economic conditions leave them diminished but stubbornly still extant. Fighting to preserve the land and traditions ranchers turn to tourism and conservation. They ensure that, though lacking its former grandeur, the cattle culture lives on. Yesterday's heroes are elevated to legend and new heroes emerge with GPS technology on their belts and no shoes on their feet.

# A new chapter in the tourism story

DONALD SINCLAIR

Last frontier; kingdom of nature; wild country; naturally wild – all familiar descriptives that permeate the brochures and travel writings that focus upon Guyana. Whatever the description, the same truth lies at the core of the perceptions – that Guyana is a place of ineffable beauty. For Herb Hiller it is a place of "rugged wilderness and raw beauty." Margaret Bacon endorses that sentiment in her description of nature in Guyana as largely "unbeholden and unexploited." It is those perceptions, images and readings of the Guyana landscape, combined with an economic imperative, that have inspired and driven the development of a tourism industry in Guyana.

It is by now both common knowledge and conventional wisdom that Guyana is the newcomer in the family of Caribbean tourist destinations. Long after the Bahamas, Jamaica, Barbados and Antigua and Barbuda had been luring sun-seeking North American and European tourists to their blue waters and sandy beaches, tourism in Guyana was barely in its infancy. That delay in the development and exploitation of tourism resources in Guyana was in large measure a result of the buoyancy of the economic trinity of sugar, rice and bauxite (therefore there was little economic pressure to diversify), and a deep-rooted, official suspicion of the social impacts of tourism. A former Prime Minister is the author of the famous and oft-quoted statement about tourism creating "false values" and leading to a "nation of waiters, sycophants and sometimes pimps". Economic buoyancy and official distrust combined to postpone, in Guyana, any significant engagement with tourism. But tourism was already happening, even as far back as the early twentieth century.

It might be that the first known official tourist guide, written in 1912 by Edith Browne, was *British Guiana as a Holiday Resort*. That remarkable, detailed work describes the holiday spots, tourist services and attractions to be found in British Guiana in the early twentieth century. Descriptions of Georgetown, the "Garden City" with its tree-lined avenues and

# ECO RESORT IS AN OASIS FOR NATURE-LOVERS

LOCATED NEAR ANNAI, IN THE BEAUTIFUL NORTH Rupununi savannahs, Rock View Lodge is a wilderness resort that is ideally suited for nature lovers, bird enthusiasts and tourists seeking a holiday with a difference.

Accessible by scheduled, internal flights and also by bus, the lodge is ideally situated for visits to the Iwokrama canopy walkways, the Amerindian village of Surama, and the Karanambu Ranch, which is famous for its giant otters and aquatic bird life.

Rock View's guest lodge has eight tastefully designed, self-contained suites located within beautifully landscaped gardens. There is also a rock pool set amid lush vegetation and in the shade of cashew trees. A working ranch offers guests the rare opportunity of riding with Amerindian cowboys (vaqueros), and nature trails and river outings present the chance to see Guyana's flora and fauna at close range.

With its tropical gardens – cooled by the north-easterly trade winds from the mountains and rainforest – Rock View Lodge resembles an oasis in the savannahs. The resort attracts bird enthusiasts and nature lovers alike as well as travellers in search of a break from the hustle and bustle of everyday life.

stately canals are sure to induce nostalgia in today's residents of the capital city. Many of those early tourists were in fact colonial officials and their families travelling to and within the colonies on business or for relaxation. Edith Browne's writing bears evidence of a very close familiarity with both the landscape and cultural diversity of the country she was visiting. She is equally at home among the mysterious first peoples of Guyana, as she is in the teeming markets of Georgetown or on the majestic Essequibo River. The chronicles of these early travellers are still with us today, creating a seamless thematic thread of celebration that extends to the pages of today's official tourist guides and publications.

Travellers continued to make their way to Guyana, more at a trickle than an avalanche, throughout the periods of the two world wars. To promote those visits and to give some form and structure to the administration of tourism, a British Guiana Tourist Committee was established. But in the absence of any over-riding national zeal for developing tourism the efforts of that committee were seen to be well-intentioned but sporadic and incoherent. The decade of the sixties was perhaps the crystallisation of official distancing of tourism when the "waiters and sycophants" statement was uttered. The decade of

# FINE LIVING AND FINE DINING AT GRAND COASTAL

ESTABLISHED IN 2001, THE GRAND COASTAL INN AND the Grand Coastal Lodge are the embodiment of style, elegance and relaxed Caribbean living.

Situated at Le Resouvenir on the east coast of Demerara, and approximately ten minutes' drive from Georgetown, Grand Coastal Inn is a well-appointed boutique hotel comprising 43 rooms which include ten one-bedroom suites, executive and deluxe rooms, and two luxury suites with private patios overlooking the waterfall pool area and the seawall. All rooms are air-conditioned and have international direct dialling, large screen cable television and complimentary high-speed Internet access.

Dining at Grand Coastal Inn is a unique experience provided by its 'Caribbean Soul' restaurant. The sophisticated menu is an eclectic mix of seasonal fresh fruits and vegetables, an array of meats, fresh seafood and fine wines. It sits alongside 'Daru', the poolside bar which also has its own outdoor dining area.

The inn is less than five minutes from the Caricom Secretariat, the Convention Centre at Liliendaal and Ogle Airport – Guyana's gateway to the interior and to the Caribbean.

The Grand Coastal Lodge is situated in the heart of the capital and offers a bed and breakfast service with long-stay apartments and kitchenettes.

ABOVE
The Baganara Island Resort occupies
the largest of more than three hundred
islands located in the Essequibo river.
The resort is a favoured escape of the
rich and famous, including Rolling
Stones front-man Mick Jagger.
Photo: I Brierley

the seventies, with sugar reigning supreme and self-reliant, socialist rhetoric beginning to be sounded, saw very little softening of the attitude towards tourism development. That softening occurred in the early eighties when economic stringencies were forcing a reassessment of economic priorities. In the new pragmatism tourism was seen as a viable economic alternative for Guyana.

As if arousing from a hundred year slumber tourism activity in Guyana quickened almost to a frenzy in the decades of the eighties and nineties. A tourism portfolio was added to the Trade Ministry and a private sector umbrella organisation – the Tourism Association of Guyana (later the Tourism and Hospitality Association of Guyana) – came into being. The First National Conference on Tourism was hosted in 1993 by the University of Guyana which introduced a programme in Tourism Studies. Meanwhile, studies of the Guyana tourism product began to proliferate as consultants produced tourism development plans and road maps for an industry rearing for take-off. Guyana joined the Caribbean Tourism Organisation and in 1996 a 'Visit Guyana Year' campaign was launched. By the decade of the nineties the Guyana tourism product was, by general

# A HAVEN FOR RECREATION AND RELAXATION

SPLASHMIN'S FUN PARK AND RESORT IS NESTLED IN the Madewini basin and is a cool 45 minutes' drive from Georgetown. Since its establishment in 2000, it has been committed to the enhancement of Guyana's tourism sector by providing a high standard of service and by promoting the country as a burgeoning tourist destination. This beautiful resort was established on four hundred acres of rainforest and comprises the Fun Park, Eco Adventure Camping Grounds and Splashmin's Hotel. The hotel is Guyana's latest, luxury accommodation and provides all the usual amenities that visitors expect for a relaxing and enjoyable stay. Constructed in March 2007, Splashmin's Hotel comprises twenty-four artistically designed, air-conditioned luxury rooms.

The camping grounds and eco wetland tours offer an adventurous outdoor experience, whether travelling through the rainforest or simply relaxing in a hammock.

# TRADITIONAL STYLE AND HOSPITALITY

COMING TO GUYANA FOR BUSINESS OR PLEASURE IS a memorable experience for guests at the Hotel Ariantze and Sidewalk Café and Jazz Club – an intimate and elegantly appointed boutique hotel that epitomises Guyanese style and hospitality. Established over a decade ago, Hotel Ariantze embodies a certain niche in the hospitality market that provides superb service, traditional quality and homely charm.

Situated in the centre of the capital, and within walking distance of the major shopping areas, this delightful getaway boasts all of the features that reflect a Georgetown of days gone by. With its colonial styling and attentive staff, guests might feel as if they were in another place and time. This said, however, the hotel also has all the usual, modern conveniences: air conditioning, television, wireless internet access in all rooms and laundry service.

Downstairs in the Sidewalk Cafe and Jazz Club, food and entertainment go hand-in-hand with a daily luncheon buffet offering Creole dishes – the names of which are synonymous with Guyanese culture: pepperpot, metem, curry and roti. A la carte dining is also available in the Bourbon Restaurant.

In the evenings, the place comes alive with all kinds of entertainment: a movie, the occasional poetry reading, dance music, and the highlight of the week, a live jazz performance by some of the Caribbean's most noted artistes.

Guest can complete their Guyana experience by purchasing authentic Caribbean arts and crafts from the hotel's Fine Art Gallery and Calabash Gift Shoppe.

ABOVE
Canopy walkways are popular attractions for visitors to Atta Rainforest Lodge, Iwokrama International Centre and Rock View Lodge.

acclamation and acknowledgement, understood to be a 'green' or 'back to nature' or 'eco-tourism' product. Black waters, jungle, wildlife, flora and fauna, all formed the elements of the mystique of Guyana's tourism. The slogans "Guyana, naturally" and the "kingdom of nature" became associated with Guyana's tourism as the country set about projecting this product image onto the screen of the global marketplace.

With the establishment of the Guyana Tourism Authority in September 2002 the administrative ground was laid for the tourism take-off. In the private sector a decade of spirited investments in hotels, resorts, nature lodges, land, river and air transport ensured that capacity existed for the numbers generated by the marketing initiatives of both the Tourism Authority and the Tourism and Hospitality Association of Guyana. Ministry and Tourism Authority supported local trips and overseas expos further extended a marketing thrust aimed at the Guyanese diaspora, prospective Caribbean visitors and first-time visitors from Europe and North America.

On the product side much imagination and more money were being applied to the diversification and enrichment of the tourism product. The Kaieteur Falls, with its sheer

# A VACATION TO MEET THE 'GIANTS' OF GUYANA

FOR ALMOST THREE DECADES, DIANE MCTURK HAS cared for orphaned giant otters at the family's Karanambu ranch. Situated along the Rupununi River, Karanambu presents an opportunity for visitors to experience Guyana's wildlife at close range. Treating guests like friends the McTurk family now shares its home with visitors from around the world. Thatched cabins provide rustic

accommodation but the experience is all about exploring various habitats, either by boat, four-wheel drive or on foot. This is the place where guests can come face-to-face with the 'giants' of the natural world: giant anteater, giant otter, capybara (the world's largest rodent), arapaima (the world's largest scaled freshwater fish) and the splendid *Victoria Amazonica* (the world's largest water lily).

# A COMPLETE TRAVEL AND TOURISM OPERATOR

### RORAIMA RESIDENCE INN

Officially opened by Guyana's President, Bharrat Jagdeo, in July 2004, the Roraima Residence Inn is located in Bel Air Park, Georgetown. The hotel was established to accompany the services offered by Roraima Airways in order to provide a complete travel and tourism operation.

This boutique hotel offers an extensive range of facilities including air-conditioned rooms, wireless internet access, swimming pool, restaurant, bar and fitness centre.

### ARROWPOINT RESORT

Opened ten years ago, the Arrowpoint Resort lies on the Pokerero Creek (a tributary of the Demerara River) and provides a secluded and relaxing atmosphere. Owned and managed by Captain Gerry Gouveia of Roraima Airways Inc., Arrowpoint is the ideal insight into eco-tourism.

Accommodation consists of four comfortable suites, two rooms in the main house, as well as a conference room with a thirty-person capacity. Activities on offer include mountain biking along the resort trails, canoeing, surf biking and swimming, and at night, guest are treated to expeditions, bonfire dinners and beach games.

drop of 741 feet, emerged as Guyana's signature attraction, challenging the technical ingenuity of celebrated German film producer Werner Herzog. The Iwokrama Rainforest Centre gained international respectability and renown as an archive and laboratory of the sustainable uses of the rainforest. Guyana's diverse bird populations were exciting the interest of serious birders, while the Rupununi in southern Guyana was making a name for itself as a living museum of indigenous vitality.

As more investors ploughed money into the tourism industry a raft of nature and leisure resorts and lodges emerged, offering weekend distraction and soft adventure as well as a more serene experience of natural beauty far from the hustle and bustle of the city. Landing at the newly renovated and welcoming Cheddi Jagan International Airport, visitors can now be whisked a short distance away to the Timehri docks where small boats wait to take visitors through the enchanted corridor of the Kamuni Creek to Timberhead Resort and Arrowpoint Nature Resort. At those resorts nature walks bring generous rewards, while Arrowpoint Resort has facilities for trail biking and an eerie, dead of night animal-spotting adventure. If

ABOVE LEFT
A warm and friendly welcome awaits visitors to Guyana.

LEFT
The Zoom Inn Hotel and Kanuku Suites are recent additions to Guyana's tourism sector.

# A HAVEN IN THE HEART OF THE CAPITAL

HOTEL TOWER LIMITED COMBINES BEST HOTEL VALUES with the most convenient location overlooking and within walking distance of the main shopping areas. It boasts a panoramic view of the capital's most historic and important buildings – the Bank of Guyana, the Cenotaph, City Hall, the National Library and St George's Cathedral.

The hotel has 73 units including suites and kitchenettes that are ideal for longer stays. They are equipped with modern amenities including TV, air conditioning, hot & cold water and telephone. Some rooms have private balconies.

Hotel Tower's Rupununi, Hibiscus and Lotus rooms are ideal for meetings, conferences, seminars, private dinners and cocktail parties and can accommodate from ten to 250 people.

The dining and bar areas represent the best of Guyana. Main Street Café offers daily buffet for breakfast and lunch and is open sixteen hours each day. The Spectrum Restaurant and Bar, which is located next to the mosaic tile swimming pool, provides entertainment on selected nights, and the Black Magic Bar and its enchanting atmosphere is the perfect place to enjoy a wide variety of cocktails.

your taste is for travel on wide rivers then the journey to the Essequibo Resorts of Shanklands and Baganara would be unforgettable. Baganara Resort is the favourite escape of Mick Jagger when he is in Guyana, offering that classy combination of elegance and remoteness. Farther down the river, along its tributaries, falls and rapids spell excitement and adventure. While up the Essequibo coast Lake Mainstay Resort sits in the midst of a lake complex that is a visual delight as well as a venue for recreation and disports.

In 2007, the country welcomed unprecedented numbers of visitors who travelled to Guyana for the World Cup Cricket competition. A new stadium and several new hotels were been built in preparation along with a new, state-of-the-art conference centre at Turkeyen. In Georgetown a new facility for upscale oriental dining and an exclusive sports bar have also been built. This surge in accommodation, leisure and convention facilities will go a long way towards enhancing Guyana's capacity to host and entertain increased numbers of visitors and business meetings in the future. The World Cup Cricket episode has driven much of this investment and has proven to be a significant chapter in the fascinating narrative of tourism in Guyana. ∎

# More reasons to visit the land of many waters

In Guyana, the tourist has many possibilities for relaxation, enjoyment and excitement. In this land of many waters, in this natural wonder, there is a profusion of delights for even the most jaded traveller. Recently, bird watching, sport fishing and yachting have captured the imagination and are fast becoming the done thing if you have an interest.

By far the most notable is the increasing number of bird tours that have been added to the itineraries of most tour operators. Guyana is home to more than eight hundred species of bird including the toucan, cock-of-the-rock, canje pheasant and harpy eagle. Visitors to Kaieteur Falls will never forget the spectacle of thousands of swallows cavorting in the mist of the crashing waters. In Georgetown, alone, more than two hundred species of bird are regularly seen, especially in the area of the newly-refurbished Promenade Gardens.

One must ask why yachting has only now become part of the things that make Guyana special, for with our numerous safe waterways it seems only natural that boating would be part of our experience. But maybe it was just too close to our vision and it took visitors here to recognise the true potential of the place for water sport. And this is not to say that we don't utilise the waters or enjoy them. For many years there were regattas both at Bartica and at Swims on the Demerara River which drew great crowds and tourists galore. What we are talking about here, though, is different: in March of 2005, four yachts visited Guyana for a trip up the Essequibo that would proclaim Guyana a fine yachting destination. In the same year, on June 13th, the government declared the township of Bartica an official port of entry with customs, immigration and health facilities to clear arriving yachts. Pleasure yachts visiting Guyana need submit only a single Customs Declaration Form specially introduced for this purpose.

Sport fishing, too, seems an almost natural choice, considering the thousands of miles of rivers and coastline in this country. Guyana boasts the world's largest, scaled freshwater fish in the world, the arapaima, and this along with a vast array of other species makes "goin' fishin'" a real treat for the dedicated angler. Add to this the quiet of unexplored nature and the vastness of the country and this might well be paradise for fishing enthusiasts.

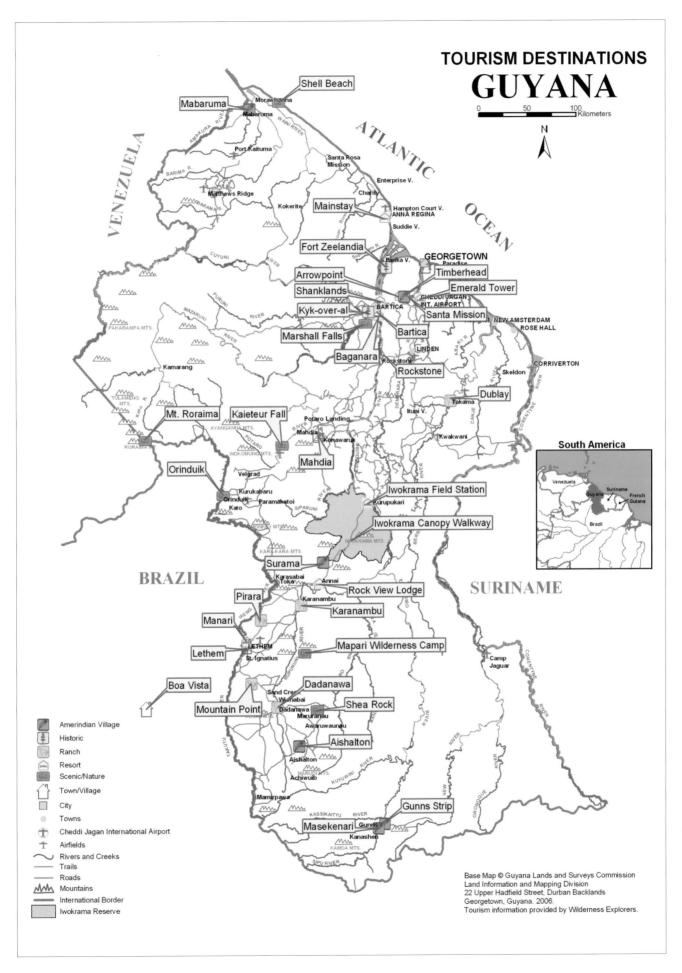

TOURISM DESTINATIONS
# GUYANA

# Cruising the waters of Guyana

C.A. NASCIMENTO

Guyana was not, until recently, considered a cruising destination. However, in 2003 a small flotilla of four yachts sailed from Chaguaramas in Trinidad to the Essequibo River and discovered that its waters offered some of the most attractive anchorages in the South American and Caribbean region.

The captain of one of the yachts, Jack Cooley, later wrote in the *Caribbean Compass*, "cruisers bored with sitting out the hurricane season in Trinidad, often look for additional areas to cruise that are out of the 'Hurricane belt'. Popular destinations include Grenada, Tobago, the delta rivers of the Orinoco and other nearby rivers ... I believe that Guyana can be added to this list of hurricane season cruising favourites." Cooley observed that the journey from Trinidad to Guyana was "not overly rigorous" and noted that "for voyages from South Africa to the Caribbean, Guyana could be a welcome respite, and in freshwater, too."

In 2005, a second flotilla of eight yachts sailed to the area. The crews were full of praise for the hospitality they received and the beauty, seclusion and security of the anchorages they found.

Today, the mining town of Bartica is the official port of entry for cruisers. Located thirty miles from the mouth of the Essequibo, and at the centre of the confluence of three great rivers (Mazaruni, Cuyuni and Essequibo), Bartica is home to a number of Guyana's leading nature resorts.

The Essequibo River now features prominently in the third edition of the *Chris Doyle Cruising Guide for Trinidad and Tobago, Barbados and Guyana*. Doyle was invited to visit the country by the government of Guyana, and was further encouraged to make the trip by former international sailor, Simon Wall, former Cabinet Minister and Public Relations Consultant, Kit Nascimento, and Trinidad and Tobago's, Donald Stollmeyer. The guide (www.doyleguides.com) provides full chart and waypoint navigational advice on approaching the Essequibo and sailing up river to Bartica, and the attractive anchorages in the vicinity off Baganara Island Resort, Hurakabra River Resort and the Shanklands Resort.

In his introduction to the guide, Simon Wall (internationally-renowned for his single-handed transatlantic crossings) noted that he first ventured into the Essequibo River in 2005 on his 50-foot sloop, and has since returned on a number of occasions. He writes, "I would urge cruisers to visit Guyana and enjoy some of its many attractions that include being outside of the hurricane belt, fresh water, exceptionally low cost of living, quality services, English-speaking and extensive safe anchorages". He also says that the more he cruises the Essequibo the more he appreciates "the spectacular beauty and many attractions that Guyana has to offer."

Navigation up the Essequibo River to Bartica, using the Doyle waypoints, is relatively simple for yachts drawing less than 15 feet. Cruisers should keep a lookout for small outboard powerboats, water taxis, fishing nets and floating debris. Cruisers must, however, take notice of the 10-foot and more tidal variations and a somewhat shifting sandbar of about 10-foot in depth at the mouth of the river. Entering on a rising tide and for sailing upriver is, therefore, recommended. The river floods at approximately

# FROM GOLD-MINING TO ISLAND RESORT

WHAT STARTED AS MANOEL CORREIA'S IDEA TO INVEST the profits he made from his small shop in the mining operations in 1926, has today evolved into one of Guyana's most dynamic and ever expanding corporations: The Correia Group of Companies. Since then, the company has grown into one of the country's most diversified conglomerates, operating in such areas as mining (Correia Mining Company Ltd), transportation (Trans Guyana Airways Ltd, Correia's Interior Transportation Services and Intraserv Inc.), aviation services (Caribbean Aviation Maintenance Services Ltd) and tourism (Evergreen Adventures Inc. and Baganara Island Resort).

Correia Mining Company is Guyana's leading mining business and is now in its third generation of family ownership and is the backbone of the group.

To further enhance its transportation capabilities, Correia's Interior Transportation Service (ITS) was created to provide a more economical and reliable form of transportation to support the development of the company's burgeoning mining operations.

Trans Guyana Airways Ltd was formed in 1956 and has matured into Guyana's leading domestic carrier. At present, the airline services more than seventy interior destinations, while also offering VIP and tourist flights.

Caribbean Aviation Maintenance Services Ltd (originally established as Caribbean Helicopters Ltd in 1991) was set up to offer maintenance for its sister company, Trans Guyana Airways, and has now expanded to become Guyana's leading, approved aircraft maintenance organisation.

Flying passengers into the interior and, below, the sprawling Baganara Island Resort

The group has diversified into the tourism sector with Evergreen Adventures Inc, a tour operator that enables visitors to experience Guyana's rich, multicultural society and diverse landscapes. The company actively promotes its Baganara Island Resort and other nature resorts as well as air tours to the magnificent Kaieteur Falls. Baganara Island Resort is one of Guyana's premier interior retreats where private and corporate guests can escape for physical and mental rejuvenation.

Today, the Correia Group of Companies has grown into a vibrant and multifaceted corporation which is a shining example of Guyanese business at its best.

1.8 knots and ebbs at about 3.5 knots. Muddy at the mouth, the river waters gradually turn a golden brown (coloured by vegetation) and the banks display some magnificent white-sand beaches.

The Baganara and Hurakabra Resorts, in particular, now cater for cruisers anchored close off-shore. These resorts are exceptionally beautiful, nature destinations which offer comfortable and well-appointed accommodation, jungle walks, birding, beach-front dining, recreation facilities, water sports and dingy docking. Cruisers can make arrangements with the resorts for support services such as fuel, laundry, ice, potable water, groceries, garbage disposal and fast boat transport to Bartica and river and road transportation to the capital. Baganara has a small, light aircraft landing strip and Hurakabra, similarly, at a nearby island.

Bartica, with a population of about 10,000, is a bustling, hinterland town servicing Guyana's flourishing gold and other mining activities in the upper reaches of its rivers. It offers a choice of local dining experiences including Creole, Chinese and Brazilian food, a wide range of fresh vegetables and meat markets, supermarket shopping, banking facilities, hardware shops, general merchandise and a popular nightlife. Boatyard facilities are not available, but Bartica has workshops capable of carrying out most running repairs.

Cruisers visiting Guyana can easily access many of the country's natural attractions – including the spectacular Kaieteur Falls – from anchor by making arrangements with Evergreen Adventures, which runs the Baganara Island Resort, or Public Communications Consultants/GEMS which runs the Hurakabra River Resort. ∎

# Searching for the gold of El Dorado

HAN GRANGER

From around midnight, 'bush trucks' (army surplus trucks) laden with food, equipment and fuel rumble down the highway leading inland from Georgetown; and at dawn, small aircraft loaded with similar supplies take off from Ogle and the international airport at Timehri. They are heading inland ("goin' in de bush") to support the hunt for gold that has been the backbone of the development of Guyana's hinterland for hundreds of years.

Though the mythical 'El Dorado' brought European treasure-hunters to the northern coast of South America in the late sixteenth century, the first major gold-seeking expedition to Guyana's hinterland on record was in 1720. Since then, countless men and women have made and lost fortunes here. With the exception of the Omai Gold Mines operation of the largest open-pit mine in South America (now exhausted and closed), most of the gold found in Guyana is from alluvial deposits – basically along old riverbeds, and extracted with suction dredges. The typical, small operation comprises three or more 'pork-knockers' (prospectors) panning for gold along rivers in the Cuyuni-Mazaruni and Potaro-Siparuni Regions of the country's north-western interior.

The Guyanese people's love affair with gold is multi-faceted. The country is a net importer of manufactured products, and gold is one of its main exports; though total production has fallen over the past five years from 455,917 troy ounces in 2001 to 262,528 in 2005 (source: gold and diamond production figures from Guyana Geology & Mines Commission). The country is also a significant source of diamonds and is sometimes listed among the top twenty producers of diamonds in the world. Though quantity is relatively small (356,950 metric carats in 2005), Guyanese diamonds are renowned for their quality.

The low cost of labour means that Guyana gold can be fashioned into jewellery by local artisans relatively cheaply; gold jewellery shines as one of the few manufactured products that can be said to be truly Guyanese, something that inspires patriotic pride. Expatriate Guyanese send money home to have their jewellery made here so they can wear "Guyana gold" – widely perceived among Guyanese to be superior to any other. In addition, the two main ethnic groups (of Indian and African decent) have a cultural attachment to gold that can border on the superstitious. Guyana's status as a developing country with a weak currency has also worked to establish the perception of jewellery as an asset and an investment.

The jewellery industry in Guyana is thriving and dynamic, with a local population of approximately 750,000 served by 301 registered goldsmiths (registered with the GGMC in 2005) and many unlicensed operators. While the lack of formal training for the majority is reflected in unscientific alloying techniques and rudimentary manufacturing methods, design is influenced by traditional Creole and Indian jewellery as well as prevailing fashion trends. For all this, the local industry thrives, with some jewellers producing well-made modern as well as conventional pieces. Successful manufacturer-retailers in the capital city and main towns range from market stalls to air-conditioned buildings, with continued patronage from residents and visitors alike drawing more and more would-be jewellers into the trade.

ABOVE
Panning for gold.

FACING PAGE
The road to the Kurupung goldmine.
Photos: I Brierley

# A QUALITY JEWELLER FOR OVER SEVENTY YEARS

FOR MORE THAN SEVENTY YEARS, L. SEEPERSAUD Maraj & Sons has built a solid reputation in Guyana's jewellery sector.

In 1935, Seepersaud Maraj commenced trading in the capital's Stabroek Market, a location from which it still operates. In 1966, the company was commissioned by the Mayor and councillors of the city of Georgetown to design a gold necklace for Queen Elizabeth II to mark Guyana's independence from Britain. Over the years, L. Seepersaud Maraj & Sons has become a household name for providing quality gold and diamond jewellery. The company is now run by the founder's sons, Heera, Sharma and Ram, who maintain their father's passion for quality and trust.

BELOW: Heera, Sharma and Ram Maraj continue their father's tradition.

TOP
A 'Bush truck' in search of gold.
Photo: I Brierley

ABOVE
Businesses associated with Guyana's jewellery industry come in many shapes and sizes.   Photo: RJ Fernandes

FACING PAGE, TOP
Mining village at Kurupung.
Photo: I Brierley

Some of the stores in Georgetown, which stock wide ranges of gold and diamond jewellery, include City Jewellers, Correia's Jewellery, De Abreu's Creations, Gaskin & Jackson, Humphrey & Co., King's Jewellery World, Sanjay's Jewellery, Sheriff's Jewellery, Steve's Jewellery and Topaz. The city's two largest markets – Stabroek and Bourda – also house jewellery stalls where traditional items of gold jewellery are made to order quickly. Established in 1935, L. Seepersaud Maraj & Sons in the Stabroek Market is the oldest and best-known of these 'market' goldsmiths. Outside of the capital, jewellers can be found in the towns of Anna Regina (Essequibo), Linden (Demerara), New Amsterdam, Rose Hall and Corriverton (Berbice), as well as in well-populated and busy areas such as Bartica, Parika, Vreed-en-Hoop and Mahaica.

Handmade local jewellery is often sold alongside imported machine-made jewellery; the latter sold at prices which compare favourably with retail prices outside of Guyana. The greatest asset of Guyana's jewellery industry, however, is the very affordable cost of handmade and custom-made jewellery. In fact, there is a strong culture of frequently "making-over" old jewellery which may be either broken or unwanted. With influences from current fashion or increased fortune, Guyanese will return to their goldsmiths to have jewellery refashioned or improved – a cheap rejuvenation that keeps local goldsmiths in work. So easy; so affordable; so quick. To residents and visitors alike, this combination of factors makes Guyanese jewellery irresistible. ■

# Investment opportunities in Guyana

Guyana is an emerging economy with enormous untapped potential. The country's geographic position at the gateway to the Caribbean and South America, combined with its natural resources, access to key export markets, English-speaking population and affordable labour, present investors with profitable opportunities to do business in Guyana. Supported by stable macroeconomic policies, attractive investment incentives, and a regulatory environment and corporate tax regime that do not discriminate against foreign investors, Guyana also provides investors favourable conditions to do business.

In the recent past, Guyana has achieved remarkable progress in its efforts to open its economy through market-oriented reforms and improvements in the investment climate, while at the same time stabilising inflation, reducing fiscal and balance of payments deficits, and strengthening infrastructure, health services and the education system. Guyana's home-grown National Development Strategy (NDS) and Poverty Reduction Strategy Program (PRSP) drive these initiatives with support from a number of bilateral and multilateral development agencies.

Despite these achievements, both private and public sector leaders understand that continued progress depends on Guyana's ability to adjust to the ever-changing global economy by responding to new challenges and taking advantage of new opportunities. As part of the NDS, Guyana is implementing a National Competitiveness Strategy (NCS) designed to further improve the investment climate and support the emergence of non-traditional export sectors, while continuing to fortify the mining, sugar, rice and timber sectors for which Guyana is so well known.

## INVESTMENT TRENDS

After a period of decline, Guyana has experienced an upsurge in investment – both foreign and domestic – in recent years. In 2005, for example, investment listed by GO-Invest exceeded US$ 340 million. Of the 141 projects, approximately one-third involved foreign investors (including joint ventures), primarily from Asia, the Caribbean and North America. According to GO-Invest, foreign direct investment exceeded US$ 250 million, or 73 percent of the total investments. The food products (including agriculture, seafood and aquaculture), mining and wood products sectors dominated, receiving nearly 70 percent of total investment. At the same time, Guyana enjoyed investment growth in Information and Communications Technology (ICT) and IT-enabled services, tourism and manufacturing.

## OPPORTUNITIES

Guyana offers potential investors – foreign and domestic alike – a broad spectrum of investment choices, ranging from more traditional industries (such as mining, sugar, rice and timber), to non-traditional export sectors (such as aquaculture, agro-processing, fresh fruits and vegetables, light manufacturing, value-added forest products), to services

# LEADING THE WAY IN WHEEL REPAIR

ESTABLISHED IN 1984 WITH A SNACK BAR, OFF-LICENSE and basic tyre repair service, RRT Enterprises has grown over the years to become one of the most sophisticated and up-to-date computerised wheel repair services in Guyana.

The company offers a complete wheel service, including vulcanising, tyre repairs, and computerised wheel balancing and wheel alignment. It is situated in the heart of the business district and, as such, is able to cater to the many vehicles that travel these routes each day. It also offers an express oil change and service centre and stocks spare parts for motor vehicles, motorcycles and bicycles.

Already considered the leading wheel repair service, RRT Enterprises is poised for the future with plans to expand its operations into Parika, East Bank Demerara, Upper East Coast Demerara and New Amsterdam.

# KEEPING GUYANA ON THE MOVE

THE GUYANA OIL COMPANY LIMITED (GUYOIL) IS A STATE-owned company that was established in 1976 to import, store, distribute and market motor gasoline, kerosene and heavy fuel oil.

As the main importer and distributor of petroleum products, this multi-billion dollar company plays a major role in the sustainability of the nation's developmental drive by ensuring that Guyana's energy needs are met. It also supplies the largest dealers' network, which includes service stations, government ministries and agencies, the police and defence forces, and other major customers such as Demerara Distillers. The company is also the national distributor for Castrol lubricants and Lake Asphalt bitumen products.

With a firm commitment to providing a consistently high level of service, Guyoil places great importance towards understanding the needs of its customers.

ABOVE
The busy streets of Georgetown are a
hive of business activity and opportunity.
Photo: H Chan

PREVIOUS PAGES 190 & 191
The Providence Stadium at East Bank
Demerara was built to host Super Eight
matches during the Cricket World Cup in
2007. The 15,000-seater complex was
built by the government of Guyana with
financial assistance from the government
of India.    Photo: I Brierley

PREVIOUS PAGE 188
A logging truck thunders its way through
the rainforests of Kurupung.    Photo: I Brierley

exports (such as tourism and Information Technology [IT]-enabled services). Many products receive duty-free or reduced-duty treatment in destination markets. Specific opportunities include:

AGRICULTURE AND AGRO-PROCESSING Guyana enjoys a number of comparative advantages – diverse agricultural environments, organic cropland, widespread irrigation, drainage and sea defences, and trainable farmers – that support a range of market opportunities for investment and export. Lucrative markets exist for producing fresh fruits and vegetables for local markets (e.g. domestic consumption, hotels and restaurants) as well as for export. There is also high demand for processed and semi-processed foods (for sale to processors), especially within the Caribbean. Promising opportunities exist in Guyana's savannahs to produce and export meat, particularly since Guyana has been declared free of foot and mouth disease. Guyana's virgin lands provide further opportunities for high-value certified organic products. Beyond Guyana's regional markets, the Guyanese and Caribbean diasporas in Canada, the US and Europe provide

# THREE GENERATIONS OF CUSTOMER SERVICE

M. BEEPAT AND SONS (GENERALLY KNOWN AS BEEPATS) is one of the more successful marketing and distribution companies in Guyana. Located in Regent Street, in the heart of the business district, it enjoys both a prime location and a loyal customer base.

The business was established in the La Penitence market in 1953 by Madho Beepat. Back then, it was a one-man operation which soon outgrew the stall in which it was housed. Mr Beepat then moved to a rented property at 95 Regent Street, which became the forerunner to the present business. He bought that property as the business continued to grow and later needed to purchase another property at 100-101 Regent Street. This premises is now home to the company head office and main wholesale/retail outlet.

As one of the first businesses on Regent Street, Beepats can be counted among those companies that were instrumental in making this part of town the hub of the business district. In 1977, the business was incorporated as M. Beepat and Sons Limited with Madho's son, Dennis, as the chief executive. Mr Beepat's son was later responsible for expanding the company's product range from basic haberdashery and general goods to a full-scale marketing and distribution operation. The company now represents a number of British and North American brands including Nestlé, Unilever and Heinz. It also has affiliations with major Far East manufacturers which supply wares, plastics and other general merchandise.

At the beginning of 2003, with Dennis Beepat at the helm and a staff compliment of one hundred employees, the company was officially renamed Beepats.

A third generation of Beepats is now involved in the business which continues to grow at a steady pace while at the same time catering for the ever-changing needs of its burgeoning customer base.

# FIRST CLASS SERVICE TO THE CONSTRUCTION INDUSTRY

THE ROOTS OF THE GAFSONS GROUP OF COMPANIES go back to the early 1950s. Today, its manufacturing operations are centralised on twenty-five acres of waterfront land at its Land of Canaan Industrial Estate, which has approximately 300,000 sq ft of covered factory space.

The company's head office, distribution service and shopping mall is located at its Houston Complex with further outlets situated in Broad Street and in the towns of Parika and Rosehall.

Gafsons Industries Limited and its subsidiaries have set high standards in the construction and building industry, supplying the

highest quality manufactured materials such as corrugated roofing sheets, PVC and aluminium windows, doors and shop fronts, and a wide range of PVC products including pipes, hoses, water tanks and chain-link fencing. The company also stocks electrical supplies, steel products, glass, mirrors, bathroom fittings and tiles, as well as lumber and quarry products.

Property development enhances the broad range of services offered by the Gafsons Group of Companies. It is also represented by sister operations in Barbados, Jamaica, Grenada and St Lucia, which all offer comparable services.

ABOVE
Paddy fields are flooded sections of
land on which rice is grown. The paddy
itself is rice before it is threshed and still
in its husk. Rice is Guyana's second
major crop and its cultivation provides
direct income for more than ten
thousand families.   Photo: I Brierley

a niche market for a number of food products. The wider US and European markets present opportunities for exporters able to meet the tough, uncompromising standards of consumers. While global pricing pressures exist in the traditional sugar and rice industries, opportunities exist for investors able to improve productivity.

SEAFOOD AND AQUACULTURE Guyana's 459 km Atlantic coastal zone and extensive network of rivers provide the ideal conditions for a dynamic marine fisheries and aquaculture industry. Already shrimp, prawn and finfish exports account for approximately 12 percent of total exports. While the shrimp and prawn sector is relatively consolidated, there are opportunities for investors able to add to the value of catches through processing and quality upgrades. Some experts suggest that virtually untapped, high-value opportunities exist among pelagic and deep-sea species further offshore on the continental slope (deepwater snapper and prawns) and in the Atlantic Ocean (swordfish and tuna). Finally, recent investments show enormous opportunities in fresh-water fish (i.e. tilapia) and shrimp farming for export, with annual income per acre exceeding US$ 3,400. At present, shrimp and fish are exported primarily to the US, but in 2004 Guyana was certified for fisheries exports to the lucrative EU market.

# A VALUABLE CONTRIBUTION TO THE DEVELOPMENT OF GUYANA

THE NEAL AND MASSEY GROUP IS ONE OF THE LEADING conglomerates in the region with enterprises ranging across a broad spectrum: automotive and industrial equipment and support services, domestic and industrial gases, financial services, security and cash services, information technology and communications and retail, distribution and shipping services.

With some thirty-nine years of business experience and acumen, the Neal and Massey Group is the representative of major international brands and is partner to many businesses throughout the country. Each of the companies in the group is well known for its high standard of operation and commitment to service and is testament to the overall values for which the group has become known.

The Neal and Massey Group is a dynamic and consolidated group which makes a valuable contribution to the country's development through quality business practices, services and products. With its sights firmly set on the future, the group is also grooming young leaders in the business arena through its scholarship programmes.

# GUYANA MICRO-PROJECTS PROGRAMME

THE GUYANA MICRO-PROJECTS PROGRAMME (GMPP) is a European Union/Government of Guyana funded programme which targets the economic and social development of vulnerable groups/communities in Guyana, by contributing to the financing of micro-projects at the community level. It is intended to support these communities to express their basic needs, to formulate the corresponding activities and to contribute to the financing of the ensuing 'project'. The overall objective of the GMPP is to reduce poverty and social inequality in Guyana.

The GMPP seeks to achieve four broad based results. Two address key issues related to the capacity building of community based organizations and micro-project funding/ implementation and the others are related to project management support and Government/Civil Society dialogue.

Micro projects implementation will be achieved through the provision of grants for approximately seventy-five micro projects at the community level focusing on the areas of Employment, Income Generation (50%); Training, Education, Communication and Good Governance (25%); and Other Socio-Economic Sectors (25%).

Implementation of micro projects will be in targeted in the following geographical areas: Georgetown and other town (30-40%); Coastal villages (40-45%); and Rural interior (20-25%).

A ceiling of Euro 30,000 (approximately GUY$6.5m) will apply for all micro-projects with the exception of projects undertaken in the hinterland where the threshold will be set at Euro 50,000 (approximately GUY$10.5m).

GMPP will fund a maximum of seventy-five percent of the eligible costs of individual micro projects. The remaining twenty-five percent is expected to be financed by the project's beneficiaries in the form of contributions in kind, services or cash.

Micro project recipients shall be local Community Based Organizations (CBOs,) and Grass Root Organizations (GROs). The major target group of the GMPP is the rural/ urban poor and vulnerable groups as described by the Poverty Reduction Strategy Paper (PRSP).

# LOCAL BUSINESS WITH SIGHTS SET ON EXPANSION

THE TWO BROTHERS BUSINESS BEGAN LIFE IN THE area of rice farming in 1976. Since then, it has developed into a group of companies with a diverse range of interests.

With rice farming still in operation, the company has incorporated rice milling to complement its original business. Its interests now comprise gas stations, fish processing, cattle rearing, ice production, restaurants, hotels, wharf facilities,

distribution and mining. The group also has plans to establish a supermarket.

In 2005, the company was incorporated in the United States as Two Brothers Corporation in order to facilitate its further expansion and development. Now an international operation, the group aims to expand its presence in Guyana and keep abreast of the growing demand for its products and services.

# JEWEL IN GUYANA'S CROWN IS A SHINING EXAMPLE

ACKNOWLEDGED AS POSSIBLY THE LEADING JEWELLER in Guyana, King's Jewellery World is a manufacturer and retailer of gold, silver, diamond and gemstone jewellery. The company, which has its headquarters in Georgetown, is also making a name for itself around the world because of its growing reputation for producing jewellery of exceptional quality and design.

As the creator of the world renowned 'Cricket Bracelet' and the first recipient of the prestigious Guyana National Bureau of Standards certificate for quality jewellery, it has been setting the standard in Guyana for nearly forty years.

King's Jewellery World was founded in 1970 by Looknauth Persaud who established the company with one goldsmith and two apprentices who made jewellery for a small number of customers and fulfilled special orders for other jewellers. Mr Persaud gained a reputation for offering superior quality, styling and service and the company flourished as a direct result.

In 1994, the company participated in GuyExpo 94, which was a national exhibition of locally manufactured products. The company received a tremendous response and prompted Looknauth to open his first showroom in June the same year. Located at Middle and Waterloo Streets, this store revolutionised the jewellery industry in Guyana with its consistent high quality and wide selection of jewellery. In 1996, another branch was opened in Pitt Street, New Amsterdam, and in November that same year, the new headquarters at King's Plaza was opened to the public. The company now has international retail affiliates in Trinidad, Bahamas and New York City.

To date, King's Jewellery World is the only jewellery company in the Caribbean that employs four graduate gemologists, one graduate diamond grader, one accredited jewellery professional and one graduate jewellery designer. It can boast that it has the region's most formidable team along with the fact that it is the largest producer of gold and gemstones in the Caribbean.

ABOVE
Buddy's Providence Hotel & Resort was
opened in 2007 to cater for the increased
arrivals during the Cricket World Cup.
Photo: I Brierley

PREVIOUS PAGE 197
City Mall is situated at the corner of
Regent and Camp Streets in Georgetown
and is the country's most modern
shopping complex. It is home to many
local and international outlets and is a
popular location for both Guyanese and
visitors to the country.   Photo: I Brierley

FOREST PRODUCTS Guyana's forests cover about three quarters of the country's land mass and contain over 1,000 tree varieties, which provide vast opportunities for the harvest and export of wood products. Forest products exports accounted for nearly 10 percent of total exports in 2005. In the past, most forestry exports consisted of processed plywood and raw or semi-processed greenheart and other valuable species (e.g. purple heart, mora, locust). There is, however, a growing interest in expanding value-added wood processing industries (e.g. furniture, flooring, doors, moulding, fencing, veneer, etc) targeting the Caribbean and US markets. Further opportunities exist for investors able to obtain Forest Stewardship Council (FSC) certification and develop products for niche markets.

IT-ENABLED SERVICES Recently, Guyana has experienced the emergence of a small, but growing IT-Enabled Services industry with both domestic and foreign investment (e.g. Canada, Mexico) in call centre and back-office processing operations. Some investors have included Guyana as part of their networks of business process outsourcing (BPO) centres located in Latin America. Although not widely known as a location for BPO, Guyana provides a number of advantages that make it an ideal location for IT-enabled services, including a fluent English-speaking workforce, skilled and trainable workers, and reasonable telecommunication costs.

# STATE-OF-THE-ART TELECOMMUNICATIONS

TOWARDS THE END OF THE EIGHTIES, THE GOVERNMENT of Guyana decided to privatise the country's telecommunications as part of its wide-ranging economic reform programme. It sought local or foreign investors with access to the necessary capital, technology and skills to revitalise the industry. It was ATN who took up the challenge.

In 1990, the parties signed an agreement in which ATN acquired eighty percent of the telephone company and the government retained twenty. This agreement heralded the creation of the Guyana Telephone and Telegraph Company Limited (GT&T), which replaced the Guyana Telecommunication Corporation.

In January 1991, GT&T commenced operations with the task of rehabilitating, modernising and expanding Guyana's telecommunications facilities and services. Since its inception, and up to December 2005, the company has invested more than US$ 250m towards the modernisation and expansion of the national telecommunications infrastructure and facilities.

GT&T's network modernisation and expansion have benefited all telecommunications consumers and, indeed, all of Guyana. Investments in the voice networks have made reliable, high-quality telephony services more ubiquitous in urban, rural and remote areas of the country. Improved and modern data networks have allowed the branches of multi-location companies such as banks, money-transfer businesses and airlines to communicate directly via a high-speed network, thereby enhancing their operational efficiency and the effectiveness of their service to customers.

Development in the mobile cellular network has not only made voice telephony more accessible but, equally important, it has spawned numerous new business opportunities for small entrepreneurs and ushered in an entirely new mode of social interaction. And investment in undersea cables, like Americas II, makes it possible for Guyana to attract international data transfer businesses such as call centres.

Today, thanks to GT&T, Guyana has a telecommunications network that is comparable to any in the developed world. Its commitment over the years has served to position Guyana to tap into the international information super-highway and become an active participant in the new E-economy.

LIGHT MANUFACTURING There is growing interest in expanding the country's light manufacturing sector. In particular, access to natural resources provides opportunities in agro processing and wood processing. Low cost labour, proximity to markets, a track record for quality, and preferential trade access, also make Guyana a good place to source apparel manufacturing, particularly production targeting the US market. Other opportunities exist in the areas of pharmaceuticals, jewellery, leather and wooden craft, basketry, and ceramics, to name a few, for both exports and domestic consumption.

MINING Guyana's mineral deposits have attracted international interest from the largest companies in the world. While the industry is relatively mature, lucrative opportunities still exist in the extraction of bauxite, gold, diamonds and other minerals. With recent investments, bauxite production is expected to grow by nearly 78 percent in coming years. In the gold sector, recent exploration suggests deposits of at least one million ounces in new resources, while the tendency for higher world prices encourages the extraction of gold deposits that previously would have been uneconomical.

## A TRULY GUYANESE COMPANY

IN SEPTEMBER 1955, BANKS BREWERIES LTD WAS established by Peter Stanislaus d'Aguiar at the newly-built Ruimveldt Industrial Estate. At the time, however, the advice from sugar company executives was that a brewery might not be such a good idea because the Guyanese were 'rum drinkers' who would not like the taste of beer.

Against this advice d'Aguiar forged ahead and created Guyana's (then British Guiana) first public company. It had a share capital of $1.5m owned by 3,420 shareholders.

In 1969, Banks Breweries Ltd was merged with D'Aguiar Bros Ltd to form Banks DIH Ltd. This event presented another opportunity for ordinary Guyanese to support and share in the company, and to date Banks DIH Ltd has more than 14,000 shareholders.

TOURISM While Guyana's tourism sector has focused primarily on business visitors or the Guyanese diaspora, Guyana's natural beauty and attractions, including Kaieteur Falls (the tallest single drop water fall in the world), Orinduik Falls, the Rupununi savannahs and the Essequibo River have been drawing increasing attention from tourists and tour operators alike. With the worldwide growth in the eco-, adventure and cultural tourism segments and narrow market niches such as bird watching, a variety of opportunities exist for the industry to develop Guyana's tourism product through investments in tourism operations/services, facilities, hotels and lodges. In the short term, there are opportunities for hospitality (hotels, restaurants and related services) as Guyana prepares to host matches during the Cricket World Cup in 2007. Up to 25,000 cricket fans from all over the world are expected to visit Guyana, providing a large boon for the industry. Other opportunities exist for business tourism, especially with the recent construction of a large conference centre in Georgetown.

LEFT
Since 1967, Farfan & Mendes has provided quality products, service and support to the agricultural and woodworking industries. The company also carries out installations of pressure water systems, solar water heaters and alternative energy systems, plus a full range of products for the mining sector.

# HAND-IN-HAND WITH TECHNOLOGY AND SOCIAL RESPONSIBILITY

TRANSPACIFIC MOTOR SPARES AND AUTO SALES HAS emerged as one of the leading automotive businesses in Guyana. The company was established approximately fifteen years ago to deal with the shortage of spare parts for the expanding number of automobiles on the roads.

In the late 1980s and early 1990s, founder and owner, Harripersaud Ramsewack began sourcing spare parts for vehicles which, at the time, could not be found in Guyana. He set up a shop at Robb and Light Streets which soon became the leading outlet for those looking for hard-to-get parts. Through its dedication to good service and affordable prices, the company has since grown into a well-known and reputable company which now occupies an impressive head office and state-of-the-art complex on the East Coast of Demerara. Expansion has also included diversification and the company, with its staff of twenty employees, is now a major importer and retailer of automobiles along with being a leading spare parts resource.

Over the years the company has always fulfilled its responsibility as a corporate citizen and contributes to the enhancement of the society through its sponsorship of sports, religious and social activities.

Transpacific Motor Spares and Auto Sales is a modern and progressive Guyanese company which offers superior products and service while keeping abreast of technology in an ever-changing marketplace.

INVESTMENT INCENTIVES In order to facilitate investment and expansion in these sectors, Guyana provides an array of across-the-board investment incentives, including a flat business tax rate, tax holidays, waivers of customs duties, export tax allowances, and unrestricted repatriation of capital, dividends and profits, as well as additional incentives in the sectors listed above. Furthermore, the Government of Guyana (GoG) has tasked GO-Invest as:

- The prime contact for investors to facilitate the investment process and expedite applications for investment concessions and government support;
- Guyana's main export promotion agency.

GO-Invest's activities, complemented by those of sector-specific agencies and organisations, provide investors with the information, support and advocacy needed to capitalise on Guyana's opportunities.

# FLOUR PRODUCTS FOR GUYANESE AT HOME AND ABROAD

NATIONAL MILLING COMPANY OF GUYANA (NAMILCO) was established in 1969 as a wholly owned subsidiary of Seaboard Corporation, which is based in Kansas City, USA. Over the years it has manufactured and sold flour solely to the Guyanese consumer, with wheat bought from the Government of Guyana, which is supplied through the PL480 Programme by the US Government.

Located at Agricola on the East Bank of the Demerara River, NAMILCO is just few minutes' drive from the centre of Georgetown. Its riverside location facilitates the delivery of wheat by ship, which is transferred by conveyor belt to silos in the mill's compound. NAMILCO produces one of the finest flours in the Caribbean, including the 'Maid Marian' range of specialty flours: Self Rising, Roti Mix, Harvest High Fibre and Wheat-up Breakfast Porridge. Recently added to these popular products was 'Pholourie Quickmix', which is also exported overseas and is in demand by Guyanese abroad who enjoy a little "taste of home".

## TRADE TRENDS

Guyana is one of the most open economies in the Caribbean and has enjoyed steady export growth since 2000. CARICOM, EU, Canada and the US continue to be Guyana's primary export markets; however, regional and bilateral trade agreements – including those involving CARICOM – with countries such as Argentina, Brazil, People's Republic of China, Colombia, Costa Rica, Cuba, the Dominican Republic, and Venezuela, present opportunities to diversify markets. Through these trade agreements and geographic proximity, Guyana enjoys easy access to 277 million consumers, and an export market in excess of US$ 130 billion with an overall purchasing power of over US$ 2 trillion.

While Guyana's traditional export products (e.g. sugar, rice, bauxite, gold and timber) continue to enjoy robust growth, Guyana's non-traditional exports (e.g. value-added wood products, non-traditional agricultural products, seafood and light manufacturing) are becoming an increasingly important source of export earnings, with their share of total exports growing consistently. This reflects progress in the country's increased emphasis towards diversifying the economy.

TOP
Bauxite plant at Linden. Bauxite is a sedimentary rock which is mined and used in the production of aluminium. The vast bauxite deposits found between the Demerara and Berbice Rivers have been one of Guyana's major exports for many years.
Photo: RJ Fernandes

ABOVE
The canopy walkway at the Iwokrama rainforest is among the many eco attractions which are helping to boost the country's tourism industry.
Photo: R Thomas

ABOVE RIGHT
Fish processing plant at East Bank Demerara.   Photo: I Brierley

LEFT
Popeye's Chicken and Seafood restaurant is one of a growing number of international restaurants operating in Guyana.
Photo: H Chan

FACING PAGE
Rice silos at Abdool Hakh & Sons in West Coast Demerara. Since 1924, the company has processed, marketed and distributed the finest quality rice produced in Guyana. The company was founded by Abdul Hakh who pioneered many standards within the country's rice industry. Today, Abdool Hakh & Sons supplies other countries in South America as well as many Caribbean and European markets.   Photo: I Brierley

# INVESTING IN PEOPLE; INVESTING IN GUYANA

ANSA MCAL IS BRINGING TOGETHER THE CARIBBEAN through commerce. Shaping the way the region does business is central to its vision. Started in Trinidad and Tobago, and with its head office there, it does not limit itself to the twin-island republic but has offices in Barbados, Guyana, Jamaica, St Kitts, Grenada, Antigua, St Lucia, St Vincent and the United States. In fact, Ansa McAl Group of Companies is one of the largest in the Caribbean region.

Ansa McAl Trading Limited is a marketing and distribution company that is also involved in manufacturing, packaging, automotive, media, insurance and financial services (including merchant banking), real estate development and shipping. After thirteen years in business, Ansa McAl now has an annual turnover of over 300 million US dollars and contributes significantly to philanthropy in the region, sponsoring everything from cultural events to scholarships.

The company is sub-divided into three main divisions: beer and beverage products, dry goods and pharmaceuticals, and administration and finance.

Carib Beer may well be the best known product manufactured and distributed by Ansa McAl, and it is well on its way to becoming the most widespread beer of the Caribbean. With a marketing and branding blitz that invokes images of sand, sea and beautiful women, it is becoming synonymous with the carefree Caribbean lifestyle. But this is just one of the many brands that Ansa McAl represents. Carib Brewery Limited also distributes Carlsberg and a host of beverage products from Grace Kennedy Export Trading Limited, headquartered in Jamaica.

The dry goods and pharmaceutical division, inclusive of Ansa Chemicals and Ansa Polymer, is partnered with

Connors Bros., Alcon, First Quality Inc., Aventis, Trinidad Match Company, Bristol–Myers Squibb, ISKO Enterprises, GlaxoSmithKline, Schering Plough Del Caribe, Novo Nordisk A/s and Misons Industries Ltd.

The administration and finance division support marketing and sales efforts, with centralised accounting and customer service facilities. Ansa McAl is continually upgrading its management information system with the objective of having fully integrated on-line facilities for control and efficiency in all key areas of operation.

Ansa McCal maintains that providing jobs and becoming integrated into the communities in which it operates is crucial to the vision of a Caribbean company that respects and rewards its human resources. Understanding the valuable contribution they make to the company's success and continued growth ensures its future development, as well as building good relationships with its customers.

LEFT
Processing plant at the Guyana Sugar
Corporation (GuySuco).   Photo: S May

# A DEPARTMENT STORE TO SUIT EVERYONE

GUYANA STORES LIMITED (FORMERLY BOOKERS Stores) was established in 1815 and has grown over the years to become the largest retail department store in Guyana with outlets in all three counties of Demerara, Essequibo and Berbice. The company was incorporated in 1976 as a state-owned enterprise to acquire the business and assets of the Booker Group of Companies, and in 2000, it was privatised.

The largest sector of this departmental store is the Universal Division, which sits in the heart of downtown Georgetown and offers products ranging from pins and needles to household furniture and appliances. The diverse range of products, available on two floors, caters for every member of the family. Guyana Stores has been a pioneer of the one-stop shopping experience in this country and continues this tradition with its diverse range of merchandise.

Within close proximity of the Universal Division are the Office Equipment and Supplies Division, situated on Main Street, and the Hardware Division, located in Water Street. The former offers an extensive selection office furniture and equipment as well as a maintenance service, and the latter stocks a variety of builders' supplies, tools, paints, fertilizers and electrical fixtures and fittings.

The company's Agency Division has the responsibility for wholesale distribution of a range of pharmaceuticals, hardware products and liquor. This division also represents a number of manufacturers worldwide. And the company's Garage Division is the authorised dealer for Mazda motor vehicles, Goodyear tires, machinery, spare parts and accessories.

Photo: H Chan

## PROSPECTS AND CHALLENGES

Alongside Guyana's opportunities come challenges for investors. Despite ongoing progress, Guyana faces problems common in many developing countries. The country's economic infrastructure – transport, energy, telecommunications and access to finance – is still developing, and this impacts profitability. The emigration of professionals often reduces the availability of management and technical skills critical for a competitive economy. Limited institutional capacity affects the implementation of legislation, policies and administrative procedures. Levels of crime, though comparable to those in other countries in the region, periodically cause concern.

These challenges do not go unnoticed by Guyana's leadership. Guyana's government, private sector and development partners have stated their common objective to do what is necessary to build upon past progress to further improve the investment environment and enhance Guyana's competitiveness. Within this respect, every major political party in the National Assembly has committed to the creation of a business climate conducive to investment.

The Government is aggressively pursuing its objectives under the country's NDS, with activities focusing on sound macroeconomic policies and economic management, strengthening investment promotion activities through GO-Invest, improving the transport infrastructure, enhancing the role of ICT in the economy, and strengthening social capital. As part of a recent initiative the Government has worked in partnership with the private sector to develop a NCS aimed at designing and executing action plans to improve the environment for investment, strengthen enterprise competitiveness for export development, facilitate fast-track development in priority sectors, and strengthen public-private cooperation in efforts to enhance Guyana's competitiveness. As part of

## GUYANESE CURRY – A NATIONAL INSTITUTION

BOTH THE DISH AND THE NAME "CURRY" HAD LONG been associated with India and most people in North America still tend to think of curry as purely Indian. In fact, curry was first introduced into Guyana in 1838 with the arrival of indentured Indian labourers. Since then, curry has developed in Guyana from a purely ethnic dish to a staple enjoyed by all ethnic communities. And in the Caribbean region and progressively in the rest of the Americas, Guyana is now regarded as a "land of curry" just as India used to be.

For most of the nineteenth century, the ingredients for curry-making in Guyana were imported from India. They included spices such as dhania (coriander seeds), sarso (mustard seed), gol mirch (black pepper), methi (fenugreek seeds) and haldi (turmeric). These ingredients were ground on marble slabs with hand-grinding stones (lohra) by housewives and blended to taste. Salt and peppers of various kinds were obtainable locally and Indian peppers were rarely imported. Until the first few decades of the twentieth century, a distinctiveness between north Indian and south Indian types of curries was still maintained. South Indian curries tended to be hotter and sometimes used tamarind as a flavour.

Quality control at Edward B. Beharry & Company

By the beginning of the twentieth century, Guyanese Indian housewives began to source local materials and other suppliers of spices were explored. For example, Morocco was discovered as a supplier of first-grade dhania (coriander) and the Gold Coast as a supplier of black peppers. India, however, still continued to be the main source for the supply of spices until the disruptions of shipping during the Second World War and the 1943 famine in India when the export of all foodstuffs was banned.

From the 1930s, many housewives, instead of using the traditional hand-grinding method, began to use small mills to grind their spices. Local entrepreneurs also used these hand mills to produce ground spices for the home market and for export to other countries of the West Indies, in particular, Barbados, St Lucia and Grenada, where curries were regarded as a delicacy. In time, the distinctiveness between north and south Indian became subsumed into a Guyanese-style curry which retained the best of India but with a Western acceptability, especially in smell and hotness.

After the Second World War, Indian curry powder began to be imported almost wholly from south India. These curry powders did quite well in the local market particularly because of the prestige of being produced in India.

At the same time, a number of local entrepreneurs ventured into the large-scale production of curry powders. They imported industrial grinding and blending machines and began to source good quality material at competitive prices. One of these companies was Edward B. Beharry & Company Ltd which, with its flagship brand, 'Indi Curry', has since taken more than an eighty percent share of the Guyanese market.

Further expansion of the company in the 1970s and 1980s resulted in a burgeoning "curry culture" with the dish itself becoming a pervasive national food, and the Indi Curry brand becoming a household name.

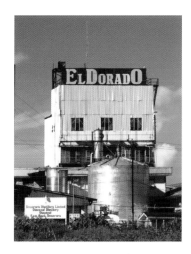

ABOVE
Demerara Distillers Ltd produces
Guyana's popular El Dorado Rum.
Photo: I Brierley

RIGHT
Demerara Bank Limited. Photo: H Chan

# AWARD-WINNING COMPANY IS AN INTERNATIONAL SUCCESS

FOUNDED IN 1983, PRECISION WOODWORKING LIMITED is today the leading added-value processor in the wood sector and a flagship company on the Guyana business landscape. Located in the Ruimveldt Industrial Estate in Georgetown, the company was established by five Guyanese men – Howard Bulkan, Gordon Forte, Hakim Rahaman, Rustum Bulkan and Ronald Bulkan – who chose not to join the exodus of talented and qualified persons that has characterised the greater part of Guyana's post-colonial history.

From humble beginnings, yet with a bold vision, the company began by exporting furniture components and household furniture within the Caribbean region. However,

since 1994, it has been exporting fully-manufactured, sophisticated hardwood outdoor-furniture to various distributors and retailers internationally, including the United Kingdom where it has a significant presence. The company boasts among its clients the prestigious British department store chain, John Lewis Plc. Its furniture is also sold extensively to the UK's contract trade, notably pubs and restaurants.

In recognition of its ground-breaking achievements and stellar performance, Precision Woodworking was the recipient of the prestigious Ernst & Young, 'Caribbean Entrepreneur of the Year' Award in 2001.

# A MAJOR PLAYER IN GUYANA'S ECONOMY

ROOPGROUP IS A DEVELOPMENT ORGANISATION MADE up of several dynamic and entrepreneurial ventures in information technology, media production, agri-business, aviation, construction and community service.

In 2004 the company opened its doors in the Guyana market with initial projects that included multi-million US dollar investment in the non-traditional agriculture sector and into the real estate markets.

RoopGroup is a major investment company; therefore, many of the projects being undertaken are long-term investments and require significant start up time. Its aim is to become one of the largest private employers in Guyana. In addition, the company has invested in communities and sports. It is credited for reviving local football in Georgetown and provided major sponsorships for other sporting organisations.

Given the limited packaging and export capacity in the country, RoopGroup built a 20,000 sq ft facility designed to process and package fresh fruit and vegetables and to provide cold storage and export of these products. The second phase of the project includes solving Guyana airlift shortage by investing into a cargo airline. This phase is expected to be completed by 2007.

The company has begun operations into the packaging of mixed chips for the export market. Utilising state-of-the-art equipment and international standard packaging material, the mixed chips will be introduced into the export market on a large scale. It has also built a factory in the Pomeroon region. The facility will be utilised as a multi-processing facility for both non-traditional agricultural products and the initiation of converting the waste materials of coconut into exportable goods such as fibre and mulch.

Major construction projects for the company properties are ongoing and construction workers have refurbished many properties for rental. The company plans to enter the market on a larger scale in 2007.

# A TRUE CARIBBEAN MULTI-NATIONAL

IN 1983, THREE YOUNG ENTERPRISING GUYANESE (JOHN La Rose, Terrence Pariaug and Glen Khan) saw a need to reconnect West Indians who were living overseas, with their families and friends in the Caribbean. The various communities in the United States, Canada and the United Kingdom needed a reliable freight service to send goods 'back home'; and, so, Laparkan was born.

The company opened its first office in Toronto followed by offices in Guyana, New York, Miami and the UK. Interest grew from other overseas communities and within six years, Laparkan had opened offices or agencies in Trinidad and Tobago, Jamaica and Barbados. By the early 1990s, Laparkan had extended its reach into the Caribbean to include Antigua, St Lucia, Grenada and St Vincent, as well as representation in Surinam. With continued success and growth, Laparkan offered its uniquely Caribbean-flavoured business brand into the larger markets of Haiti and the Dominican Republic. As the company developed its Caribbean operations, it simultaneously expanded its presence in North America. Its offices flourished within the communities they served and became an integral part of their customer base. Today, Laparkan can be found in the midst of the Caribbean communities in North America and the UK.

Laparkan later diversified its interests to acquire major companies in Guyana and now owns the long-established Fogarty's Department Store, and is the major shareholder in Guyana's oldest and largest engineering company, the Guyana National Industrial Corporation. The company's diversification also includes the formation of Laparkan Financial Services and the Laparkan Office Equipment & Supplies Division.

Through its network of offices in North America and the UK, Laparkan Ocean Freight provides consolidated as well as full container shipment to the Caribbean. This operation includes the transhipment of commercial cargo, personal

Far right: Glen Khan with five young recipients of Laparkan Bursaries

effects and a door-to-door service. Air freight is handled by Laparkan Air Freight, an IATA-registered cargo airline. This service supports the company's Express Courier Service, which provides direct delivery of packages as well as an airport-to-airport service. The company also provides bonded and secure warehousing facilities throughout its network.

Money transfer is another area in which Laparkan has been able to make a difference. This service is provided by Laparkan Money Transfer.

Since its creation – and as the company approaches its 25th year of service to the Caribbean – Laparkan has become a household name and continues to live up to its motto: "We make the difference".

these activities, GO-Invest's capacity to promote Guyana and attract investment will be strengthened, and priority bureaucratic processes will be streamlined, starting with business registration and customs import and export procedures. These initiatives, coupled with recent legislative accomplishments such as the introduction of a Value-added Tax (VAT) and the passing of an Investment Act, Small Business Act and Competition and Fair Trading Bill, will likely present an opportunity for Guyana to accelerate investment, trade and economic growth.

Many of Guyana's opportunities for investment and business development are only now being realised. With ongoing efforts to address competitiveness issues, the conditions for investment are constantly improving. As a result, new investors can benefit from 'first mover' status and choose the most promising projects, while at the same time establishing a platform for long-term growth and profitability. ■

FACING PAGE, TOP
The Harbour Bridge crosses the Demerara river and is the world's longest pontoon bridge. This elevated section allows river traffic to navigate the waters unhindered.   Photo: Hansib

# AN AGENCY TO PROMOTE AND FACILITATE INVESTMENT

GUYANA IS A COUNTRY AND ECONOMY IN TRANSITION. Modernisation is underway in all sectors and the country is now emerging as an attractive destination that offers investors immense opportunities – vast natural resources; stable and open financial markets; attractive fiscal incentive regime; duty-free access to Caricom markets; a political environment that fully supports a market-oriented approach to economic growth.

Over the last five years the country has attracted a number of investments in such sectors as mining, forestry, agriculture, information and communication technology, tourism and services. While some of these investments were local business ventures, a large percentage involved foreign-owned companies from such countries as United States, Russia, Canada, Malaysia, France, Israel, China, Brazil, South Africa, Holland, Jamaica and Trinidad and Tobago.

In support of investment and business activities, the government has passed a number of Acts in Parliament – Investment Act; Small Business Act; Fiscal Enactments (Amendments) (No. 2) Act 2003. The government has also tasked the Guyana Office for Investment (GoInvest) as the prime contact for investors to facilitate the investment process and expedite applications for investment concessions and Government support.

GoInvest was created in 1994 as a semi-autonomous agency and comes under the direct purview of the Office of the President. The CEO answers to a Board of Directors, which is composed of representatives of both the public and private sectors. GoInvest is divided into two divisions – Investment Facilitation and Promotion; Export Promotion.

Since May 2002, GoInvest has organised investment and export promotion missions (Guyana Trade and Investment Expositions) in Antigua and Barbuda, St Lucia, Barbados, Trinidad and Tobago, Suriname, Canada and the United States. Over 160 companies have participated in these expositions and this is partly responsible for the twenty percent increase in exports from 2001 to 2004.

GoInvest has also facilitated a number of new and expanding investment projects (domestic and foreign) in all sectors and in all sizes – micro, small, medium and large. These projects are located in all ten administrative regions of Guyana. The investment facilitation services of the Agency include – providing investors with information relevant to their projects; assisting with the acquisition of land and factory space for business purposes; organising business meetings and site visits for foreign delegations; and processing applications for fiscal concessions. In a nutshell, "doing all that is necessary to ensure the investment is successful."

Photo: I Brierley

# Reasons to invest in Guyana

**NATURAL RESOURCES** Guyana is a country of vast, often untapped, natural resources. Endowed with extensive savannahs, productive land and forests, rich mineral deposits of gold, bauxite and diamonds, abundant water resources and Atlantic coastline, the country presents dynamic business opportunities across multiple sectors of the economy. While recognised globally as a sugar and rice producer, much of its agricultural potential is yet to be realised, especially with regard to fresh and processed fruits and vegetables. Its forestry potential is just beginning to be realised, particularly in the realm of value-added wood products. Its extensive network of rivers and Atlantic coastline provide ideal conditions for both seafood and aquaculture. Finally, its pristine environment, unspoiled rainforest and exotic fauna and natural attractions, which include the famous Kaieteur Falls, the highest single drop waterfalls in the world, makes Guyana a highly attractive location for eco- and adventure tourism.

**LOCATION** Guyana's unique geographic positioning and its socio-political heritage put it at the gateway of South America and the Caribbean. On one hand, its Caribbean and English-speaking heritage enables Guyana to be part of the Caribbean Community (CARICOM), while on the other, it is a South American country, neighbouring two of the most important economies on the continent – Brazil and Venezuela. As a result of

THE BUSTLING STREETS OF GEORGETOWN.    Photo: I Brierley

its geographic proximity, Guyana has easy access to 277 million consumers, and a US$ 130+ billion export market with an overall purchasing power of over US$ 2 trillion.

**Duty Free Market Access** Through a combination of regional, bilateral and preferential agreements, about 75 percent of Guyana's exports enter destination markets duty free, with many others receiving duty-reduced access. This is achieved through Guyana's membership of CARICOM, which provides duty-free access to the 15-nation CARICOM market, CARICOM agreements with the Dominican Republic, Colombia, Costa Rica, Cuba and Venezuela, partial scope agreements with Brazil and Venezuela, and bilateral agreements with Argentina, China and Turkey. Guyana also benefits from preferential duty-free or reduced-duty access to major developed country markets through CARIBCAN (Canada), the US Caribbean Trade Partnership and the European Union's (EU) ACP Contonou Agreement.

## ENTREPRENEURIAL PROGRAMME IS A FIRST FOR THE CARIBBEAN

CONSIDER AN ENVIRONMENT WHERE YOUNG entrepreneurs have the skills needed to make their businesses work, the correct attitude to succeed in the most difficult of circumstances, the will to continue even under the stiffest pressures – and they were not born with these behaviours but managed to acquire them through training. Of course, not your usual kind of training, but an intense ten-day interactive workshop that is being hailed around the world as revolutionary in its effects on entrepreneurial behaviour.

Introducing the Empretec Training Workshop, an innovative and instructive approach that really changes the way business people look at themselves and the way they function. Operated by the United Nations Conference on Trade and Development (UNCTAD), this workshop is now operational in over twenty-five countries and is dramatically changing the business landscape with its hands-on and practical structure. And Guyana is the first Caribbean country to benefit from the training. An initiative of the Government of Guyana, the United Nations Development Programme and the Guyana Manufacturers Association, Empretec was established in Guyana some three years ago as a pilot project to examine how it might contribute to progress in the region.

And no one who has attended these workshops will tell you what they entail. If you are interested you must attend one yourself, but the results are being seen in the entrepreneurs who have taken the training. They talk of a new understanding of themselves as entrepreneurs and feel that every person who owns or operates a business should become "empretecos", the name given to all participants who have successfully completed the workshop. What is immediately apparent is there is changed behaviour, and talking with Executive Director Judy Semple-Joseph, it soon becomes clear that this is the objective of the programme. "Our aim is not to make people better managers, provide them with monies, or to tell them how their business works – they must look for the expertise in those areas in other environments. We aim to create a new perspective, to encourage behavioural change, to make participants aware of the behaviours successful entrepreneurs exhibit and let them find ways in which these behaviours can be inculcated so they become a natural part of your functioning," the Executive Director explained. And according to her, what makes this programme different are the methods used during the ten days to make this possible. Those she would not discuss.

Follow-up is through the Post Training Workshops which integrates the skills learned during the ten days with the more formalised approaches that are necessary for the survival of a business. There is the health check that is a diagnostic of the current state of the business and in-depth communication with the empreteco to advise and structure programmes to help the business to function better.

Over 200 participants have already benefited from the programme and there is a waiting list of others across the country who would like to participate. The workshop has been run in Georgetown, New Amsterdam and Linden and there are plans to take it to Essequibo, Bartica and Lethem in the near future. A network of Empretecos has been set up to allow for interaction that will lead to synergies in the business environment. The Caribbean is already expressing interest and with the introduction of the Caribbean Single Market and Economy (CSME) the need for new approaches and pioneering efforts are becoming more and more apparent. As the engines of growth in any economy, the private sector must look for fresh ways to enervate itself and in Empretec they think they've found a jewel. RUSSEL LANCASTER

## Investing in LDCs: Risk and Return

*"Why would anyone invest in a less-developed country?" a presumably hard-headed investor might ask. "Aren't the risks too high and the profits precarious?"*

This perception, though unfounded, seems widespread in some business circles. When it comes to profits, the evidence is that the rate of return on FDI in less-developed countries (LDCs) is often much higher than investment in developed countries, or even more developed emerging economies. Often the negative perception of LDCs results in an enormous untapped potential. As such, investors able to do their homework and distinguish between perception and reality may find abundant and lucrative investment opportunities. These investors can benefit from 'first mover' status. As opposed to locations where everyone wants to be investing, first movers can pick the most promising opportunities. If they are able to navigate the challenges that come with doing business in LDCs, investors will find their experience quite rewarding.

SOURCE: UNCTAD

*Doing Business in Guyana* is a comprehensive and informative guide for potential investors.

## THE GUYANA SMALL BUSINESS ASSOCIATION

The Guyana Small Business Association was established in 1988 to provide its members with the orientation and technical know-how to help them consolidate their various businesses. This includes a study of the needs of its members and the creation of a consultancy service to respond to those needs.

President of the association, Patrick Zephyr is of the strong opinion that the small business sector has an invaluable contribution to make to the development of the country but it is only with the commitment of its members and the input from government that this can be fully realised.

Membership has quadrupled since the floods of January/February 2005. The gravity of the situation allowed the organisation to interact with many new and potential members and this has created a new impetus within the organisation to forge a place for itself and to move ahead with plans to strengthen the structure and programmes needed.

Funding is one of the primary problems of the organisation and to date most has come from international sources like the United States Agency for International Development (USAID), the International Labour Organisation (ILO) and the Canadian International Development Agency (CIDA). According to Mr Zephyr, small business associations in other CARICOM countries all have close relations with their respective governments and receive funding from the state for their activities. He was called recently to sit on the National Small Business Council set up by the government to draft legislation relating to small businesses, the preparation of a Small Business Policy and the maintenance of a Small Business Register.

One of the proposals to be implemented by the Small Business Association is the establishment of a credit union, which will be available to all members in financial standing within the organisation. Small businesses can function in almost any environment since they are more flexible, more adaptable and therefore tend to show more resilience than larger businesses in the face of difficult economic circumstances. The Guyana Small Business Association wants to offer a resource to these businesses to help them grow and prosper within the framework of Guyana's economy.

**Language** Guyana is the only English-speaking nation in South America. Investors contemplating the installation and operation of service enterprises will find this a distinct advantage. This is especially true for those involved in the growing IT and business process outsourcing (BPO) markets in North America, as well as businesses conducting operations to support the activities of large corporations worldwide, and those serving English-speaking tourism markets.

**Affordable Labour** Guyana has one of the most competitive wage rates when compared to Latin America and the Caribbean. The labour force is well educated, with literacy estimated at close to 99 percent, and is regarded as trainable and hard working.

**Openness to Investment** Both public and private sector leaders have declared Guyana 'open for business'. Foreign investors receive the same treatment as domestic investors. Guyana provides an array of across-the-board investment incentives, including a flat business tax rate, tax holidays, waivers of customs duties, export tax allowances, and unrestricted repatriation of profits, as well as additional incentives in priority export sectors. Furthermore, Guyana's investment promotion agency, GO-Invest, provides effective support to investors before, during and after an investment has been realised. ∎

SONNENUNTERGANG AM ESSEQUIBO-FLUSS. Foto: I Brierley

# Guyana – das Geheimnis offenbart sich

Willkommen in Guyana, dem „Land der vielen Wasser", dem einzigen englischsprachigen Land des südamerikanischen Kontinents und dem südlichsten Staat der Karibik. Guyana ist von drei anderssprachigen Nachbarn – Venezuela (spanisch), Brasilien (portugiesisch) und Suriname (holländisch) – umgeben und verbindet diese mit der englisch sprechenden Welt.

Guyana ist ein Land der Widersprüche und Superlative. Hier gibt es den Kaieteur-Fall, den höchsten Wasserfall der Welt, sowie einen ihrer riesigsten unerforschten und unberührten Regenwälder, der mehr als drei Viertel der 215000 Quadratkilometer des Landes überzieht. Die Bevölkerung von Guyana steht mit nur 750.000 Menschen im umgekehrten Verhältnis zur Größe des Landes und setzt sich zusammen aus Einwanderern aus Afrika, Indien, Europa und China sowie den Amerindianern, die sich vor Tausenden von Jahren als erste Siedler hier niedergelassen haben.

Von Sir Walter Raleigh als Ort des legendären El Dorado berühmt gemacht, wurde „Guiana" bis zu seiner Unabhängigkeit vor 40 Jahren abwechselnd von den Holländern, Franzosen und Briten regiert, die alle darauf aus waren, seine reichen Diamanten-, Gold- und Bauxitvorkommen sowie sonstige, noch unbekannte Schätze in die Hand zu bekommen. Im Mittelpunkt der Geschichte von Guyana stand jedoch vor allem der Anbau von Zuckerrohr – das nahezu fünfhundert Jahre lang eine wichtige Grundlage des europäischen Reichtums bildete.

Doch was macht Guyana zu einem solch besonderen Ort, und warum ist es dem Rest der Welt so lange ein Geheimnis geblieben? Die Antwort liegt in seiner einzigartigen Schönheit und seiner eigentümlichen Geschichte – den Herausforderungen, denen es sich im Laufe der Jahre ausgesetzt sah, während verschiedenste politische Bewegungen sich darum bemühten, seine ungewöhnliche Mischung fundamentaler Merkmale in den Griff zu bekommen, und dabei feststellten, dass es nicht immer einfach war, angemessene Lösungen zu finden. Ist dies das Paradies – diese erstaunliche Landschaft von atemberaubender Schönheit und bezwingender Macht, zu der nur der ernsthaft Strebende gelangt, wenn er es nach langer Suche nach ihrem ephemeren Kern wirklich verdient hat? Viele erblicken nur das von den übereifrigen Medien erstellte äußerliche Bild und übersehen die wahren Eigenschaften, für die Guyana berühmt geworden ist: seine Gastfreundschaft, die weiterhin als eine der besten auf der Welt gilt, seine Frische, seine unverdorbene natürliche Schönheit, seine widersprüchlichen Menschen, die gleichzeitig naiv und hoch entwickelt sind und zu den kreativsten und zähesten der Welt gehören. Der oberflächliche Betrachter übersieht die sinnliche Energie, die die Atmosphäre von Guyana durchzieht, und bemerkt nicht, dass hier der Himmel blauer und die Sterne heller zu sein scheinen und die Luft mit einem ambrosischen Duft angereichert ist, der die Sinne anregt und das Gemüt beschwichtigt, so dass es die Sorgen des Alltags vergisst, während sich der Lebensrhythmus verlangsamt und die restliche Welt eine ferne Erinnerung wird. Wenige, die Guyana besuchen, wollen es wieder verlassen, und alle, die je hier waren, sehnen sich danach zurückzukehren.

Es steht außer Zweifel, dass Guyana etwas Besonders ist – das wird ihm jeder Besucher bescheinigen. Das Land ist fast so groß wie Großbritannien und durchzogen von einem weit verzweigten Netz von Flüssen, Stromschnellen und Wasserfällen, die sich jeder Katalogisierung entziehen und in so undurchdringlicher Landschaft liegen, dass viele nur den unerschrockensten Besuchern zu Gesicht kommen.

Eine typische Reise durch dieses Land beginnt in der Hauptstadt Georgetown, einer gelungenen Mischung aus altertümlichen Charme und überraschender Modernität. Hier offenbaren sich die ersten Widersprüchlichkeiten – in einem täuschend simplen Bauplan mit Holzhäusern und üppiger Begrünung, in dem historische Stätten Seite an Seite mit modernen Gebäuden anzutreffen sind. In dieser Hauptstadt befindet sich auch die St. Georgeskathedrale, das höchste Holzgebäude der Welt. Die Stadt ist zudem der Sitz des Sekretariats der CARICOM, des obersten Entscheidungsorgans der karibischen Region.

Kokosnussplantage. Foto: H Chan

Hier in Georgetown ist die Bevölkerung des Landes am stärksten konzentriert. Und hier scheint es gelegentlich geradezu unmöglich, die verschlungenen Wege des bürokratischen Labyrinths erfolgreich zu navigieren. Diese Hauptstadt ist der Knotenpunkt, von dem alles ausgeht und der den oft weit entlegenen regionalen Gemeinschaften des riesigen Landes seinen Stempel aufdrückt. Die in der Hauptstadt angesiedelte Zentralregierung schafft den Rahmen, innerhalb dessen der bunt gemischte Staat funktioniert. Der größte Teil der Bevölkerung lebt im Küstengürtel, wo der fruchtbare kontinentale Boden eine Fülle von einheimischen Gemüse- und Obstsorten produziert und schon seit hunderten von Jahren Reis und Zucker angebaut werden. Es ist dieser Gegend zu verdanken, dass Guyana der „Brotkorb der Karibik" genannt wird.

Bis vor nicht allzulanger Zeit war Guyana durch seine drei Hauptregionen Demerara, Essequibo und Berbice definiert, doch heute werden seine Verwaltungsbezirke als ein zweckmäßigere Methode zur Beschreibung des Landes angesehen. Es gibt zehn Verwaltungsbezirke mit eigenen demokratisch gewählten Regionalräten, die lokale Angelegenheiten regeln. Doch die wichtigsten Städte sind weiterhin New Amsterdam in der „uralten Region" Berbice und Anna Regina in der „Aschenputtel-Region" Essequibo. Weitere bedeutende Städte sind Bartica, Corriverton, Linden und Lethem. Bei Lethem verläuft die Grenze zu Brasilien, und hier ist eine Brücke im Bau, die Guyana mit Brasilien verbinden soll. Diese wird – zusammen mit einer Allwetterstraße, die in Zusammenarbeit mit der brasilianischen Regierung entsteht – in einigen wenigen Jahren das Gesicht Guyanas merklich verändern.

Doch Guyanas wahre Schönheit und den einmaligen Geist des Landes kann man nur voll erleben, wenn man sich ins Landesinnere begibt – in eine verlorene Welt, die von magischer Energie pulsiert und die in ihren noch unerforschten Tiefen die Geheimnisse universeller Rettung birgt. Hier in Iwokrama eröffnen sich uns auf weit über 400000 Hektar, die dem nachhaltigen Leben gewidmet sind und dem Rest der

Pavillon im Botanischen Garten von Georgetown. Foto: I Brierley

Guyana ist für seine atemberaubenden Wasserfälle bekannt. Foto: I Brierley

Welt zum Geschenk gemacht werden, verborgene Geheimnisse, während wir mehr darüber erfahren, wie wir die Ressourcen unserer Welt auf eine Weise nutzen können, die sie für künftige Generationen bewahrt. Iwokrama auf Guyana ist gewissermaßen ein Labor, das womöglich zur Rettung der Erde beitragen kann, da hier Antworten auf die Fragen nach der Beziehung des Menschen zur Natur und nach seiner symbiotischen Wechselbeziehung mit ihren Geschenken gesucht werden. Auf Guyana sind auch die Riesenotter und das Dreifinger-Faultier zu Hause. Ebenfalls hier anzutreffen sind der größte Süßwasserfisch der Welt – der Arapaima – und eine der größten Katzenarten, der Jaguar.

Guyana ist der Traum eines jeden Touristen: ein Ort, den man schon immer gesucht hat, aber den man sich nie wirklich vergegenwärtigen konnte – bis man hier eintrifft und der Traum zur Wirklichkeit wird. Mit vielen verschiedenen Regenwald-Resorts für jeden Geschmack steht Guyana im Begriff, zum neuen Mekka für alle zu werden, die ein wirklich energetisierendes Erlebnis suchen. Aber denken Sie nicht etwa, dass es auf Guyana an Prosaischem fehlen würde, denn wir sind begeisterte Cricket-Fans und haben im Laufe der Jahre sechs Kapitäne des Westindischen Cricket-Teams gestellt. Und weil das Land so reiche Goldvorkommen besitzt, ist es nichts Ungewöhnliches, wenn Guyaner neben Ketten, Ohrringen und Ringen aus dem edlen Metall auch einen oder zwei Goldzähne blitzen lassen. Guyanas Besucher erhalten ebenfalls Gelegenheit, diese kostbare Quelle zu nutzen und in den vielen Schmuckläden des Landes erlesene Stücke zu erstehen.

Für den, der Augen für Echtes und Tiefgründiges hat, stellt Guyana eine *tabula rasa* dar – ein unbeschriebenes Blatt, auf das er seine Vorstellung vom Paradies projizieren kann, wodurch sich seine Sicht der eigenen Existenz auf Erden dramatisch verändert. Besuchen Sie Guyana und machen Sie sich darauf gefasst, dass es Sie für immer verändern wird. Bleiben Sie hier, und lassen Sie sich für alle Zeiten verwandeln. Bei uns finden Sie kein Idyll für Zaghafte, sondern eine lebensverändernde Erfahrung, die Ihnen Erneuerung bringt. Guyana ist in Bewegung, und es ist nur eine Frage der Zeit, bis sich seine besonderen Qualitäten der ganzen Welt offenbaren. ■

# Guyana – el secreto revelado

EL COMPLEJO TURISTICO DE TIMBERHEAD TIENE SU PROPIO NIDO EN LAS SELVAS TROPICALES.  Foto: I Brierley

Bienvenidos a Guyana, tierra de muchas aguas, y el único país en el continente suramericano de lengua inglesa, además de ser el estado más al sur de toda la región caribeña.  Circundada por tres vecinos – la hispanohablante Venezuela, el Brasil de lengua portuguesa y el Surinam, donde se habla el holandés - Guyana ofrece a sus vecinos su enlace al mundo anglohablante.

Guyana es una tierra llena de contradicciones y superlativos.  En Guyana se encuentran las Cataratas de Kaieteur, la catarata de una sola caída más alta en todo el mundo; una de las mayores selvas tropicales inexploradas, aún en estado virgen, en la que vienen cubiertos más de los tres cuartos de los 215.000 kilómetros cuadrados de la superficie del país; y una población desproporcionada a la dimensión del país, de apenas 750.000 habitantes, representando la diversidad cultural proveniente de África, India, Europa, y China además de su propia gente indígena, los amerindios, quienes se establecieron en estas tierras hace miles de años.

Celebrada por el inglés Sir Walter Raleigh, como la legendaria ciudad de El Dorado, 'Guiana' ha estado bajo el control de los holandeses, franceses e ingleses y, en los últimos 40 años por su propio pueblo.  Y todo esto como parte de una misión para aprovecharse de su vasta riqueza natural de diamantes, oro y bauxita, además de las riquezas que por ahora, permanecen sin descubrir.  Es importante destacar que su historia se revuelve alrededor de la cultivación de azúcar de caña, ese alimento de primera necesidad de la abundancia europea para más de medio milenio.

Pero ¿que será lo que tiene Guyana que hace de ella un lugar tan especial? y ¿cómo ha logrado mantener su secreto tan bien guardado del resto del mundo por tanto tiempo? La respuesta se encuentra en su magnificencia única y en su curiosa historia - los desafíos que ha enfrentado a lo largo de los años, en cuanto sucesivos movimientos políticos han intentado comprender la combinación rara de características fundamentales, sólo para darse cuenta de que sus problemas no son siempre fáciles de resolver.  ¿Puede que esto sea el paraíso, este paisaje irresistible, de un poder sorprendente, cuya belleza nos deja sin aliento y al que llegan sólo los verdaderamente dedicados y meritorios después de una larga y ardua búsqueda de su centro efímero?  Muchos de los que van en busca de ello ven sólo la imagen externa creada por unos medios de comunicación demasiados apasionados, y así pierden las calidades verdaderas que han hecho de Guyana una tierra renombrada: su hospitalidad, que sigue siendo considerada entre las más admiradas del mundo, su fresquera, su belleza natural preservada, su pueblo contradictorio, curiosamente cándido y al mismo tiempo sofisticado, y entre los más creativos y resistentes de todo el mundo.  Ellos no ven la energía sensual que permanece en el ambiente y tampoco se dan cuenta de que en Guyana el cielo se ve más azul, las estrellas parecen ser más brillantes, y el aire está enriquecido con un aroma deleitoso que sosiega los sentidos haciendo que uno se olvide los problemas del día a día, a medida que se desacelera el ritmo y el mundo externo se convierte a un recuerdo distante.  Son muy pocos entre los que vienen a Guyana que no desean quedarse, y todos los que pasan por esta tierra hermosa desean regresar de nuevo.

Que Guyana sea una tierra especial no quepa duda alguna, como atestarían todos los que por aquí pasan. Casi el mismo tamaño que Gran Bretaña, Guyana puede presumir de una vasta red de ríos, rápidos y cataratas demasiado numerosos para catalogar, y en general un paisaje tan difícil de penetrar, que sólo los más duraderos han llegado a poder contemplarla.

Uno empieza su aventura por este país en Georgetown, la ciudad capital, una mezcla de ranciedad antigua y modernidad sorprendente. Y es aquí donde primero se le notan las contradicciones en una engañosamente sencilla composición de edificios construidos de madera y verdura floreciente, donde lo histórico se sienta al lado de la contemporaneidad. En esta ciudad capital se encuentra la Catedral de San Jorge, la construcción de madera más alta del mundo. Y es aquí en Guyana donde el Secretariado de la Caricom, el mayor organismo decisorio del Caribe tiene sede.

Es aquí en Georgetown, donde la mayor concentración de los ciudadanos tiene su domicilio. A veces uno se pierde, intentando navegar las complejidades del laberinto burocrático. Esta ciudad capital es el nexos desde el cual todo se extiende para imprimirse sobre la presencia desparramada de las comunidades regionales a través de la inmensidad que ofrece este país. Un gobierno centralizado, que funciona desde su sede en la capital, brinda una estructura en la cual funciona el órgano nacional. La mayoría de los habitantes vive en la zona costal, donde la tierra continental fértil ofrece una riqueza de verdura nativa y donde el arroz y el azúcar han sido cultivados durante cientos de años. Y es precisamente esta riqueza que le ha proporcionado a Guyana el nombre de "el cesto del pan caribeño".

En el pasado, Guyana se definía por tres condados: Demerara, Essequibo y Berbice hasta hace poco tiempo, cuando las regiones administrativas se convirtieron en la manera más funcional de describir el país. En total hay diez regiones administrativas, cada una con su propio consejo democrático regional que se encarga de asuntos locales. A pesar de esto, los mayores pueblos siguen siendo Nueva Ámsterdam en el "condado antiguo" de Berbice y Anna Regina en el "Condado Cenicienta" (llamado así porque se considera pequeña) de Essequibo. Otros pueblos de gran importancia incluyen Bartica, Corriverton, Linden y Lethem. En Lethem se encuentra la frontera con Brasil, y es el lugar en que un puente, actualmente en proceso de construcción, establecerá una conexión con su vecino. Esto, además de una carretera resistente a todo tipo de clima que será completada en colaboración con el gobierno brasileño, cambiará para siempre la cara de Guyana en un futuro próximo.

La pesca tradicional de los amerindios.
Foto: I Brierley

Bartica está situada donde confluyen los ríos de Essequibo y Mazaruni. Foto: I Brierley

El lujoso complejo turístico de Isla Baganara. Foto: I Brierley

Pero la belleza verdadera de Guyana y su espíritu sutil sólo pueden ser experimentados yéndose al más allá, por el interior hacía un mundo perdido que vibra con una energía mágica llena de los secretos de la creación universal en sus entrañas inexploradas. Es aquí, en Iwokrama, en un área de un millón de acres dedicado a un modo de vivir sostenible, y presentado como un regalo al resto del mundo, que misterios incontables se desarrollan para que podamos aprender más sobre cómo aprovecharnos de los recursos naturales de este mundo, para que se puedan preservar para futuras generaciones. Aquí en Guyana, en Iwokrama, preside el laboratorio natural que tal vez sea la salvación de esta tierra, a medida que nosotros vayamos en busca de respuestas según la cuestión de la relación del hombre con la naturaleza y su interacción simbiótica con los regalos que ésta nos ofrece. Guyana también es el hogar de la nutria gigantesca y del perezoso de tres dedos, y en Guyana también se puede encontrar el Arapaima, el pez de agua dulce más grande del mundo, además del jaguar, el mayor felino del mundo.

Guyana es la fantasía de cada turista: ese lugar en la imaginación el que siempre se ha buscado pero el que no se conseguía concebir, hasta que aquí llegan y conocen la verdadera satisfacción. Con varios balnearios en las selvas tropicales dedicados a satisfacer todo tipo de gusto, Guyana se está convirtiendo rápidamente en la nueva Meca, ofreciendo una experiencia totalmente enervadora. Y no se creen que por eso se pierdan la Guyana pragmática, pues somos aficionados del críquet y a lo largo de los años nada menos de seis capitanes del equipo de críquet nacional de las Antillas han sido guyaneses. Y como el oro es tan abundante por aquí, no es poco común encontrar a guyaneses demostrando un diente o dos de oro, además de collares, pendientes, y anillos hechos de metales preciosos. Nuestros visitantes también pueden aprovecharse de esta fuente natural con artículos exquisitos que puedan añadir a sus colecciones, en las numerosas joyerías existentes en todo el país.

Para ustedes que van en busca sólo de lo real y de lo profundo, Guyana ofrece una *tabula rosa*, una pizarra limpia en la que escribir su visión del paraíso, transformando de modo milagroso la manera en que uno ve a su propia existencia en esta tierra. Visite Guyana y quede asegurado que usted nunca más será el mismo. Quédese aquí y será continuamente trasformado. Lo nuestro no es un mundo idílico para los pusilánimes, sino una experiencia que cambiará completamente su vida, dejándole totalmente renovado. Guyana está en movimiento y sólo el tiempo le permitirá revelar sus calidades al mundo. ■

NUAGES FLOTTANT AU-DESSUS DE LA VASTE FORÊT TROPICALE DU GUYANA. Photo : I Brierley

# Guyana – Secret au grand jour

Bienvenue au Guyana, « Land of many waters » (contrée des mille cours d'eau), seul pays anglophone sur le continent sud-américain et l'état à l'extrême sud de la région des Caraïbes. Le Guyana constitue le trait d'union entre le monde anglophone et ses trois voisins : le Venezuela hispanophone, le Suriname néerlandophone et le Brésil où l'on parle portugais.

Le Guyana est un pays de contradictions et d'exceptions. Il s'enorgueillit des cascades de Kaieteur, la plus haute chute d'eau au monde; de l'une des plus larges forêts tropicales restée inexplorée et intacte, et couvrant plus des trois quarts de la superficie du pays (215 000 kilomètres carrés); ainsi que d'une population en disproportion directe avec sa taille, à peine 750 000 habitants, rassemblant des individus d'origine africaine, indienne, européenne, chinoise et les indigènes, les Amérindiens, qui s'y sont installés il y a plusieurs milliers d'années.

Rendu célèbre par Sir Walter Raleigh le décrivant comme le légendaire Eldorado, 'Guiana' est passé aux mains des Hollandais, des Français et des Anglais avant de devenir indépendant il y a quarante ans. Tous désiraient leur part du gâteau, de vastes ressources naturelles en diamants, or et bauxite, tout comme le fruit encore inconnu de la nature abondante de cette contrée. Son histoire tourne autour de la culture de la canne à sucre, culture à la source de la richesse européenne pendant près de cinq cent ans.

Quels sont ces détails qui font du Guyana une contrée si particulière et pourquoi ce pays est-il resté si longtemps secret pour le reste du monde? Ces questions trouvent une réponse dans son unique splendeur et sa curieuse histoire ; les défis qu'il a dû relever au fil des ans, alors que les divers mouvements politiques, qui se sont succédés, ont essayé de s'atteler aux tâches qu'impliquait sa combinaison inhabituelle de caractéristiques fondamentales et découvert qu'il n'est pas toujours facile de remédier aux divers problèmes. Serait-ce le paradis, ce paysage d'une beauté à vous couper le souffle et d'une puissance saisissante, auquel seuls les plus dévoués et méritants peuvent accéder après une recherche longue et acharnée de son cœur éphémère ? Nombreux sont ceux qui ne voient que l'image superficielle, produit d'un monde médiatique trop zélé, et ne perçoivent pas les vraies qualités auxquelles le Guyana doit son renom : son hospitalité, toujours considérée comme l'une des plus chaleureuses au monde, sa fraîcheur, sa beauté naturelle préservée et intacte, sa population contradictoire, curieusement naïve et sophistiquée à la fois et comptant parmi les plus créatrices et déterminées au monde. L'énergie sensuelle imprégnant l'atmosphère leur échappe, tout comme le fait qu'au Guyana le ciel semble plus bleu, les étoiles plus étincelantes et que l'air jouit d'une succulence divine qui stimule les sens et apaise l'esprit jusqu'à lui en faire oublier les soucis du quotidien, alors que le rythme ralentit et le monde extérieur se transforme en un souvenir lointain. Peu nombreux sont les visiteurs qui veulent quitter le Guyana après l'avoir découvert et tous rêvent d'y retourner.

Comme toute personne l'ayant visité en témoignera, il n'y a aucun doute quant au caractère extraordinaire du Guyana. Pratiquement de la taille du Royaume Uni, le pays s'enorgueillit d'un réseau de rivières, rapides et chutes d'eau tellement vaste qu'il est impossible de les cataloguer. En outre, ces joyaux sont pour la plupart enfouis au sein d'un paysage tellement impénétrable que seuls les plus téméraires peuvent les admirer.

Une visite typique de ce pays commence à Georgetown, une capitale combinant le charme de l'ancien monde à une modernité surprenante. C'est ici que se dessinent les premières contradictions, dans un paysage trompeusement simple caractérisé par des constructions de bois et une verdure abondante, où les édifices modernes avoisinent les sites historiques. La cathédrale St George, le plus haut bâtiment en bois au monde, est l'une des grandes attractions de cette capitale. Le Guyana héberge le Secrétariat de la CARICOM, foyer de l'organe de décision suprême de la région des Caraïbes.

C'est ici, à Georgetown, que l'on enregistre la plus haute densité de population du Guyana. C'est ici aussi qu'il relève parfois de l'impossible de retrouver son chemin dans les subtilités du labyrinthe bureaucratique. Cette capitale est le système nerveux du pays qui se ramifie et imprègne les diverses communautés régionales tentaculaires à travers l'immensité que ce pays représente. Un gouvernement centralisé, basé dans la capitale, fournit le cadre selon lequel l'ensemble du pays fonctionne. La majeure partie de la population vit dans la région côtière, où la terre fertile et continentale produit une pléthore de fruits et légumes du pays, et où les cultures de riz et de sucre font partie du paysage depuis des centaines d'années. C'est cette nature abondante qui a donné au Guyana son nom de « grenier des Caraïbes ».

Avant d'être réorganisé en régions administratives pour des raisons pratiques, le Guyana était défini par trois grands comtés: Demerara, Essequibo et Berbice. Aujourd'hui, le pays compte dix régions administratives dotées de leur propre conseil démocratique régional gérant les affaires locales. Mais les villes principales restent toujours New Amsterdam dans « l'ancien comté » de Berbice et Anna Regina dans le « modeste comté » d'Essequibo. D'autres villes comme Bartica, Corriverton, Linden et Lethem sont aussi à mentionner. C'est à Lethem, avoisinant la frontière brésilienne, que l'on trouve l'endroit où un pont, qui reliera le Guyana au Brésil, est en cours de construction. Ce pont tout comme une route résistante à toutes les intempéries, qui sera bâtie en collaboration avec le gouvernement brésilien, changera le visage du Guyana dans un avenir très proche.

Mais la beauté véritable et l'esprit subtile du Guyana ne peuvent être réellement vécus qu'en s'aventurant dans l'arrière pays, dans un monde perdu vibrant d'une énergie magique et détenant les secrets de la délivrance universelle en son coeur encore inexploré.

Guyana est une contrée aux mille cours d'eau. Photo: I Brierley

Eglise catholique romaine Santa Rosa.
Photo: I Brierley

Le marché de Stabroek est un centre
très animé dans la capitale du Guyana.
Photo: I Brierley

C'est ici, à Iwokrama, sur un million d'acres dédiés au développement durable, et présentés comme un cadeau au reste du monde, que de grands mystères sont dévoilés alors que l'on apprend à utiliser ces ressources naturelles de manière à ce qu'elles puissent être préservées pour les futures générations. Iwokrama au Guyana offre un laboratoire qui pourrait bien se révéler être le salut de la planète dans notre recherche de réponses quant à la relation de l'homme avec la nature et son interaction symbiotique avec ses joyaux. Le Guyana abrite également la loutre géante et le plus grand paresseux à trois doigts, ainsi que l'arapaïma, le plus grand poisson d'eau douce du monde, et l'un des plus gros félidés, le jaguar.

Le Guyana est le rêve de tous les touristes. Cette contrée imaginaire qu'ils recherchent depuis toujours mais n'avaient jamais pu visualiser avant de mettre les pieds au Guyana et d'y ressentir une impression de plénitude. Avec ces nombreuses stations tropicales pourvoyant aux goûts de tous, le Guyana est en passe de devenir la nouvelle Mecque offrant une expérience réellement enivrante. Et n'allez pas vous imaginer que le prosaïsme du quotidien en viendra à vous manquer au Guyana, car nous sommes fans de cricket et six capitaines guyanais ont mené l'équipe des Antilles au fil du temps. L'or y coulant à flot, il n'est pas rare de voir un guyanais arborer une ou deux dents en or en outre des traditionnels bracelets, boucles d'oreille et bagues de ce métal précieux. Les visiteurs, dénichant des pièces exquises à ajouter à leur collection dans les nombreuses bijouteries du pays, peuvent eux aussi repartir avec leur part du trésor naturel du pays.

Pour ceux que seules les profondeurs et réalités de la vie intéressent, le Guyana offre une *tabula rasa*, une ardoise vierge attendant votre vision du paradis, transformant miraculeusement votre manière de concevoir votre existence sur la terre. Venez visiter le Guyana et sachez que ce voyage vous changera à jamais. Restez-y et préparez-vous à une transformation permanente. Nous ne vous proposons pas une idylle pour natures sensibles, mais une expérience qui changera votre vie et vous donnera une sensation de renaissance. Le Guyana est en pleine évolution et seul le temps révélera ses qualités particulières au reste du monde. ∎

# Guiana – o segredo revelado

A GUIANA É UM PAÍS COM VEGETAÇÃO LUXURIANTE.   Foto: H Chan

Seja bem-vindo à Guiana, terra de muitas águas, o único país do continente sul-americano de língua inglesa e o estado caribenho mais ao sul da região. Cercado por três vizinhos – a Venezuela de língua espanhola, o Brasil de língua portuguesa e o Suriname de língua holandesa – a Guiana é a ponte de comunicação entre estas nações e o mundo de fala inglesa.

A Guiana é um país de contradições e superlativos. Ali estão a Cachoeira de Kaieteur, a maior cachoeira do mundo de uma só queda d'água; uma das maiores florestas tropicais ainda inexploradas e intocadas que cobre mais de três quartos dos 215.000 k² da área do país; uma população desproporcional à dimensão do país, de apenas 750.000 habitantes, representando a diversidade cultural proveniente da África, Índia, Europa e China, além do seu próprio povo indígena, os Ameríndios, que ali se estabeleceram há milhares de anos.

Tornada famosa por Sir Walter Raleigh como o local do mítico El Dorado, a Guiana esteve sob o controle dos holandeses, franceses e ingleses e, nos últimos quarenta anos, do seu próprio povo, todos motivados pela busca de suas vastas riquezas naturais de diamantes, ouro e bauxita, além das riquezas ainda desconhecidas, cuja história se desenvolveu em torno do cultivo da cana de açúcar, o produto básico da riqueza européia durante quase meio milênio.

Mas, por que a Guiana é um país tão especial e por que permaneceu um segredo tão bem guardado do resto do mundo por tanto tempo? A resposta está na sua magnificência única e na sua curiosa história – os desafios que o país enfrentou ao longo dos anos enquanto sucessivos movimentos políticos tentaram compreender sua combinação incomum de características fundamentais até descobrirem que as soluções para suas complexidades nem sempre são fáceis de encontrar. Poderia ser isso o paraíso, esta intensa paisagem de uma beleza emocionante e de uma força surpreendente, para a qual só os verdadeiramente dedicados e merecedores podem afluir depois de uma longa e difícil busca de seu âmago efêmero? Muitos daqueles que olham vêem apenas a imagem externa gerada por uma mídia ultraentusiasta e não percebem as qualidades que fizeram da Guiana uma terra renomada: sua hospitalidade, ainda considerada uma das mais admiráveis do mundo, seu frescor, sua beleza natural preservada, seu povo contraditório, curiosamente ingênuo e, ao mesmo tempo sofisticado, e um dos mais criativos e maleáveis do mundo. Eles não vêem a energia sensual que envolve o ambiente, e deixam de perceber que, na Guiana, o céu parece mais azul, as estrelas mais brilhantes e o ar transparente abençoado por uma deliciosa suculência que mexe com os sentidos e leva a mente a esquecer as preocupações do dia a dia, à medida que o ritmo desacelera e o mundo exterior se torna uma memória longínqua. Poucos entre aqueles que visitam a Guiana querem sair e aqueles que estão de passagem não vêem a hora de retornar à este país.

Acima de qualquer dúvida, a Guiana é uma terra especial, como podem confirmar todos os que por aqui passaram. Quase do tamanho da Grã-Bretanha, a Guiana oferece uma vasta rede de rios, corredeiras e quedas-d'água numerosas demais para serem catalogadas, numa paisagem em sua maior parte tão impenetrável que somente os mais persistentes têm a oportunidade de contemplar.

A aventura por este país começa em Georgetown, capital federal, que combina o charme do velho mundo com uma surpreendente modernidade. É aqui que as contradições começam a se tornar aparentes num desenho enganosamente simples onde se vêem construções de madeira e exuberantes áreas verdes e onde o passado convive lado a lado com o contemporâneo. Nesta capital, encontra-se a Catedral de São Jorge, a mais alta construção de madeira do mundo. É na Guiana que o Secretariado do Caricom, a mais alta organização decisória do Caribe, está localizada.

É aqui, em Georgetown, que se encontra a maior concentração da população guianense. E é aqui que, algumas vezes, achamos quase impossível navegar entre o emaranhado labirinto da burocracia. Esta cidade capital é o nexo do qual tudo se irradia, imprimindo-se na vasta ocorrência das comunidades regionais através da amplidão deste país. O governo centralizado representa a rede na qual toda a multiplicidade nacional funciona. A maioria da população vive no cinturão costeiro onde o solo fértil e continental oferece uma abundância de vegetação e frutos nativos e onde o arroz e a cana de açúcar são cultivados há séculos. E é esta abundância que levou a Guiana a ser conhecida como "o celeiro do Caribe".

Antes, a Guiana se definia por três condados: Demerara, Essequibo e Berbice até há pouco tempo, quando as regiões administrativas se tornaram a maneira mais funcional de se descrever o país. Há dez regiões administrativas com suas próprias prefeituras democráticas regionais que administram as questões locais. Mas as cidades mais importantes ainda são Nova Amsterdã, no "condado antigo" de Berbice, e Anna Regina, no "Condado Cinderela" de Essequibo. Outras cidades de importância são Bartica, Corriverton, Linden e Lethem. Em Lethem encontra-se a fronteira com o Brasil e o local onde uma ponte, em processo de construção, irá ligar os dois países. Isto, além de uma estrada resistente a todas as estações, que será completada em colaboração com o governo brasileiro, transformará a face da Guiana num futuro bem próximo.

Mas a verdadeira beleza da Guiana e seu espírito sutil só podem ser experimentados viajando-se pelo interior para um mundo perdido que vibra com uma energia mágica e

Escolares na Main Street em Georgetown
Foto: I Brierley

Caminhão transportando toras de madeira em Karapung. Foto: I Brierley

As ruas movimentadas da capital da Guiana, Georgetown.   Foto: H Chan

que guarda os segredos da criação universal em suas entranhas ainda inexploradas. É aqui, em Iwokrama, numa área de um milhão de acres dedicados à economia sustentável, e presenteado ao resto do mundo, que incontáveis mistérios se desenrolam à medida que aprendemos mais sobre as maneiras de utilizar os recursos deste mundo para que ele seja preservado para futuras gerações. Na Guiana, em Iwokrama, encontra-se o laboratório natural que poderá vir a ser a salvação deste planeta, à medida que buscamos respostas para a questão da relação do homem com a natureza e sua interação simbólica com suas dádivas. A Guiana é também o mundo da lontra gigante e da maior preguiça de patas rachadas, e na Guiana pode ser também encontrado o Arapaima, o maior peixe de água doce do mundo, bem como um dos maiores felinos do planeta, a onça.

E a Guiana é a fantasia dos turistas: o lugar em suas imaginações que eles sempre desejaram encontrar mas que não conseguiam vislumbrar até aqui chegar e desfrutar sua auto-realização. Com inúmeros resorts na floresta tropical satisfazendo a diferentes gostos, a Guiana está se tornando rapidamente a nova Meca de uma experiência verdadeiramente extraordinária. E não pense que você deixará de experimentar a Guiana do mundo 'real', pois amamos o nosso críquete e, ao longo dos anos, tivemos seis guianenses como capitães da seleção de críquete das Índias Ocidentais. E como o ouro é tão abundante por aqui, não é incomum deparar-se com guianenses exibindo um ou dois dentes de ouro além de colares, brincos de orelha e anéis deste precioso metal. E os visitantes, também, têm a oportunidade de usufruir deste recurso natural com maravilhosas peças para suas coleções nas inúmeras joalherias existentes em todo o país.

Para aqueles que só estão em busca do verdadeiro e do profundo, a Guiana oferece a *tabula rasa*, uma placa na qual você pode registrar sua visão de paraíso, o que transformará milagrosamente a visão que você tem da sua existência na terra. Visite a Guiana e saiba que você nunca mais será o mesmo. Fique e será continuamente transformado. O nosso idílio não é para os de coração fraco mas uma experiência de mudar a vida para sempre que o deixará renovado. A Guiana existe em movimento e só o tempo permitirá que suas qualidades especiais sejam reveladas ao mundo. ■

## GOVERMENT OFFICES

**Office of the President**
New Garden Street, Bourda
Tel: 225-1301-3 / 1335. Fax: 226-3395

**Prime Minister's Office**
Wights Lane, Kingston
Tel: 227-3101-2 / 226- 6955. Fax: 226-7573

**Ministry of Agriculture**
592 Regent Street, Bourda
Tel: 223-7844. Fax: 225-0599

**Ministry of Culture, Youth and Sport**
71-72 Main Street, S. Cummingsburg
Tel: 226-3665 / 3788. Fax: 225-5067

**Ministry of Education**
26 Brickdam, Stabroek
Tel: 223-7900. Fax: 225-5570

**Ministry of Finance**
Main Street, Kingston
Tel: 225-6088 / 227-1114. Fax: 226-1284

**Ministry of Fisheries, Crops and Livestock**
Regent Road, Bourda
Tel: 226-1565. Fax: 227-2798

**Ministry of Foreign Affairs**
254 South Road, Bourda
Tel: 226-1606-9. Fax: 223-5241

**Ministry of Foreign Trade and International Co-operation**
154 South Road, Bourda
Tel: 226-1606-9 / 1600. Fax: 226-8429

**Ministry of Health**
Brickdam, Stabroek
Tel: 226-5861-5. Fax: 225-4505

**Ministry of Home Affairs**
Brickdam, Stabroek
Tel: 226-2444-5 / 1717. Fax: 227-4806

**Ministry of Housing and Water**
41 Brickdam, Stabroek
Tel: 225-7192 / 226-0498. Fax: 227-3455

**Ministry of Labour, Human Services and Social Security**
1 Water Street, Stabroek
Tel: 226-6115 / 6076. Fax: 227-1308

**Ministry of Legal Affairs**
95 Carmichael Street, North Cummingsburg
Tel: 226-2616. Fax: 225-4809

**Ministry of Local Government**
Fort Street Kingston
Tel: 226-5071-3. Fax: 226-5070

**Ministry of Public Works and Communication**
Wights Lane, Kingston
Tel: 225-5540 / 226-2505. Fax: 225-6954

**Ministry of Tourism, Industry & Commerce**
229 South Road, Lacytown, Georgetown
Tel: 226-2392 / 2505 / 8695. Fax: 225 9898

**Parliament Office**
Brickdam, Stabroek
Tel: 226-8456-9. Fax: 225-1357

**Public Service Ministry**
164 Waterloo Street, North Cummingsburg
Tel: 227-1193. Fax: 227-2700

## GUYANA CONSULATES OVERSEAS (HONORARY)

**ANTIGUA AND BARBUDA**
Honorary Consulate of Guyana
PO Box 1159, Coolidge, St John's
Tel: 268-462-4320. Fax: 268-461-4864

**BARBADOS**
Honorary Consulate of Guyana
#10 Belle Main Road, Belle District, St Michael
Tel: 264-426-0861. Fax: 264-426-0861

**BELIZE**
Honorary Consulate of Guyana
3 Barrack Road, Belize City
Tel: 501-232-469. Fax: 501-235-164

**BOTSWANA**
Honorary Consulate of Guyana
P.O Box 1478 Gaborne
Tel: 267-312-655. Fax: 267-374-039

**BRAZIL**
Honorary Consulate of Guyana
Av. Benjamin Constant, No 1020 – E
Centro, Boa Vista, Roraima
Tel: 55-95-224-1333

**CYPRUS**
Consulate General of Guyana
Limasso Avenue No. 2, Office no39
2220 Laxia, Nicosia
Tel: 357-248-6800. Fax: 357-242-5375

**DOMINICAN REPUBLIC**
Honorary Consulate of Guyana
JF Kennedy Avenue, Bonanza Bldg., Santo Domingo
Tel: 809-567-3843. Fax: 809-567-6974

**GREECE**
Honorary Consulate of Guyana
206 Syngrou Avenue
Tel: 301-0958-5064. Fax: 301-0958-5149

**GRENADA**
Honorary Consulate of Guyana
Mt Parnassus, St George
Tel: 473-440-2031. Fax: 473-440-4129

**JAMAICA**
Consulate of Guyana
66 Slipe Road, Kingston 5
Tel: 876-968-5983
Fax: 876-929-4028

**JAPAN**
Honorary Consulate of Guyana
Iberia Building 6P, 6-5-3 Jingu-mae,
Shibuya-ku, Tokyo 150-0001
Tel: 813-3406-3363. Fax: 813-3406-5575

**JORDAN**
Honorary Consulate of Guyana
24 Sharif Abdul Hamid Sharaf St,
Shmeisani Amman, PO box 222-Amman 11118
Tel: 962-6-560-9500. Fax: 962-6-560-4664

**LEBANON**
Honorary Consulate of Guyana
Selim Bustros Str., 1st floor E1 Dar Bldg,
Achrafteh, Beirut
Tel: 961-1-202-220. Fax: 961-1-336-711

**PAKISTAN**
Honorary Consulate of Guyana
12 Ebrahim Building, West Wharf Road
PO Box 5486, Karachi-7400
Tel: 9221-231-2255. Fax: 9221-213-0205

**SOUTH AFRICA**
Honorary Consulate of Guyana
PO Box 1877, Randburg 2125
Tel: 27-11-789-9760. Fax: 27-11-789-9763

**ST LUCIA**
Honorary Consulate of Guyana
PO Box 2003, Gros Islet
Tel: 758-453-0309. Fax: 758-451-7029

**TRINIDAD AND TOBAGO**
Honorary Consulate of Guyana
15 Grey Street, St Clair, Port of Spain, Trinidad
Tel: 868-622-1967
Fax: 868-622-1779

**UNITED STATES – California**
222 West Florence Avenue, Inglewood
California 90-301
Tel: 310-320-3370. Fax: 310-320-3370

**UNITED STATES – Florida**
Honorary Consulate of Guyana
3550 SW 124 Avenue, Miramar, Miami 33027
Tel: 954-432-7079
Fax: 305-693-9313

**UNITED STATES – Texas**
Honorary Consulate of Guyana
1810 Woodland Park Drive, Houston,
Texas 77077
Tel: 281-497-4466. Fax: 281-497-4476

**CONSULATES, EMBASSIES & HIGH
COMMISSIONS OVERSEAS**

**BRUSSELS (European Union)**
12 Avenue du Bresil, 1050
Tel: 322-675-6312. Fax: 322-672-5598

**BRAZIL**
Embassy of Guyana
SISH Q 105 Conjunto19, Cassa 24, Lago
sul, CEP 71615-190, Brasilia
Tel: 55-61-3-248-0874-5. Fax: 55-61-3-248-
0886

**CANADA**
Guyana Consulate
505 Consumers Road, Suite 206,
Willowdale, Ontario, M2J4V8
Tel: 416-494-6040

Guyana High Commission
151 Slater Street, Suite 305, Ottawa, KIP
5H3
Tel: 613-235-7240. Fax: 613-235-1447

**CUBA**
Guyana Embassy
Calle 18, No 506, Entre 5ta y 7ma,
Miramar, Havana
Tel: 537-204-2094. Fax: 537-204-2294

**CHINA**
Guyana Embassy
NO1 Xiu Shui Dong Jie, Jian Guo Men Wai
Beijing
Tel: 8610-6532-1601. Fax: 8610-6532-5741

**SURINAME**
Guyana Consulate
Doorga Shaw Straat #29, Nickerie
Tel: 597-021-0266. Fax: 597-023-1687

Guyana Embassy
Gravenstraat No. 82, P.O Box 785,
Paramaribo
Tel: 110-597-477-895. Fax: 597-472-679

**UNITED KINGDOM**
Guyana High Commission
3 Place Court, Bayswater Road, London
Tel: 44-207-221-6144. Fax: 44-207-727-
9809

**UNITED STATES – New York**
Guyana Consulate
370 7th Avenue, Room 402, New York
Tel: 212-947-5115. Fax: 212-947-5163

Guyana Permanent Mission
801 Second Avenue, Fifth Floor, New York
10017
Tel: 212-573-5828. Fax: 212-573-6225

**UNITED STATES – Washington**
Guyana Embassy
2490 Tracy Place, N.W. Washington, DC
20008
Tel: 212-265-3834. Fax: 212-232-1297

**VENEZUELA**
Guyana Embassy
Quinta Roraima, Avenida El Paseo,
Pradosdel Este, Caracas
Tel: 58-212-977-1158. Fax: 58-212-976-3765

**FOREIGN EMBASSIES, HIGH
COMMISSIONS & CONSULATES**

Bolivarian Republic of Venezuela
296 Thomas Street, South Cummingsburg
Georgetown
Tel: 226-6749 / 226-7543. Fax: 225-3241

British High Commission
44 Main Street, North Cummingsburg,
Georgetown
Tel: 226-5881-4. Fax: 225-3555

Canadian High Commission
Young and High Streets, Kingston,
Georgetown
Tel: 227-2081-5. Fax: 225-8380

Commission of European Communities
11 Sendel Place, Stabroek, Georgetown
Tel: 226-4004 / 5424. Fax: 226-2615

Consulate General of the Netherlands
53-55 Access Road, Georgetown
Tel: 225-9311-4. Fax: 227-1032

Embassy of the Federative Republic of Brazil
308 Church Street, Georgetown
Tel: 225-7970 / 7971. Fax: 226-9063

Embassy of the Peoples Republic of China
Tract "B" Durban Backlands, Georgetown
Tel: 227-1651 / 1951. Fax: 225-9228

Embassy of the United States of America
100 Young Street, Kingston
Tel: 225-4900 / 4909. Fax: 225-8497

Indian High Commission
307 Church & Peter Rose Streets,
Queenstown, Georgetown
Tel: 226-3996 / 8965. Fax: 225-7012

Republic of Cuba
46 High Street, Kingston
Tel: 225-1881-3. Fax: 226-1824

Republic of Suriname
171 Peter Rose Street, Queenstown
Tel: 226-7844 / 225-2631. Fax: 225-0759
Email: surnmeb@gol.net.gy

The Russian Federation
3 Public Road, Kitty
Tel: 226-9773 / 225-2179. Fax: 227-2975

**GENERAL**

CARICOM
P.O. Box 10827, Georgetown
Tel: 226-9281. Fax: 226-7816
Email: webmaster@caricom.org

Consultative Association of Guyanese
Industry
157 Waterloo Street, Georgetown
Tel: 226-4603
Email: caig@guyana.net.gy

Guyana Manufacturers' Association
Exhibition Site, Sophia, Georgetown
Tel: 223-4295
Web: www.gma.org.gy

**Guyana Office for Investment
(GO-INVEST)**
190 Camp & Church Street, Georgetown
Tel: 225-0658
     227-0653
Fax: 225-0655
Email: goinvest@goinvest.gov.gy
Web: www.sdnp.org.gy/goinvest

**Guyana Small Business Association**
Salod Building, 156 Charlotte Street,
Lacytown, Georgetown
Tel: 225-1192
     227-0685
     227-0677
Fax: 227-0759
Email: zephent2000@yahoo.com

**Guyana Tourism Authority**
National Exhibition Centre, Sophia,
Georgetown
Tel: 223-6351
Fax: 231-6672
Web: www.guyana-tourism.com

Private Sector Commission
157 Waterloo Street, Georgetown
Tel: 225-0977. Fax: 225-0978
Email: pscentre@guyana.netgy

Tourism & Hospitality Association of
Guyana
157 Waterloo Street, Georgetown
Tel: 225-0807
Fax: 225-0817
Email: thag@networksgy.com

## DIALLING CODES

**International dialling code:**
**592**

**Dialling from the Caribbean and North America: 011-592**

**Dialling from the United Kingdom: 00-592**

## EMERGENCY NUMBERS

POLICE        911
FIRE          912
AMBULANCE  913

## AIRLINES

**Caribbean Airways**
63 Robb Street, Georgetown
Tel: 226-5272
Fax: 227-3052
Email: cdefour@bwee.com

Caribbean Star Airlines
5 Robb Street
Georgetown
Tel: 226-8676 / 227-6770
Web: www.flycaribbeanstar.com

LIAT
63 Robb Street
Georgetown
Tel: 227-8281
Fax: 226-5048
Email:
Li_geo@solutions2000.net

North American Airlines
126 Carmichael Street
South Cummingsburg
Georgetown
Tel: 227-5805 / 227-5838
Fax: 227-4164
Email:
Guyana@northamericanair.com

**Roraima Airways Inc**
R8 Eping Avenue
Bel Air Park
Georgetown
Tel: 225-9648
Fax: 225-9646
Email: ral@roraimaairways.com

Trans Guyana Airways Ltd
Ogle Aerodrome
East Coast Demerara
Tel: 222-2525
Fax: 222-5462
Email: tga@transguyana.com

## AIRPORTS

Cheddi Jagan International
Airport
Timheri
Tel: 261-2300
Flight Information
Tel: 261-2245

Ogle Municipal Airport
Ogle Aerodrome
East Coast Demerara
Tel: 222-2525

## AIR SERVICES & CHARTERS

Air Services Ltd
Tel: 222-4357 / 4368

CariAir
Tel: 227-1053

**Caribbean Airways**
Tel: 226-5272

Caribbean Star Airlines
Tel: 227-6770 / 226-8676

LIAT
Tel: 227-5805 / 5838

North American Airlines
Tel: 227-5805

**Roraima Airways**
Tel: 225-9647 / 8

Suriname Airways
Tel: 225-3473

Trans Guyana Airways
Tel: 222-2525

Universal Airlines
Tel: 226-9262

Wings
Tel: 222-6513 / 226-9098

## APARTMENTS (see Hotels, Resorts, Apartments)

## AUTOMOTIVE (SALES & PARTS)

**K Rahaman & Sons (Spare Parts)**
51 Russell & Evans Streets
Charlestown, Georgetown
Tel: 226-1778
Fax: 225-2289
Email:
raheemarahaman@yahoo.com

**R.R.T. Enterprises**
W ½ 107 Regent Road
Bourda, Georgetown
Tel: 225-2237 / 231-7287
Fax: 225-1290
Email: rrt@networksgy.com

**Trans Pacific Motor Spares & Auto Sales**
Lot 5 Good Hope
East Coast Demerara
Tel: 220-9293 / 9284 / 0985 / 0986
Fax: 220-9796
Email:
transpms@guyana.net.gy
Email:
geetaramsewack_25@hotmail.com

**Trans Pacific Motor Spares & Auto Sales**
45 Robb & Light Streets
Georgetown
Tel: 225-7448 / 226-2103

## BANKS

Bank of Baroda
10 Avenue of the Republic
Georgetown
Tel: 226-4005. Fax: 225-1691

Bank of Nova Scotia
104 Carmichael Street
Georgetown
Tel: 225-9222
Fax: 225-9309

Citizens Bank
201 Camp Street, Georgetown
Tel: 226-1705. Fax: 226-1719

Demerara Bank
230 Camp & South Street
Georgetown
Tel: 225-0610 / 9
Fax: 225-0601

**Global Bank of Commerce Ltd**
Global Financial Centre
PO Box W1803
Friars Hill Road
St John's, Antigua
Tel: (268) 480-2329
Fax: (268) 462-1831
Email:
customer.service@gbc.ag

Guyana Bank for Trade & Industry
47 Water Street, Georgetown
Tel: 226-8430-9
Fax: 227-1612

National Bank of Industry & Commerce Ltd
38-40 Water Street
Georgetown
Tel: 226-4091. Fax: 2267-2921

## BOOKSHOPS

**Austin's Book Services**
190 Church Street
North Cummingsburg
Georgetown
Tel: 227-7395
Fax: 227-7396
Email:
lloydaustins@guyana.net.gy

Bread of Life Book Store
C&F Mall, 9-10, Bagotstown
East Bank Demerara
Tel: 233-5496

Literacy Book Store
307 East Street, North
Cummingsburg, Georgetown
Tel: 223-6401. Fax: 225-9019

New Era Bookshop
162-163 Lamaha Street, N /
Cummingsburg, Georgetown
Tel: 226-2355

The Bookseller
78 Church Street, Georgetown
Tel: 227-1244

## BUSINESS / COMMERCE

**Abdool Hakh & Sons**
Rice Milling & Marketing
Complex
Harlem
West Coast Demerara
Tel: 269-0027
Fax: 269-0028
Email:
a.hakh&sons@solutions2000.net

**Ansa McAL Trading Ltd**
60 Betervertwagting
East Coast Demerara
Tel: 220-0455 / 0505 / 0268
Fax: 220-0796
Email: paul.chan-a-
sue@ansamcal.com

**Ansa McAL Trading Ltd**
Farm East Bank
Demerara
Tel: 265-2265

**Ansa McAL Trading Ltd**
New Amsterdam
Tel: 333-5891
Fax: 333-4061

**Banks DIH Ltd**
Thirst Park
Georgetown
Tel: 226-2491-8
Fax: 226-6523

**Buddy's Investments**
Corporate Office
Brickdam, Stabroek
Georgetown
Tel: 226-8162
Tel: 225-3983
Email:
buddyshotel@guyana.net.gy

Consultative Association of
Guyanese Industry
157 Waterloo Street
Georgetown
Tel: 226-4603
Email: caig@guyana.net.gy

**Correia Group of Companies**
159 Charlotte Street
Lacytown, Georgetown
Tel: 226-0605
Fax: 225-1171
Email: info@correiamining.com

**DIDCO (Friendship Hotel & Restaurant Holdings Ltd)**
Lot 1, Public Road, Ruimveldt
Georgetown
Tel: 226-8863 / 225-2475 / 225-1994
Fax: 225-2316
Email: didcokfc@guyana.net.gy

**Edward B. Beharry & Company Ltd**
191 Charlotte Street
Lacytown
Georgetown
PO Box 10485
Tel: 227-1349 / 2526 / 0632 / 5
Fax: 225-6062
Email:
ebbsec@beharrygroup.com

**Etegra Inc – Peter Ramsaroop (Roop Group)**
34 King & North Road
Lacytown
Georgetown
Tel: / Fax: 227-1053
Email: media@roopgroup.com

**Farfan & Mendes Ltd**
45, Urquart Street
Georgetown
Tel: 226-8130 / 6401
Fax: 225-8651
Email: fml@networksgy.com

**Farfan & Mendes Ltd**
35 High Street
Georgetown
Tel: 225-7373

Forest Producers Association
of Guyana
157 Waterloo Street
Georgetown
Tel: 226-9848

**Gafsons Group of Companies**
Plantation Houston
East Bank Demerara
Tel: 227-5886 / 7
Email: nil@guyana.net

Guyana Bar Association
39 Brickdam
Stabroek
Georgetown
Tel: 226-0478

Guyana Diamond Trading
Company
35 New Market Street
South Cummingsburg
Georgetown
Tel: 227-5575

**Guyana Lottery Company**
357 Lamaha Street
North Cummingsburg
Georgetown
Tel: 226-0753
Fax: 225-9633
Email: tlewis@cbnco.com

Guyana Manufacturers'
Association
Exhibition Site, Sophia
Georgetown
Tel: 223-4295
Web: www.gma.org.gy

**Guyana Marketing Corporation**
87 Robb & Alexander Streets
Lacytown
Georgetown
Tel: 226-8255
227-5809
225-7808
Fax: 227-4114
Email:
newgmc@guyworksgy.com

**Guyana Office for Investment (GO-INVEST)**
190 Camp & Church Street
Georgetown
Tel: 225-0658 / 227-0653 / 225-0653
Fax: 225-0655
Email:
goinvest@goinvest.gov.gy
Web: www.sdnp.org.gy/goinvest

**Guyana Oil Company**
166 Waterloo Street
North Cummingsburg
Georgetown
Tel: 225-1595-8 / 7161
Fax: 225-2320
Email: BadrieP@guyoil.com
Email: guyoil@gol.net.gy

Guyana Rainforest Herbs
335 Cummings Street
Cummingsburg, Georgetown
Tel: 223-8013. Fax: 223-6355

Guyana Rice Millers' & Exporters
Development Association
216 Lamaha Street
Georgetown
Tel: 592-5353

Guyana Rice Producers
Association
126 Parade Street, Kingston
Tel: 226-4411

**Guyana Small Business Association**
Salod Building
156 Charlotte Street
Lacytown
Georgetown
Tel: 225-1192 / 227-0685
Fax: 227-0759
Email:
zephent2000@yahoo.com

**Guyana Stores Ltd**
Lot 19 Water Street
Georgetown
Tel: 226-6171
Fax: 226-3685
Email:
tonyyassin@telsnetgy.net

**Guyana Sugar Corporation Inc.**
Ogle Estate
East Coast Demerara
Tel: 222-6044 / 220-6030
Email: info@guysuco.com
Email:
marketing@guysuco.com
Web: www.guysuco.com

Guyenterprise
234 Almond & Irving Streets
Queenstown, Georgetown
Tel: 227-1770 / 226-9874
Email: netshop@guyana.net.gy

Institute of Private Enterprise
Development
253 South Road, Bourda
Georgetown
Tel: 225-8949
Email: iped@solutions2000.net

**John Fernandes Group of Companies**
24 Water Street, Georgetown
Tel: 225-3501 / 2
Fax: 226-1881
Email: enquiries@jf-ltd.com

**Karanambu Cattle Co Ltd**
A102 Issano Place, East Bell
Air Park, Georgetown

**National Milling Company of
Guyana Inc.**
Agricola
East Bank Demerara
Tel: 233-2462
Fax: 233-2464
Email:
bert_sukhai@namilcoflour.com

**Neal & Massey Guyana Ltd
(Geddes Grant Guyana Ltd)**
5 Ruimveldt
Georgetown
Tel: 226-7291-5
      227-2031-8
Fax: 226-0310
      225-7676
Email:
ainlim@solutions2000.net
Email:
geddesgrant@solutions2000.net

**New GPC Inc.**
A1 Farm, East Bank Demerara
Tel: 265-4261
Fax: 265-2229
Email: limacol@newgpc.com or
marketing@newgpc.com

**Pharmagen Enterprises**
Lot 1F Area L
Bel Air, Georgetown
Tel: 226-0776 / 227-4833
Fax: 225-6961
Email:
pharmagen@networksgy.com

Parika Marketing Centre
Parika, Essequibo
Tel: 260-4471

**Pritipaul Singh Investment, Inc.**
McDoom Village
East Bank Demerara
Tel: 226-9934 / 223-7638-9
Fax: 226-7753 / 0006
Email: priti@networksgy.com

**Roop Media Productions**
**Architect of Communication**
34 King Street & North Road
Lacytown, Georgetown
Tel: / Fax: 227-1053
Email: media@roopgroup.com

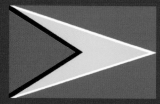

Twins Manufacturing Chemist
P.O. Box 10108, 30 Industrial
Estate, Ruimveldt, Georgetown
Tel: 225-6321. Fax: 227-7651
Email:
twinchem@guyana.net.gy

**Two2 Brothers Corp**
17 Vergenorgen
East Bank Essequibo
Tel: 260-2282
      260-2014
      260-4014
      260-4023
Fax 260-2037
Email:
info@two2brotherscorp.com
Email: tbatc@hotmail.com

**CHAMBERS OF
COMMERCE**

Berbice Chamber of Commerce
12 Chapel Street
New Amsterdam
Tel: 333-3324

Essequibo Chamber of
Commerce
6 Anna Regina
Tel: 771-5032

Georgetown Chamber of
Commerce & Industry
156 Waterloo Street
North Cummingsburg
Tel: 225-5846
Fax: 226-3519

Linden Chamber of Industry &
Commerce
97-98 Republic Avenue
Linden
Tel: 444-2901

Rupununi Chamber of
Commerce
Phase 2, Lethem
Tel: 772-2213

**DEPARTMENT STORES /
SHOPPING**

**M Beepat & Sons**
100-101 Regent Street
Lacytown
Georgetown
Tel: 226-1292
      226-7380
      227-0637
      225-7630
      223-6192
Fax: 226-1930
Email:
mbeepat@networksgy.com

**W M Fogarty's Ltd**
34-37 Water Street
Georgetown
Tel: 225-6870
      225-5678 / 6877
Fax: 227-6381
Email:
fogartystore@inetguyana.net

**The Lingerie Shop**
101, Cummings Street
Georgetown
Tel: 231-3837
Fax: 227-6798
Email: saytls@networksgy.com

**FURNITURE
MANUFACTURERS**

Ayube Hamid & Daughters
Furniture
35 East Canefield Settlement
East Canje
Tel: 327-7367. Fax: 326-0480

Furniture Designs International
23 Blossom Scheme
Enmore, East Coast Demerara
Tel: 256-3538 / 622-4760
Email:
furniture_design@hotmail.com

Melsha & Lyndill Furniture
15 Public Road, Mon Repos
South, East Coast Demerara
Tel: 220-9429

Modern Furniture
24 Hill & James Street
Albertown, Georgetown
Tel: 225-6810

**Precision Woodworking**
35 Industrial Estate, Ruimveldt,
PO Box 10 1546
Georgetown
Tel: 225-2366
Fax: 225-6448
Email:
precision@networksgy.com

Shiva Woodworking
Establishment Ltd
5a Public Road
Enmore
East Coast Demerara
Tel: 256-3709
Fax: 270-6573

Summersons Furniture
66 Sixth Street, Albertown
Georgetown
Tel: 226-0874
      231-7288

**HOSPITALS / MEDICAL**

**Guyana Association of
Alternative Medicine
Bakja Health Movement**
32-33 Dr Miller Street
Triumph
East Coast Demerara
Tel: 220-2130 / 2254
Fax: 220-5821
Email:
bakja_h_m@hotmail.com

Davis Memorial Hospital
121 Durban Street, Durban
Backlands, Georgetown
Tel: 227-2041-3
Fax: 225-2041
davismemorial@yahoo.com

Dr Balwant Singh's Hospital Inc.
314 East Street
South Cummingsburg,
Georgetown
Tel: 226-5783 / 4279
Fax: 227-1616

Georgetown Medical Centre Inc.
Prasad's Hospital
258-259 Thomas & Middle
Streets
Tel: 226-7210-9
Fax: 227-2215
gmcinc@networksgy.com

Bandstand in the botanical gardens in Georgetown  Photo: I Brierley

**Georgetown Public Hospital Corporation**
New Market Street,
Georgetown
Tel: 226-1839
Fax: 226-6249

Medical Arts Centre
265 Thomas Street, North
Cummingsburg, Georgetown
Tel: 225-7402. Fax: 226-5220

St Joseph Mercy Hospital
130-132 Parade Street
Kingston, Georgetown
Tel: 227-2072-9 / 225-3185
Fax: 225-0260
Email: sjmh@solutions2000.net

**HOTELS, RESORTS, APARTMENTS**

Annie Sezz' Efficiency Suites
23 Lamaha Street
Queenstown
Georgetown
Tel: 227-4454
Email:
bernapes2000@yahoo.com

Arabian Atlantic Hotel
44 Henrietta Village, Essequibo
Coast
Tel: 771-4365 / 4748
Email: Arlantel2002@yahoo.com

Arlington Apartments
93 Smyth & Hadfield Streets
Georgetown
Tel: 225-8981 / 227-0830
Fax: 225-1059

**Arrowpoint Nature Resort**
R8 Epping Avenue, Bel Air
Park, Georgetown
Tel: 225-9647. Fax: 225-9646
Email: ral@roraimaairways.com

Atlantic Inn
56 First Ave & Church Road
Subryanville, Georgetown
Tel: 225-5826 / 5827 / 5815

**Atta Rainforest Lodge**
Wilderness Explorers
176 Middle Street, Georgetown
Tel: 227-7698 / 2011
Fax: 226-2085
Email:
info@iwokramacanopywalkway.com

**Baganara Island Resort**
C/o Evergreen Adventure
158 Charlotte Street
Lacytown
Georgetown
Tel: 226-0605
Fax: 225-1171
Email:
evergreenadventures@webworksgy.com

Blue Wave Apartments
8 North Road, Bourda
Georgetown
Tel: 227-8897 / 226-1417-8
Fax: 226-2742
Email:
bluewave@networksgy.com

Brandsville Apartments
89 Pike Street, Campbellville
Tel: 226-1133 / 223-6323
Fax: 231-7001
Email: brandsville@gol.net.gy

**Buddy's International Hotel Inc.**
Public Road, Providence, EBD
23 Brickdam, Stabroek,
Georgetown
Tel: 265-7001 / 7002
Fax: 265-7002

Cara Lodge
294 Quamina Street
Georgetown
Tel: 225-5301-5
Fax: 225-5310
Email:
caralodge@carahotels.com

Cara Suites
176 Middle & Waterloo Streets
Georgetown
Tel: 226-1612 / 1684
Fax: 226-1541
Email:
carasuites@carahotels.com

Church View Hotel
3 Main & King Streets, New
Amsterdam, Berbice
Tel: 333-2880. Fax: 333-4151
Email:
churchviewhotel@networksgy.com

Club 28 Motel & Lounge
Malgre Tout, West Bank
Demerara
Tel: 264-2945
Fax 264-2948
Email:
club28motel@hotmail.com

Crimson Bat Hotel & Discothèque
632 Industrial Area, Makenzie
Demerara River
Tel: 444-6221

Dadanawa Ranch (South
Rupununi via Lethem)
C/o Wilderness Explorers
176 Middle & Waterloo Streets
Tel: 227-7698
Fax: 226-2085
Email: teri@wilderness-
explorers.com

Double 'B' Exotic Gardens
58 Eastern Highway
Tel: 225-2023

Delux Guest House
5-19 Coburg Street, New
Amsterdam, Berbice
Tel: 333-3004
Fax: 333-6626
Email:
cdenobrega@hotmail.com

Demico Hotel
Brickdam
Stabroek
Georgetown
Tel: 225-7400

'D' Factor 2 Interior Guest House
Lot 2 Triangle Street, Bartica
Essequibo
Tel: 455-2544 / 0061
Email:
silkyshomia@hotmail.com

Double Day Hotel
Lot 30 Block 20 Tuschen
East Bank Essequibo
Tel: 260-2209

Ease Chalet
118 Aubrey Barker Road
South Ruimveldt Park
Georgetown
Tel: 218-4954 / 4955 / 2014
Email:
easeauto@networksgy.com

El Dorado Inn
295 Quamina & Thomas Streets
Georgetown
Tel: 225-3966 / 3967
Fax: 225-3943
Email: francia@eldorado-
inn.com

El Tropico Sea-View Hotel
22 Richmond Village
Essequibo Coast
Tel: 771-5291. Fax: 771-5291
Email:
Granville@networksgy.com

Emba Sea Breeze Hotel
8 Pere Street, Kitty
Georgetown
Tel: 225-0542. Fax: 225-0622
Email:
seabreeze_hotel@hotmail.com

**Emerald Tower**
74-75 Main Street, Georgetown
Tel: 227-2011
Fax: 225-6021
Email:
hotel.tower@solutions2000.net

Florentene's Hotel, Restaurant
& Bar
3 North Road, Bourda
Georgetown
Tel: 226-2283

Glow International Hotel Co. Ltd.
23 Queen Street, Kitty
Georgetown
Tel: 227-0863. Fax: 226-8705

**Grand Coastal Lodge**
144 W1/2 Regent Street
Bourda
Georgetown
Tel: 231-7674
Fax: 231-7074
Email:
grandcoastal_lodge@yahoo.com

**Grand Coastal Suites**
2 Area M Plantation
Le Ressouvenir
East Coast Demerara
Tel: 220-1091
Fax: 220-1498
Email:
reservations@grandcoastal.com
Email: ceo@grandcostal.com

Herdmanston Lodge
65 Peter Rose & Anira Streets
Queenstown, Georgetown
Tel: 225-0808
Email:
stay@herdmanstonlodge.com

**Hotel Ariantze and Sidewalk
Café & Jazz Club**
176 Middle Street, Georgetown
Tel: 226-9555 / 623-8924
Fax: 227-0210
Email:
ariantze@networksgy.com
Web:
www.ariantzesidewalk.com

Hotel Purple Heart
Charity, Essequibo
Tel: 771-5209. Fax: 225-2535

Hotel Sunset View
Lot 1 David & Stanley Place
Tel: 612-0250 / 223-6416

**Hotel Tower Ltd**
74-75 Main Street, Georgetown
Tel: 227-2011-14
Fax: 225-6021 or 223-6019
Email:
hotel.tower@solutions2000.net

**Iwokrama International Centre**
High Street, Kingston
Georgetown
Tel: 225-1504
Fax: 225-9199
Email:
iwokrama@wokrama.org

Jubilee Resort
86 First Street, Albertown,
Georgetown
Tel: 223-7847. Fax: 223-0739

Kanuku Suites
123 Section M, Campbellville
Georgetown
Tel: 226-4001

**Karanambu Ranch**
(Rupununi via Lethem)
A 102 Issano Place
East Bel Air Park, Georgetown
Tel: 226-5180
Fax: 226-2085
Email:
mcturk@networksgy.com

La Belle Apartments,
Restaurant & Bar
64 Norton Street
Lodge, Georgetown
Tel: 225-3128-9. Fax: 231-4247
Email: labelleapt@yahoo.com

Lake Mainstay Resort
216-217 Lamaha Street, North
Cummingsburg, Georgetown
Tel: 226-2755
Fax: 226-2755
Email: lm_resort@mail.com

Le Chalet Country Club
Plantation Estate
Linden / Soesdyke
Demerara
Tel: 261-5237 / 261-5238
Fax: 261-5237
Email: lechaletcc@yahoo.com

**Le Meridien Pegasus**
Seawall Road
Kingston
Georgetown
Tel: 225-2853 / 2859
Fax: 225-3703
Email:
reservations@lemeridien-
pegasus.com

Little Rock Hotel
67 Vrymans Erven, New
Amsterdam, Berbice
Tel: 333-4445 / 333-4758
Email: irtvs@guyana.net.gy

Lords Hotel
25 Maria's Lodge
Essequibo Coast
Section A Anna Regina
Tel: 774-4280 / 771-4280
Fax: 774-4480
Email:
jupiter2171@hotmail.com

Mahogany on the River
50 Corriverton, Corentyne,
Berbice
Tel: 335-3037. Fax: 335-3525

Malimar Hotel & Restaurant
13 Public Road, 78 Corriverton
Berbice
Tel: 335-3409. Fax: 335-3328
Email:
hotelmalinmar@yahoo.com

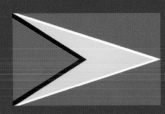

Melbourne Inn
29 Sheriff Street, Campbellville
Georgetown
Tel: 226-7050 / 223-9708
Email:
Melbourne@caribsurf.com

Morocco Hotel & Restaurant
14 First Avenue, Baritca
Tel: 445-2946

M's Ville Apartments
230 Anaida Avenue
Eccles
East Bank Demerara
Tel: 233-2409-11
Fax: 233-2724
Email:
mvilleapartment@yahoo.com

National Parks Commission
Thomas Lands
Georgetown
Tel: 225-8016
Fax: 223-5379
Email:
natpark@networksgy.com

The New Modern Hotel &
Nightclub
Lot 9, First Avenue
Bartica
Tel: 455-2301 / 0052
Fax: 455-2301

New Safari Inn Hotel
13 Friendship
East Bank Demerara
Tel: 266-2323

Ocean View International Hotel
Lilliedaal
East Coast Demerara
Tel: 225-5429
Fax: 222-4722
Email:
ovihotel@networksgy.com

Paraton Inn
Number 78 Village, Corriverton
Berbice
Tel: 333-2292

Parkway Hotel
4 Main Street, New Amsterdam
Berbice
Tel: 333-3928
Fax: 333-2028

Platinum Inn International
Lot 7 First Avenue, Bartica
Tel: 445-3041 / 3042

Prairie International Hotel
11 South Half Coverden
East Bank Demerara
Tel: 261-5007 / 5032-35
Fax: 261-5359
Email:
Prairie.hotel@networksgy.com

Raddison Suites
83 Laluni Street
Queenstown, Georgetown
Tel: 226-2145
Fax: 226-2145
Email:
raddison2000@yahoo.com

Rainbow River Safari Guyana
Ltd
Lot 6 Best Road
Best Village, West Coast
Demerara
Tel: 644-7646
Email: tedsabat@yahoo.com

Regency Suites
98 Hadfield Street
Georgetown
Tel: 225-4785 / 226-0621
Fax: 226-0531
Email:
regencyhotel3@yahoo.com

Rits Hotel
171 Springlands
Corriverton
Berbice
Tel: 335-4051
Fax: 335-3605

**Rock View Lodge**
Annai, North Rupununi
Tel: 226-0605
Fax: 225-1171
Email:
evergreen.adventures@webworksgy.com

**Roraima Residence Inn**
R8 Eping Avenue
Bel Air Park
Georgetown
Tel: 225-9647-8
Fax: 225-9646
Email:
ral@roraimaairways.com

Savannah Inn
Lethem
Tel: 772-2035 / 623-3270
Fax: 772-2035

Shanklands Rainforest Resort
232 Middle & Camp Street
Georgetown
Tel: 226-8907
Fax: 226-9738
Email: forest@networksgy.com

Sleeping Guest House
151 Church Street
Albertown
Georgetown
Tel: 223-0991

**Splashmins Fun Park &
Resort**
48 High Street, Werk-en-Rust
Georgetown
Tel: 225-8066 / 223-7301 / 624-
9266
Fax: 225-6052
Email:
deslyn.jack@splashmins.com
Email: infl@splashmins.com

Star Bonnet Hotel
671 Industrial Area, Linden
Demerara
Tel: 444-6505

Surama Village
Surama, North Rupununi
Tel: 226-2085
Fax: 226-2085
Email: teri@wilderness-
explorers.com

Timberhead Resort
Tropical Adventures Guyana Inc
8-10 Providence
East Bank Demerara
Tel: 233-5179 / 5108
Fax: 225-0549
Email:
timberhead@solutions2000.net

**Toucan Guest House &
Heritage Museum**
17 Kastev
Metenmeerzorg
West Coast Demerara
Tel: 275-0028
Email: toucan-
s@networksgy.com

Waterchris Hotel & Bar
184 Waterloo Street
South Cummingsburg
Georgetown
Tel: 226-5257 / 227-1980
Fax: 227-3266
Email: waterchris@mail.com

Windjammer International
Cuisine & Comfort Inn
27 Queen Street, Kitty
Tel: 227-7478
Fax: 223-6583
Email:
info@windjammergy.com

Zen's Plaza Hotel, Restaurant
& Bar
43 Second Avenue
Bartica
Essequibo
Tel: 455-2441
Fax: 455-2956
Email: zensplaza@yahoo.com

**JEWELLERS**

Aria Jewellers
64B Middle Street, Georgetown
Tel: 223-6100
Fax: 223-6101

Bharat's Jewellery Store
33 Robb & Orange Walk
Bourda, Georgetown
Tel: / Fax: 225-9245
Email:
bharatjewellery@yahoo.com

Bravo's Jewellery
Stall 55 W1/2 Section 1
Stabroek Market
Georgetown
Tel: 226-6139

City Jewellers & Pawn Brokers
Ltd
16 Robb & Hinck Streets
Georgetown
Tel: 226-1936

**Correia's Jewellery Inc**
5 Robb Street
R/Town, Georgetown
Tel: 226-1556
Fax: 225-9499
Email: corrjew@guyana.net.gy

D & T Nandalall Jewellery
Stall A5, Section 1, Stabroek
Market, Georgetown
Tel: 227-3167

De Abreau's Creations
E 1/4 224 New Market Street
North Cummingsburg
Georgetown
Tel: 225-2589

Doodnauth's Jewellery
173 Pike Street
Kitty, Georgetown
Tel: 226-7260
Email: haresh@guyana.net.gy

Elegance Jewellery
Lot 1 Durban Street, Werk-en-
Rust, Georgetown
Tel: 223-6331

Gaskin & Jackson Jewellers
226 'B' Camp Street
North Cummingsburg
Georgetown
Tel: 225-7201
Fax: 227-5022
Email:
dean@solutions2000.net

Gem's Jewellers
7B La Union
West Coast Demerara
Tel: 254-0366

Hillaire's Jewellery
Stabroek, Georgetown
Tel: 225-0244

Humphrey & Company
5 Avenue of the Republic
Georgetown
Tel: 226-1906

**King's Jewellery World**
176 Middle Street, Georgetown
Tel: 225-8575
Email: kjw@solutions2000.net

**King's Jewellery World**
141 Quamina Street,
Georgetown
Tel: 225-8570 / 226-0704 / 226-
0984
Fax: 225-2524
Email:
admin@kingsjewelleryworld.com

Kumar Alli Jewellery Est
Lot 4 First Street
Alexander Village, Georgetown
Tel: 225-5949

**L Seepersaud Maraj & Sons**
Stabroek Market (under the
clock)
Georgetown
Tel: 226-3469
Fax: 226-1141
Email:
ramaraj@ewireless.gy.com

Mohamed's Enterprise
29 Lombard Street
Werk-en-Rust, Georgetown
Tel: 227-7952
Fax: 225-9019

N.H. King Jewellery
190 Church Street, South
Cummingsburg, Georgetown
Tel: 226-3048

R. Sookraj Jewellers
76 Robb Street
Lacytown, Georgetown
Tel: 223-6156
Email:
sookraj2000@yahoo.com

Rakesh R & R Jewellery
333 East Street
South Cummingsburg,
Georgetown
Tel: 226-5750

Raymond's Jewellery
297 Independence Blvd
La Penintence
Tel: 225-8462

Rennie's Exotic Jewellery
19-22 Stabroek Market,
Georgetown
Tel: 227-4912

Robert's Jewellery
72 Brummel Place
Stabroek, Georgetown
Tel: 231-7602

Royal Jewel House
137 Regent Street
Lacytown, Georgetown
Tel: 226-2708
Fax: 225-2764

Sanjay's Jewellery Store
17-18 America Street,
Georgetown
Tel: 225-4537

Seeram's Jewellery
133 Church Street, Georgetown
Tel: 227-8122

Sheriff's Jewellery
17 Brickdam, Georgetown
Tel: 223-7600

Steve's Jewellery
301 Church Street
South Cummingsburg,
Georgetown
Tel: 223-9641
Fax: 223-9642

Sunflower Jeweller
92 West Ruimveldt Estate H/
Scheme
Tel: 223-4982

Tony's Jewellery
22 First Street, Alexander
Village
East Bank Demerara
Tel: 225-8432

**Topaz**
143 Crown & Oronoque Streets
Queenstown
Georgetown
Tel: 227-3968
Email: topaz@networksgy.com

## LEGAL

**Mohabir A Nandlall &
Associates**
'Bhagwati Chambers'
217 South Road
Lacytown
Tel: 227-2712 / 223-7487
Fax: 223-7486
Email:
anil_nandlall@hotmail.com

## MUSEUMS

**Guyana Heritage Museum**
17 Kastev, M/Zorg
West Coast Demerara
Tel: 275-0331

## NEWSPAPERS

Berbice News Weekly
16 New Street, New Amsterdam
Tel: 333-2687

Catholic Standard
222 South Road
Lacytown, Georgetown
Tel: 226-1540

Guyana Chronicle
Lama Avenue
Bel Air Park, Georgetown
Tel: 226-3243-9
Email: khan@guyana.net.gy

Kaieteur News
Saffon Street, Charlestown
Georgetown
Tel: 225-8458. Fax: 225-8473
Email:
kaieteurnews@yahoo.com

The Mirror
8 Industrial Estate
Ruimveldt, Georgetown
Tel: 226-2471 / 2089
Email:
ngmirror@guyana.net.gy

New Nation
Congress Place
Sophia, Georgetown
Tel: 225-7852
Email:
pnc_reform@hotmail.com

Stabroek News
46 Robb Street
Lacytown, Georgetown
Tel: 226-8981 / 225-1530
Fax: 225-4637
Email:
stabroeknews@stabroeknews.com

**RESORTS (see Hotels,
Resorts, Apartments)**

## RESTAURANTS &
TAKEAWAY

Audrey's Tasty Snackette
176 Charlotte Street, Lacytown
Georgetown
Tel: 226-4512

Barrows Restaurant and Lounge
82 Manni Street, Linden
Tel: 444-6790-99

Belvedere Inn No. 1
Belvedere Settlement,
Corentyne, Berbice
Tel: 322-3406

Belvedere Inn No. 2
72C Independence Avenue
Rose Hall Town
Corentyne, Berbice
Tel: 337-4025

Bottle Bar and Restaurant
294 Quamina Street
Georgetown
Tel: 225-5301
Fax: 225-5301
Email:
Caralodge@carahotels.com

**Browns Café**
Le Meridian Pegasus
Seawall Road
Kingston, Georgetown
Tel: 225-2853 / 9
Fax: 225-3703

**Buddy's Mei Tung Restaurant**
137 Sheriff Street
Georgetown
Tel: 231-4100

Caribbean Rose Restaurant
25 Middle Street, Georgetown
Tel: 225-1687 / 226-8462
Fax: 227-3762

**Cazabon at Hotel Tower**
74-75 Main Street
Georgetown
Tel: 227-2011-4
Fax: 225-6021

**El Dorado Restaurant at Le
Meridian Pegasus**
Seawall Road
Kingston, Georgetown
Tel: 225-2853-9
Fax: 225-2316

**Demico Qik Serve**
Camp Street & South Road
Georgetown
Tel: 225-4387

Dutch Bottle Café
10 North Road, Bourda
Georgetown
Tel: 231-6561
Email:
dutchbottlecafe@yahoo.com

Faheeda's Halaal Restaurant
147, No 78 Corriverton
Berbice
Tel: 335-3830

Foodtime
16 Main & New Streets, New
Amsterdam, Berbice
Tel: 333-6658

Francine's Absolute Taste Fish
Shop & Bar
47 Sheriff & Garnett Streets
Campbellville
Georgetown
Tel: 227-2753

Garden State Restaurant
170 Barr Street, Kitty
Georgetown
Tel: 227-8440

German's Restaurant
8 New Market & Mundy Streets
Georgetown
Tel: 227-0079

Glow International Hotel Co Ltd
23 Queen Street
Kitty, Georgetown
Tel: 227-0863

Golden Coast Restaurant
62 Main Street, Georgetown
Tel: 231-7360

Golden Eagle Restaurant
7-12 Main & Charlotte Streets
New Amsterdam, Berbice
Tel: 333-2033

Hack's Halaal Restaurant &
Take Away Service
5 Commercial Street,
Georgetown
Tel: 226-1844

Hilton Restaurant
1 Garnett & Middleton Streets
Georgetown
Tel: 226-5818

Howard's Restaurant
68 Old Road, Eccles
East Bank Demerara
Tel: 233-2386

**Idaho Health Bar**
Demico House
Brickdam
Tel: 225-7400

J R Burgers
3 Sandy Babb Street
Kitty, Georgetown
Tel: 226-6614

Kamboat Restaurant
51 Sherrif Street, Campbelville
Tel: 225-8090 / 8323

KFC Bagotstown
Bagotstown
East Bank Demerara
Tel: 233-6800

KFC Mandela Avenue
Mandela Avenue
Georgetown
Tel: 226-8400

KFC Stabroek
23 Water & Croal Streets
Stabroek, Georgetown
Tel: 227-3110

KFC / Pizza Hut
Vissengen Road
Georgetown
Tel: 225-3909

La Caribe Diner
1 Main Street, New Amsterdam
Berbice
Tel: 333-5540

**Le Meridien Pegasus**
Seawall Road
Kingston
Georgetown
Tel: 225-2853
Email: enquiries@lemeridien-
pegasus.com

Lucky House Chinese
Restaurant
17 Main Street & Lad lane
New Amsterdam
Berbice
Tel: 333-4287

**Main Street Café @ Hotel
Tower**
74-75 Main Street
Georgetown
Tel: 227-2011
Fax: 225-6021

Muffin's Fried Chicken & Fast
Food
133 Regent & Cummings
Streets, Bourda, Georgetown
Tel: 231-7402

New Thriving Restaurant
Camp Street and Brickdam
Georgetown
Tel: 226-5492 / 227-5104
Fax: 227-7662

Oasis Café
125 Carmichael Street
Georgetown
Tel: 226-9916

Pizza Hut Guyana
Barima Avenue & Vlissengen
Road
Georgetown
Tel: 226-6888
Email: didcokfc@guyana.netgy

Popeye's
1E Vlissengen Road & Duncan
Street
Georgetown
Tel: 223-6226

**Qik Serve**
Demico House
Brickdam
Georgetown
Tel: 225-7400
Fax: 226-7852

Ridley's Fast Food
106 Brickdam, Georgetown
Tel: 225-7245

Royal Castle
52 Sheriff and Garnett Street
Campbellville
Tel: 227-0108 / 227-0136
Email: royal@networksgy.com

Salt & Pepper Food Court
14-15A Croal & Longden Street
Georgetown
Tel: 223-6172

Salt & Pepper Restaurant &
Bakery
38 Robb Street, Georgetown
Tel: 226-2518

Secret End Diner
21 Main & Saint Magdelene
Streets, New Amsterdam,
Berbice
Tel: 333-4884

**Sidewalk Café & Jazz Club**
176 Middle Street
Georgetown
Tel: 227-0152
Fax: 227-0210

Sue Brothers Restaurant
Main & Saint Ann's Street
New Amsterdam, Berbice
Tel: 333-2408

The Garden City Café
45 High Street
Kingston, Georgetown
Tel: 223-7312
Email:
viviene122002@yahoo.com

The Guinness Bar, Restaurant
& Creole Food
67 Joseph Pollydore Street
Lodge
Georgetown
Tel: 223-5373
Email: barman@yahoo.com

The New Court Yard
35 Main Street
South Cummingsburg
Georgetown
Tel: 231-7362

The Original Dairy Bar
42 Croal and UN Place
Stabroek, Georgetown
Tel: 225-5995
Fax: 227-4456

Upper Level Restaurant & Bar
42 First Avenue, Bartica
Tel: 455-3115

Upscale Guyana Restaurant
32-33 Regent & Hinck Street
Georgetown
Tel: 225-4721
Email: joel.cole@wtgeorge.com

VIP Kids Zone
279 Sheriff & John Smiths
Streets, Campbellville
Georgetown
Tel: 227-6596

VIP Pizza Plus
164 Barr Street
Kitty
Georgetown
Tel: 227-0781

Waterchris Hotel & Bar
184 Waterloo Street
South Cummingsburg
Georgetown
Tel: 226-5257
Email: waterchris@mail.com

White Castle
236 Albert & Forshaw Streets
Queenstown
Georgetown
Tel: 223-0921

Windjammer International
Cuisine & Comfort Inn
27 Queen Street
Kitty
Georgetown
Tel: 226-3407
Email:
info@windjammergy.com

## SHIPPING & FREIGHT
## FORWARDING

**Laparkan (Freight
Forwarding Division)**
2-9 Lombard Street
Georgetown
Tel: 226-1095-7
Fax: 227-6808
Email:
infoguyana@laparkan.com

## SPORT & SPORTS CLUBS

Georgetown Cricket Club
Regent and New Garden Street
Georgetown
Tel: 226-3404 / 3130

Georgetown Football Club
North Road, Bourda
Tel: 226-2001

Georgetown Squash Club
208 Camp Street, Georgetown
Tel: 226-1239 / 4656
Fax: 226-4810

Guyana Football Association
17 Dadananawa Street, Section
K, Campbellville, Georgetown
Tel: 227-8758

**Le Meridien Pegasus (Tennis)**
Seawall Road, Kingston
Tel: 225-2856

Lusignan Golf Club
Lusignan
East Coast Demerara
Tel: 220-5660

## TELECOMMUNICATIONS

**Guyana Telephone &
Telegraph Company**
69 & 79 Brickdam, Georgetown
78 Church Street
Georgetown
Tel: 225-1315

## TIMBER PRODUCERS /
## EXPORTERS

Demerara Timbers Ltd
Lot 1 Water Street & Battery
Road, Kingston, Georgetown
Tel: 225-3835

Premier Lumber
27 Lombard Street, Werk-en-
Rust, Georgetown
Tel: 225-2471

Toolsie Persaud Ltd
10-12 Lombard Street
Georgetown
Tel: 226-4071

## TOURS & TOUR
## OPERATORS

Amazon Adventures
212 Duncan Street
Lamaha Gardens, Georgetown
Tel: 231-7141
Fax: 231-7141
Email:amazon@guyana.net.gy

**Correia Interior
Transportation**
158 Charlotte Street, Lacytown
Georgetown
Tel: 226-0605. Fax: 225-1171
Email: cmcl@networksgy.com

Dagron Tours
35 Main Street, Georgetown
Tel: 223-7921. Fax: 227-1166
Email:
dagron@solutions2000.net

**Evergreen Adventures**
159 Charlotte Street
Georgetown
Tel: 226-0605 / 222-6114
Fax: 225-1171
Email: sales@evergreen-
adventures.com

Nature Tours
238bb Eccles
East Bank Demerara
Tel: 233-2454 / 2280
Email:
Naturetours60@hotmail.com

Outdoor Expeditions
307 "1" Stone Avenue,
Campbellville, Georgetown
Tel: 225-2315
Email:
outdoors_expeditionsguyana@yahoo.com

**Rainforest Tours**
Hotel Tower
Main Street, Georgetown
Tel: 227-2011
Fax: 227-5632
Email:
rainforesttours@networksgy.com

**Rock View Lodge**
159 Charlotte Street
Georgetown
Tel: 226-0605
Fax: 225-1171
Email:
info@rockviewlodge.com

Shanklands Rainforest Resort
Adventure Tours
232 Middle and Camp Street
Georgetown
Tel: 226-8907
Fax: 226-9738
Email: forst@networksgy.com

The Maichony-Abary Water Conservancy reservoir    Photo: RJ Fernandes

**Shell Beach Adventures**
Seawall Road, Kingston
Georgetown
Tel: 225-4483

Torong Guyana Company Ltd
56 Coralita Avenue, Bel Air
Park, Georgetown
Tel: 225-0876. Fax: 225-0749
Email:
Toronggy@networksgy.com

Tourism and Hospitality
Association of Guyana
Private Sector Building
Waterloo Street, Georgetown
Tel: 225-0807
Fax: 225-0817
Email: thag@networksgy.com
Website:
www.exploreguyana.com

**Wilderness Explorers**
Cara Suites
176 Middle Street
Georgetown
Tel: 227-7698 / 226-2085
Fax: 226-2085
Email: Info@wilderness-
explorers.com

Wonderland Tours
158 Waterloo Street
Georgetown
Tel: 225-3122. Fax: 225-9795
Email:
Rousman2002@yahoo.com

**TOURISM**

Guyana Tourism Authority
National Exhibition Centre
Sophia, Georgetown
Tel: 223-6351
Fax: 231-6672
Web: www.guyana-tourism.com

**TRAVEL AGENCIES**

Angellina's Travel Agency
1995 Parika Highway
Tel: 260-4536 / 7
Email:
angellinastravel@hotmail.com

Expedia Travel N Tours
4c New Road, Vreed-en-hoop
Tel: 254-0359-61
Email: expedia@guyana..net.gy

Constellation Tours Ltd
140'A' Quamina Street
South Cummingsburg
Tel: 223-7276-8. Fax: 223-7280
Email:
contours@networksgy.com

Frandec Travel Service
29 Main & Holmes Streets
Georgetown
Tel: 226-3076
Fax: 225-2526

Friends Travel Service
82 Robb Street
Lacytown
Tel: 225-8537-8
Fax: 227-0193
Email:
friendst@networksgy.com

Guyana Association of Travel
Agents
R8 Eping Avenue
Bel Air Park
Georgetown
Tel: 223-7221
Fax: 227-2999
Email:
connections@networksgy.com

Jim Bacchus Travel Service
34-37 Water Street
WM Forgarty's Building
Tel: 227-7225

**Roraima International Travel
Agency**
R8 Eping Avenue
Bel Air Park, Georgetown
Tel: 225-9648. Fax: 225-9648
Email: ral@roraimaairways.com

Spready's Travel Agency
10 Freeyard, Port Mourant
Corentyne, Berbice
Tel: 336-6476. Fax: 336-6476

**WILDLIFE /
CONSERVATION**

Guyana Amazon Tropical Birds
Society
77 C1 Light Street, Albertown
Georgetown
Tel: 225-2190

Guyana Marine Turtle
Conservation Society
Tel: 227-7377